THE PROFESSIONAL DECISION-THINKER

THE PROFESSIONAL DECISION-THINKER

America's New Management and Education Priority

BEN HEIRS
WITH PETER FARRELL

DODD, MEAD & COMPANY
NEW YORK

For Meiko, my mother, father and sister,
and the memory of
Maggie and Dae

   2   3   4   5   6   7   8   9   10

Library of Congress Cataloging-in Publication Data

Heirs, Ben J.
   The professional decision-thinker.

   Originally published: Great Britain : Sidgwick & Jackson,
1986.
   Bibliography: p.
   1. Decision-making.   I. Farrell, Peter.   II. Title.
HD30.23.H445 1986   658.4'03   87-15575

ISBN 0-396-09203-9

Contents

Acknowledgements

Consistent with the philosophy which is put forward in this book, I have benefitted from the help and advice of many people in the course of writing and preparing it for publication. My first debt, however, is to my clients. If they had not invited me to participate in some of their important thinking efforts, I would never have accumulated the experience upon which the book is based.

Next, I would like to express my appreciation for the work which Peter Farrell has put into this project over the past two years. It is not just that he has helped me to express my ideas in written form; our regular weekly discussions have also encouraged me to develop and articulate thoughts which were previously only vague or half-formed.

Many friends, with experience in fields ranging from international business to scientific research, medicine, the law, government and the media, have also contributed to the preparation of the book. The time they gave to reading various sections of draft and the diversity of opinions expressed in their comments have been of inestimable value. I should, therefore, very much like to thank the following: Willis Culver, Robert Ducas, Dr. Barry Frank, Peter Giblin, Tony Hallatt, John Hobson, David Hodara, David Hood, Mark Howell, Jay Leary, Colin McIver, Brian Nicholson, Hugh Palmer, Tim Razzall and Joy Sterling. I want also to acknowledge my debt to the late Gordon O. Pehrson, whose thinking continues to exercise a powerful influence upon my own.

If, over the past twenty five years, I have come to understand something of 'the Japanese way', it is largely thanks to the patience and help of a few individuals: above all, of course, my wife Meiko, but also Professor Jun-ichi Kyogoku, formerly of the University of Tokyo, Takeo Masuda of the C. Itoh Group, Shigeru Uemura of Daiwa Securities, Yoshiro Ide, art dealer, and Shintaro Shiiya, acupuncturist.

Like every other author, I also owe considerable debts of gratitude to the authors of the books and papers which I have read over the years, and I want to express my particular appreciation to the authors, past and present, whose works are listed in the Selected Bibliography at the end of the book.

Finally, I would like to pay tribute to Jonas Salk, who has contributed so much to my thoughts about thinking in the course of conversation and debate over the last three years, and to William Armstrong of my British publishers, Sidgwick and Jackson, whose insights and enthusiasm have guided and encouraged me through the final stages of this enterprise.

This book has been some five years in the writing. Throughout that period Anne-Marie Simonet has patiently typed and retyped a long succession of drafts. For all the hard work involved, as well as the meticulous care she has shown, she has my heartfelt thanks.

But, although the book might never have been written were it not for the help of others, I am in no doubt about where the responsibility for its content lies. The ultimate responsibility is mine, and I accept it willingly.

Ben Heirs
Geneva, Switzerland
May 1987

Author's Note

The word 'manager' is one that I use with some misgiving. It seems so often to mean different things to people in different professions, or even in different organizations within the same profession. Unfortunately there are no satisfactory substitutes, and the only way of guarding against misunderstanding is to make it clear at the start what I mean when I use the word.

A manager, in the context of this book, is an individual, man or woman, who has the responsibility for taking major decisions and for determining policy and plans within any organization. In these terms, the president of the United States is a manager; so, too, is the owner of a corner store, the chief executive of a business enterprise, the officer in charge of a corporate division, the head of a government department, the president of a university or the head of a family. The manager's desk is where both the planning and the decision making bucks stop.

★

This book, while specifically addressed to an American audience, was first published in Britain in 1986 as an 'out of town' presentation in preparation for its US publication. In finalizing this new edition I have therefore been able to take account of the reactions of British readers.

One of the features that many of them found useful was the questionnaire designed to help the reader construct a profile of his own strengths and weaknesses as a decision-thinker and as a manager of other decision-thinkers, which appeared as an integral part of Chapter 12 – 'Know Thy Thinking Self'. They did, however, point out that when spread out over three pages in the middle of the book the questionnaire was not as accessible as they would have liked. In order to meet this point it has now, in addition to appearing in Chapter 12 on pp. 173–175, also been reproduced at the end of the book as an Appendix, where it can easily be referred to or, if the reader wishes, detached without causing any damage to the main body of the book.

It was also noted that the questionnaire can be used by a manager as an effective aid in evaluating the decision-thinking strengths and weaknesses of the people who report to him.

★

Throughout the book, when referring to a manager, I use masculine pronouns. This usage is for convenience and reading ease, and I ask women managers not to take offense; none is intended.

We have been so busy tracing the tangible aspects of evolution in the forms of animals that our heads, the little globes which hold the midnight sky and the shining, invisible universes of thought, have been taken about as much for granted as the growth of a yellow pumpkin in the fall.

Loren Eiseley

Don't they want America to be strong and healthy? Sure they do. But they want it to happen without any planning. They want America to be great by accident.

Lee Iacocca

We still do not teach people how to think.

Sir John Hoskyns

AMERICA'S FUTURE—A DECLARATION ON BEHALF OF OUR BRAIN

—To face our day-to-day responsibilities, how should we best manage our brain?

—In practical terms, what does it mean to "think"?

These are questions to which all of our managers should know the answer, but few do.

★ As a consequence, this failure is causing many of our most important managers and leaders in the United States to make a fundamental mistake. They are not taking practical *thinking* anywhere near as seriously as they should—that is, the kind of thinking we have to use to operate and guide into the future our government organizations, business corporations, educational systems and private lives.

★ This kind of thinking can usefully be identified as: decision-thinking.

★ Today, we need individual brilliance in decision-thinking, but we need collective brilliance within our organizations and corporations even more.

★ We are all decision-thinkers by default; there is no other way to get through life. The misfortune is that we are not taught how to do such thinking, let alone how to do it brilliantly.

★ Nor do we know *consciously* and *precisely* what it means to manage professionally our own practical decision-thinking or to manage professionally other decision-thinkers.

★ As a result, the alarming truth is that we Americans are also sending our young people into life's practical thinking battles untrained, unprepared, and largely unarmed.

★ This situation must change and our thinking practices must
  evolve. Before the modern escalation of nuclear weapons,
  complexity and change, our managers and leaders could perhaps take for granted the brain and one of its most vital
  functions—practical decision-thinking. But to continue to do
  so today is irresponsible and highly dangerous, both for our
  country and for our planet.

★ The rules and process of effective decision-thinking are deceptively simple. But the barriers in our society to such thinking
  are formidable. The task now is to so popularize the rules and
  process of effective decision-thinking that the barriers are
  overcome.

★ Dr. Jonas Salk recently observed: "The question remains as to
  whether or not we can influence human destiny constructively.
  It seems evident that if anything can be done, it will require that
  the human mind act upon itself, in the sense that the minds of
  human beings act upon each other." In practical terms, I believe
  this means that we have to learn to respect, care for and manage
  more effectively our brains and their decision-thinking efforts.

★ We in the United States are at a crossroads in our history. We
  can either become individually and collectively better and
  wiser in decision-thinking or we can decline.

The Setting – Our Thinking Challenge

America is usually surprised.

James Reston

There are many gifted and intelligent people in America. This individual brilliance – our most important natural re-source – is, however, often being under-utilized or wasted when employed *within* our organizations by inadequate, destructive or simplistic 'bottom-line' management practices.

Not only are brilliant individuals and the organizations for which they work suffering because of certain management failures – so, increasingly, is our country. For the organizations concerned – the government bodies and public institutions that formulate and implement policy and the corporations that fur-nish our prosperity – are the basis upon which American influ-ence and American power rests.

When it comes to facing up to the two greatest thinking challenges of our time, ever-growing complexity and constant change, our country is making a major strategic error. We now need, urgently, to establish a new personal priority for our present and future managers. This book is about correcting that error and creating that priority.

★

Ancient Egypt, the Roman Empire and the British Empire were the superpowers of their time. Now they are one with Nineveh and Tyre. Today the United States is a superpower, upholding and defending Western values and the way of life we all cherish.

But will our power endure? There is no God-given law that says it will.

Power fades not so much by the action of external forces but more often by the way its protection affords a country the debilitating luxury of wasting the practical thinking talents and energies of its people on problems that are secondary or even trivial. To do this over the long-term is fatal, for it is like taking a drug that enfeebles while giving the user the short-term illusion of strength.

In this book I wish to address one of the most important questions now facing our nation: How can we improve the thinking that *precedes* the decisions made within our government organizations and business corporations – in the setting of agendas, the development of strategies, the creation of alternatives and the anticipation of consequences?

This is the fundamental challenge that must now be met by our business, government and educational leaders, and by all those who aim to make American corporate and public management more competitive and competent.

★

Ours is an age of specialization. We respect the authority of the expert. We reward it, often handsomely, and allow the expert's writ to run through most of those areas that directly affect our professional and private lives.

Is it not then strange that when it comes to the most critical management jobs in our society – political leadership, the running of our public institutions, and the direction and future development of our business enterprises – we seldom require or even expect that those who fill these positions should have a definable expertise? Rather, what we tend to look for are personal characteristics like 'judgment', 'perseverance' and 'strength of character'. While these qualities are certainly vital, by themselves they are no longer sufficient.

If, as it often appears, the last opportunity open to a non-expert is to be a boss, then this seems to me to be not just inconsistent but absurd. After all, few of us would want to entrust our lives to an airline pilot, our health to a physician, our children to a teacher or our tax returns to an accountant unless we were satisfied that the individual concerned was professionally qualified. Why should we ask any less of those to whom we entrust our future?

It is often claimed that managers should be generalists, not specialists. But, while that is true as far as it goes, I believe that we can no longer afford to close the discussion there.

In the United States, where so much faith is rightly placed upon the value of expertise, there are now very good reasons emerging as to why we need to carry our ideas through to their logical conclusion and insist that those who hold executive power should also attain a standard of professionalism that matches their responsibilities.

As we have struggled to come to terms with the repercussions of superpower parity and global stalemate, and as we have felt our economic position threatened by the rise of Japan and Western Germany, by OPEC arm-twisting and by the destabilizing problems of Third World debt, so the need for more professional management of our political and economic affairs has become increasingly obvious.

It is, however, one thing to want our managers and leaders to go about their tasks more professionally. It is quite another to define exactly what we want them to be more professional *at*.

Do we want them to become even more expert at politicking for votes and popularity? Should we urge them to become even better at rewarding and promoting themselves in the short term, on the grounds that the benefits will, in due course, filter down to the rest of society? Or do we want them to display even more charisma and produce even more inspiring rhetoric? I do not think so – not if we want to stay on top.

Rather, we should expect those who direct our corporations and public institutions to be – in addition to possessing their other important skills and qualities – *professional thinkers.* For the battles we have been losing since 1960 have been, above all, *thinking* battles.

To put it bluntly, it is not just that we have often been out-thought by our enemies and competitors, we have not even begun to face up to the complex *collective* thinking efforts that will be required to overcome many of the formidable social, educational and financial problems that we now face or are in the process of inflicting upon ourselves.

But to stand on the sidelines and urge, as many people are now beginning to do, that those charged with managing our affairs should think better is, by itself, no more helpful than yelling 'Go faster!' at a runner or 'Fight harder!' at a boxer. If we want our managers to think better, then we must say how and to what end.

In this book I wish to demonstrate that there is a unique and manageable process of thinking that is essential to the manager's most important task – reaching the best possible decisions about future courses of action. I also wish to show that this kind of thinking, 'decision-thinking' as I will call it, must be for the manager what logic is for the mathematician and what the scientific method is for the physicist – *the basic foundation of his professionalism.*

Decision-thinking differs from mathematical or scientific thinking, because it deals, specifically, with the practical aspects of human life: with the problems of political economy; with war and peace; with profits and jobs; with crime and welfare; with human action and interaction. It takes us into those areas of life where clear cut answers seldom exist. It is concerned with making plans, predictions and judgments about the always uncertain future; with trade-offs in priorities; with deciding, as often as not, between the lesser and greater evil.

Despite the complexities and inexactitudes of decision-thinking, it is nevertheless a learnable skill, one which can be mastered by managers and applied in the ordinary course of work. While there are certainly subjective and creative aspects to decision-thinking, I will argue that it is within the capacity of managers at all levels of business and government to learn how to become both better decision-thinkers and better managers of other decision-thinkers.

Far too much of our current decision *making* is dominated by the need to react to events. Better decision-*thinking* can help us to anticipate and shape events, rather than constantly struggling to improvise piecemeal and short-term responses to each new crisis.

Our country was built on the practical faith that tomorrow could be better than today, and no public occasion in America is complete without a speech about the American Dream. If we remain serious about our Dream and about the precious moral and political values that we proclaim, then the time has come to stop talking so much about our tomorrow and start thinking more about it and planning more for it.

★

We in the United States have never lacked confidence in our ability to respond successfully to a challenge, *once* we have seen clearly the true nature of the challenge. We did it when we decided to win World War II and later when we decided to land some of our citizens on the moon.

This time however the challenge – a precise individual and collective decision-thinking challenge – is far more important and demands a far more *enduring* response than any of those we have faced before. If we refuse to recognize the nature and scope of the challenge and refuse to do something about it, we will inevitably pay the price.

How we produce better and more professional decision-thinking is a priority to which many of us can respond. The American Dream will not, henceforth, be achieved by some lucky chance or brought about by some grand national design.

It can only be achieved by millions of Americans discharging daily their own thinking responsibilities more efficiently and by their making and implementing better plans for themselves and for the organizations for which they work. I believe that this can happen and America can become the first *durable* superpower

if we now concentrate on creating an appreciation for professional decision-thinking in every important stage of our educational process and in every phase of our management
practices.

★

In my business career I have had the opportunity to observe
at first hand the tangible benefits that can accrue to an organization from well-managed decision-thinking and the disasters
that can result from thoughtless or short-sighted decisions. I
have written this book to identify the ways in which you, the
actual or aspiring manager, public administrator or political
leader, can train yourself *consciously* to think better and more
wisely and also *consciously* to manage the thinking efforts of
other people better and more wisely.

I do not claim to have said the last word on the subject nor
to have invented a formula that will cure all decision making
problems. But I do believe that the proposals set forth in this
book can help create a wave in favor of professional decision-
thinking that will sweep away those weaknesses in thinking that
are causing the competitive decline with which we are now
threatened.

Sweeping away those weaknesses is the new thinking
challenge we Americans must now accept. We can no longer
afford to be 'usually surprised' or out-thought.

PART I

The Theory and Rules of Decision-Thinking

1

A New Perception of Management: The Pre-eminent Role of Thinking

When it comes to creating the best decisions, what will matter henceforth is collective brilliance – not individual brilliance.

Anon.

Is it possible to point to one factor which, above all others, determines whether an organization will survive and prosper? Successful managers know the answer: an organization will excel tomorrow only if those who manage it make the right decisions today.

Every manager must, of course, be capable of taking effective short-term decisions when he finds himself obliged to react to a new development or to an urgent crisis. But, in the long run, the decisions which will prove most important are the creative ones which involve a manager in initiating events and leading his organization into the future – those decisions that are required to set goals, determine policy, make plans and ensure that those plans are correctly implemented. This point does not need emphasis or explanation; it is now widely understood.

But to see the manager essentially as a decision maker is to oversimplify his true role. It implies that his *thinking* responsibilities are confined to selecting one course of action out of a range of options presented to him, rather as a customer in a restaurant chooses a dish from the day's menu. The definition of the manager that I want to propose is quite different. I see him, to continue the analogy, not merely as the customer who scans the menu and makes a choice, but also as the restaurateur whose duty it is to give direction to the menu, as the *chef de cuisine* who ensures that only top-quality raw materials come into the kitchen and only excellent dishes leave it, and as the head waiter who oversees the efficient and agreeable service of the meal.

In other words, decision making, properly seen, is just *one* stage in a mental process which begins when a manager determines what problems and issues his organization should be addressing and which ends only when he has done everything possible to ensure that his decisions will be effectively carried out.

Most management literature and management education and training seem to concentrate on what might be called the executive aspects of management – the decision-making stage and the implementing one which follows it. In this book I will maintain that, important as these functions obviously are, they can only be dealt with successfully if they have been *preceded* by well-managed, imaginative and rigorous thinking. In management we now need to take one step back and focus first on thinking – the submerged nine-tenths of the iceberg, of which decision making is only the visible tip.

The manager's professional responsibilities must now be redefined, and his role as *both* a thinker and a manager of the thinking efforts of other thinkers should be recognized as being pre-eminent. Set out in summary form, my thesis is as follows:

1. The manager's most vital responsibility is to *manage* the thinking efforts of his organization in such a way as to ensure that it makes the best decisions about its future.

2. Unless he gets the important decisions right, *all* the manager's other skills – as an organizer, administrator and leader – will be exercised in vain.

3. A manager will only – can only – make a correct decision if he has *first* done everything within his power to ensure that the correct issue has been addressed, that there are no alternative courses of action which have been overlooked, that a serious effort has been made to foresee the consequences of each available alternative and that, finally, the chances of success and the balance between risks and rewards of each alternative have both been clearly and honestly calculated.

4. In order to achieve these considerable objectives, the thinking of both a manager and his organization must follow a *four-stage process* that begins with the posing of a question, proceeds via the asking and answering of a series of further questions, and culminates in the making of the decision.

5. The type of thinking that a manager is responsible for is *different* from, but certainly today no less important than, the other uses of human thought, such as scientific or mathematical thinking.

6. This different branch of thinking can accurately and usefully be identified as *decision-thinking.*★

7. The overriding need at each stage of the decision-thinking process is for clarity and objectivity. The manager must recognize that such clear and dis-

★ This does not mean that we do not often use scientific and mathematical thinking to help make a contribution to our decision-thinking, but rather that their processes are different, in some vital ways, from the mental process that we need to follow in management to arrive at the best possible decision.

interested thinking – what could be called *pure* thinking – rarely comes naturally to people working within a managerial hierarchy, and he must work hard and with subtlety to overcome the forces of complacency, arrogance and corporate politics, which can so easily distort or destroy the mind of an organization.

8. A manager has *two* fundamental tasks – to manage a decision-implementing team and a decision-thinking team. The composition of the two teams may or may not be different; what needs to be clearly understood, however, is that managing these two teams requires different skills and different leadership qualities.

9. Because decision-thinking is a discipline which must be applied not only to the *mind of the individual manager*, but also to the *collective mind of the organization* which he leads, it will only be effective if all the individuals chosen to participate in the process of decision-thinking think *together* as a team.

10. The manager, consequently, has a dual mental role. He must function, like a player-manager in baseball, both as a contributing *member* of his thinking team and as its *coach* – selecting, inspiring, cajoling and, where necessary, disciplining the other members to ensure that they give of their best.

11. To be an effective decision-thinker a manager must first understand the mental skills, principles and rules he needs *consciously* to call upon at each stage of the decision-thinking process, and then come to know his 'thinking self' by making an honest appraisal of his own capabilities both as a thinker and as a manager of other thinkers.

12. Thus, the professional management of decision-thinking demands *specific* skills, attitudes and percep-

tions and requires, above all else, that a manager should perceive his colleagues not only as implementers of policy, but also as a *team* of fellow thinkers.

★

There may be some readers who will feel that reducing the complicated mental processes that lead to the making of a decision to a formula of any kind is either, somehow, to over-simplify them or to attempt, naively, to analyze something that is automatic, instinctive and intuitive. Others may say, 'I know all about that process; I use it all the time; so what else is new?' I would like to forestall this sort of criticism right at the start by taking an analogy from a very different field, that of sport.

All of us who are reasonably sound in wind and limb can run well enough to catch a bus or fool about with the kids in the yard. We do it quite automatically, without considering how we control and coordinate the movement of our limbs. But if we went in for running seriously, then, whatever our natural talent, we would have to understand the process of running at quite a different level. We would have to become *conscious* – with the aid of coaches and trainers – of what we were doing with our limbs and lungs, capable of analyzing our movements, identifying the faults and putting them right, all with the intention of *managing* our bodies *and* minds to produce the best possible performance. We would, moreover, have to train long and hard if we wanted to compete successfully in track events at, say, the national or international level.

The same logic, I believe, applies to our managers and leaders. *We can no longer afford to depend upon their natural thinking talents alone.* In the long term we need to seek out managers who have the potential, in terms of natural talent, of a Jesse Owens, a Mary Decker Slaney or a Sebastian Coe, and then ensure that they receive the best coaching and undergo the most rigorous training in order to develop their thinking abilities to the full.

In the meantime those of us who seek to be expert managers

must strive – both as thinkers and managers of other thinkers – to improve on our strengths, analyze and remedy our weaknesses and, thereby, bring our minds to a higher level of professionalism. Chapter 12 and the Appendix, if dealt with candidly, will assist in this regard.

In addition, we need to supplement our conventional academic education with a practical and comprehensive program for developing a manager's thinking talents. The model, rules and practices of decision-thinking proposed in this book are intended to provide a basis for such a development program – both for present-day managers and for the managers of the future.

More specifically, as far as you, the reader, are concerned this book is intended to be of help to you whether you are already a manager or aspiring to become one. If you have people reporting to you and you want to make sure that you get the best thinking out of them, not simply for yourself but for your organization, then I believe you will find the proprosals that are contained herein relevant to that aim. If, on the other hand you feel that you are not contributing as much as you could to the thinking efforts of your organization, or that your ideas are not getting the attention they deserve, then again, you should find recommendations and insights here which can help you to contribute more effectively and also help you to ensure that more of your thoughts are acted upon.

★

Until we come to grips with the fact that when we want to make a decision, which will lead to (or avoid) action in the practical world, we need to call upon a very special and unique use of our thinking skills, the vital role of thinking in our practical life will remain unclear – and, hence, neglected. And all our mental efforts – whether scientific, religious, mathematical, artistic or action-oriented – will continue to be lumped together and analyzed under the all too vague and now, therefore, meaningless heading of 'thinking'.

Instead, when it comes to the complex subject and practice of decision-thinking, as with *all* uses of thinking, we need consciously to understand what we are doing and why we are doing it. In other words, as managers we need to understand how our decision-thinking should be managed just as a scientist needs to understand how his scientific thinking should be managed.

In summary, it is the purpose of this book to help you to become a professional decision-thinker. For that, I believe, is the crux of the matter. In what follows I will argue that henceforth, given the magnitude of the complexities and uncertainties with which America's managers must now cope, only a manager who becomes a professional decision-thinker can become a professional manager.

2

The Manager Is Also a Thinker

We insist that all of our employees contribute their minds.

Akio Morita of Sony

To be decisive is comparatively easy. The real problem, today, is to decide what to be decisive about.

Anon.

To be an excellent thinker does not necessarily make one an excellent manager. Who, after all, would suppose that the Swiss civil service lost a major executive talent when Albert Einstein resigned from his position as a clerk in the Zürich Patent Office? But I believe serious dangers arise if, conversely, it is assumed that an excellent manager need not be an excellent thinker.

Unfortunately, 'thinker' and 'manager' are words which, in our Western world, evoke completely contrasting images. Thinkers, however intelligent, are seen as passive, inward-looking and impractical, living a life more or less divorced from everyday reality. Managers, on the other hand, are perceived as being active, extrovert and, above all, concerned with finding solutions to practical problems.

These perceptions are, at least in part, accurate. Many of

those who are commonly considered to be thinkers tend to stand aside from – or, as they too often see it, above – the down-to-earth tasks of creating jobs, budgets and profits with which managers must contend. It is also true that far too many managers view thinking as an abstract, theoretical activity, having little to do with the world they work in. They see themselves as doers, men and women of action.

In the United States, in particular, we seem to admire 'action' for its own sake. We enjoy 'action movies'; we seek out 'a piece of the action'; our heroes are 'men of action'. It is hardly surprising, then, that 'active' qualities like drive, efficiency and leadership should come high on most people's list of management virtues. But few would rank imaginative thinking or, more importantly, skill in stimulating and managing other people's thinking efforts anywhere near the top of the list. Thinking, it seems to be assumed, is something we do naturally, like breathing and walking. And in management, as elsewhere, a preoccupation with thinking is often viewed as the choice of the weak and indecisive, those who lack the strength or courage to decide and act.

This emphasis on 'doing' at the expense of 'thinking' seems to me to be fundamentally wrong and, if left unchallenged, potentially fatal. What, after all, is the key function of management? Is it not to take information relating to the past and the present circumstances of an organization and its environment, and to process that information in order to create decisions and action plans relating to the future development of that organization?

But how is that information to be processed into wise decisions and effective plans, if not by thinking with and about it? To imagine that a management which refuses to face up to its thinking responsibilities can be successful is like expecting workers in a factory to take delivery of raw materials and, without using any energy or applying any skills, to transform them into marketable products.

Nor should it be imagined that the thinking skills and efforts which are, or should be, demanded of management represent an easy option or an academic exercise. Thinking is not a function that can be safely shoved aside into some backwater of organizational life and left in the hands of the impractical or the second rate. On the contrary, as an organization goes forward into the hazardous waters of the future, it is the expert thinkers who must be up there on the bridge, charting the course and manning the helm.

Over the years my work has brought me into contact with many different businesses, and it has taught me to recognize one where excellent thinking is being practiced. Coming into the offices of such an organization for the first time is a bit like meeting someone who you know, almost instantly, is going to be a stimulating companion, with interesting things to say and an entertaining way of putting them. You get a feeling of excitement, open-mindedness and anticipation.

This atmosphere almost always emanates from the top. For *nothing* is more influential in setting the mood of an organization than the manager's attitude to thinking, and very little good thinking will get done unless the manager encourages it, stimulates it and sets an example for others to follow. In the end, you will find, every manager gets the thinking he deserves.

The next time you are in a really lively office where people are buttonholing each other in the corridors, dropping into one another's offices to exchange ideas, sending out for coffee and sandwiches so that a meeting can continue through the lunch hour, pause and consider that what you are witnessing is not just a lot of physical activity, but the *collective mind of that organization*★ in action.

If the organization where you work has corridors that are hushed, if it is a place where people only talk with, or at, each other when they get together for scheduled meetings, and if everyone's office door is shut because they are busy 'working', then maybe your organization has a pretty dull mind. And maybe, if you are the manager, it is time you rethought your

★ This is a perception which was first developed in a previous book, *The Mind of the Organization*, by Gordon Pehrson and myself, Harper & Row, revised edition, 1982.

definition of your responsibilities. If you are not, then perhaps it is time you tried, with subtlety, to change things.

★

From now on anybody who wants to consider himself a professional manager not only needs to perform competently both as a thinker and a manager of thinkers – something which already many, though still not enough, American and European managers clearly do. He must also, *consciously*, understand and apply the rules and practices which underlie his own thinking competence, and be capable of communicating those rules and practices to the people who work and think for him.

The management skills involved can no longer be taken for granted or based only upon intuitive abilities. They need to be brought out into the open, analyzed, defended and, yes, even periodically audited. Nor can we afford to continue to rely on just basic brainpower, business school degrees and good fortune to see us through.

Three factors have emerged during the last few decades which have rendered traditional concepts of management incomplete. They are: the rising number of possible social, political, commercial, environmental and legal *consequences* associated with any important decision; the growing *complexity* of the information and assumptions that need to be considered before a decision can be taken; and the ever-increasing rate of *change* which obliges us to make more and more decisions. Any one of these factors would be serious enough to undermine traditional ideas about the way in which organizations are managed. In combination, they make it necessary to re-think entirely our approach to planning, decision making and management priorities.

It would have been possible to argue, perhaps as recently as half a century ago, that the sort of practical knowledge and good judgment that enables us to cope with everyday life was adequate for dealing with the challenges which a manager faced. Troubled though the 1930s were, people lived then in a less crowded world – one which was, by today's standards, far simpler and slower moving. That world was also more forgiving of errors, even large ones. People could survive without so much thought and concern about the consequences and inter-relationships of their actions.

If, for example, lumber was needed to build houses, people simply cut down the nearest trees. The future results, in terms of land erosion, ecological imbalance and the destruction of a natural resource which could not easily be replaced were only beginning to be contemplated. Reactive thinking and short-term budgets, rather than foresight and careful planning, seemed to be enough.

Up to about 1950, maybe even later, learning how to be a manager was still rather like learning to drive a car. Special skills were involved, to be sure, and experience and natural aptitude were vital advantages, but most people could 'get the hang of it' given the chance. Today cars have, of course, become easier to drive. A motorist from the 1930s might find the appearance of a 1987 model unfamiliar and would certainly be surprised at the scale of the new super highways and the amount of traffic they carry. But he or she would quickly realize that the basic business of driving had changed little, and that the vehicle was designed to be handled in much the same way as its predecessors.

But to take a manager of the pre-war era and confront him with the problems of today's world would be like plucking the driver from a 1936 Studebaker and depositing him in the cockpit of a Boeing 747. He would find himself at the controls of a complex and terrifying machine, traveling in a strange medium at an unbelievable speed, and nothing short of a miracle could avert disaster.

We should now no more expect the thinking practices which allowed the managers of the 1930s (or indeed the forties, fifties and sixties) to get by or prove adequate in the circumstances of the 1980s and 1990s, than we should expect the skills of the average motorist to qualify him to take over the piloting of a jet airliner. And, as tragic incidents like those at Bhopal and Chernobyl or the disastrous failure of our own Challenger space shuttle show, 'thinking' failures at even the middle-management level can have consequences more far-reaching than a mistake in the cockpit of a 747.

Furthermore, when the pace of change was slow, one truly significant new idea was enough to assure the success of a manager or even a whole enterprise. The application of mass production to automobile manufacturing, for example, was an innovation that sufficed to secure the fortune of Henry Ford and the prosperity of the Ford Motor Company for thirty years.

Today even a highly successful manager cannot count on being so fortunate. The founders of Apple, for example, did for the computer industry very much what Henry Ford, with his Model T, did for the automobile industry, but within a decade the company's meteoric success had peaked and it faced near collapse.

In a business or government career the professional manager will now confront far more occasions when a right or wrong decision is crucial than were faced by a person in a similar position thirty or fifty years ago. This is simply because the accelerated rate of change is bound to mean that there will be *more* make-or-break decisions to be made within the time frame of one career. Mr Ford needed to be exceptionally brilliant once in thirty years. Mr Jobs, formerly of Apple, will, if he is to do as well, probably have to be exceptionally brilliant at least ten times in thirty years.

Paradoxically, the more pressing our immediate problems and the more rapidly the waves of crisis and change break upon us, the more we need to find the time and energy to raise our sights to look further ahead into the future. With each new technological, financial and social revolution coming hot upon the heels of the last, no manager can now afford to rest upon his thinking laurels.

★

I can imagine, to digress for a moment, that there are some readers who are beginning to frown and to murmur to themselves, 'This is all fine in theory. We would all like to have more time to think and we would all like to be able to afford the luxury of setting medium- and long-term objectives for our organizations and creating the plans necessary to achieve them. But in the too real world, the world in which I must operate, things just are not like that. How, facing one crisis now, and two or three crises that may break within the next ninety days, am I supposed to find the time or energy to think about next year, let alone the years after that?'

The reply to that, not uncommon, question is, I am afraid, quite straightforward. Today a manager is either a professional or he is a danger to himself and his organization. Of course every manager faces the problem of keeping a host of balls in the air; but the truly professional manager will be the one who recognizes that, even as he juggles, he and his organization are balanced on a tightrope which stretches ahead into the future. If he wants to stay on that rope, he has got to keep his eyes fixed firmly to the front.

So when I stress the overriding importance of finding the time and energy to carry out careful thinking, it is not because I underestimate or fail to recognize the urgency of the need for tactical thinking to cope with the problems that clamor for any manager's immediate attention. Nor do I for a moment underrate the tremendous pressure of political forces and P/E ratios, as well as corporate incentive schemes, that channel his thinking towards the short-term problem and the short-term solution. I have experienced these things personally and I have watched, almost daily, as they take their toll of my clients' and my own mental resources. I know how tempting it is to concentrate on them to the exclusion of all else – but I also know that the success, even the survival, of an organization depends upon the ability of its managers to resist these temptations.

The fact that short-term pressures are now so intense just makes it all the more urgent that we recognize them, resist them, and indeed avoid them when we can. No one would suggest that it is easy. As Lyndon Johnson once said with his customary pungency, 'When you are up to your ass in alligators, it is sometimes hard to remember why you started draining the swamp.' But unless managers can learn how to fend off the snapping alligators which constantly distract their attention and to concentrate, also, on their medium- and long-term thinking responsibilities, the swamp will not only remain undrained, it will just get deeper and more treacherous.

★

Given our complex challenges and problems, the need for our managers to learn, and to learn quickly, how both to think more professionally themselves and to manage more professionally the thinking efforts of their colleagues – whether they concern the short-, medium- or long-term – should be obvious. But this does not mean that they need to excel in disciplines, such as physics or philosophy, which are traditionally considered to be the province of Thinkers with a capital T.

On the contrary, one of the main objectives of this book is to identify and focus on those thinking challenges and skills which are unique to management and practical decision making. For there is no doubt that managers are right in believing that many of the thinking methods appropriate to the contemplation of, say, scientific or mathematical issues are *not* sufficient for dealing with the kind of problems they must face.

Where they go wrong is in underestimating or playing down the importance of the special skills involved in their own particular branch of thinking. I will argue that the specific use of thinking we shall be considering in this book is a discipline in its own right, as valid a field for study and analysis as the thinking which is done by logicians or mathematicians – with the all important difference that the success or failure of those who practice it is crucial to all our futures. Just because it is different from the thinking required in other fields does not mean – and this is the key point – that it is any less definable, difficult or demanding.

If anything, the reverse is true. Managers must often think in circumstances and under pressures of time, stress and contingency which do not normally apply to our other uses of thinking. Moreover, for managers, along with a few other professionals such as doctors and engineers, thinking and the mental disciplines they employ are only a means to an end, never an end in themselves. No manager can afford the luxury of leaving a question open or an issue unresolved. And no manager can be satisfied with an elegant paradox, an abstract truth or a conclusion which is of purely academic interest.

A manager is concerned with reaching decisions – to act or not to act, to stop, change directions or continue on course. The thinking a manager does relates to the world of possibility and probability, to the world of predicting and shaping the future, to the stage where much of the human story is, and will be, enacted.

Because the need for a decision is an imperative – the focus upon which every manager's thinking must concentrate – I have chosen to use the term *decision-thinking* to describe the special use of thinking which I believe managers must master and practice, with the intention that it should find – quickly – a permanent place in the everyday language of management.

★

Before moving on to analyze and explain the principles and rules of decision-thinking, there are two points which need to be disposed of to avoid any misunderstanding. First, decision-thinking should not be confused with decision making. The term decision-thinking covers a four-stage process which is more complex and wider in scope than that usually covered by the words 'decision making'. Indeed, decision making, properly seen, is no more than the fourth and final stage of decision-thinking.

Secondly, although most of what follows will concentrate on the ways in which the decision-thinking process should be applied to business, it should not be viewed solely in a business context. Decision-thinking is not a technique, like 'discounted cash flow' or 'management by objectives', which is applicable only on restricted fronts such as financial management or management control. On the contrary, we now need to make explicit

– and, therefore, capable of analysis and improvement – a mental process which has been implicit in *all* action-related thinking throughout human history.

The need to make decisions has, after all, been with the human race from the start. And the exceptional individual may now unconsciously adopt, for his own use, the modern techniques appropriate to the decision-thinking process without explicit analysis of that process.

But today a manager can neither think nor decide in isolation. He creates the organizational environment for the thinking processes of his subordinates, whether he is aware of doing so or not. The professional manager must, therefore, *consciously* structure the context in which his organization's thinking and deciding take place. And this context cannot be efficiently created without a clear understanding of the decision-thinking process and the specific rules that govern each stage of that process. Within organizations, excellent thinking will not happen by chance.

Summary

Thought should come before action and planned thought should come before planned action. Managers must therefore be thinkers first, doers second – and *equally* competent at both.

Careful and creative thought is a prerequisite for effective action. An organization's future success, therefore, depends on the quality of its collective mind and how well that mind is managed. Some managers may have muddled through in the past, but from now on they will need to recognize that:

when they and their organization think about making a decision, they need, consciously, to employ and

manage a unique human thinking method – the decision-thinking process;

problems of complexity, change and contingency can only be dealt with by professional decision-thinkers;

to achieve professional status, managers must first analyze their own decision-thinking skills and strive to improve them;

they must then do the same for their organization;

decision making is only the final stage of decision-thinking – the tip of the iceberg; to be a professional manager, one must be responsible for the whole iceberg.

3

The Whole Iceberg: The Model of the Decision-Thinking Process

What is discovered by man is never the 'universal' or cosmic 'truth'. Rather, the process by which the mind brings about a 'discovery' is itself the 'universal'.

Joseph Chilton Pearce

If, in your imagination, you step back for a moment from our planet to observe how we human beings go about our daily work, one of the first patterns you will perceive is that, both individually and in groups, we are continually involved in making and implementing decisions. We are a decision-thinking, decision-making, decision-implementing animal – living through time. That is the essence of our practical, material life on earth.

Individually and collectively, privately and professionally, we shape our lives by the decisions we make and by the skill, energy and persistence with which we put them into effect. If we aspire to live better lives, then we must learn to make better decisions and to implement them more effectively. But no matter what daring or courage we bring to the making of a decision, or how great the drive and determination with which we carry it out, that decision can only be as good as the thinking, the decision-thinking, leading up to it. The single most important step we can take to improve the quality of our decisions is, therefore, to improve the quality of the thinking which precedes them.

Yet, it is one which we have been strangely reluctant to take. In political life we at least pay lipservice to the idea that important decisions must be preceded by thorough thinking. Laws arrived at without full public debate are, we believe, likely to be bad laws. The various elements composing the mind of a democracy – the executive and the legislature, the media and public opinion – must all be brought to bear upon a social or economic issue, before we will be satisfied that it has been thoroughly thought through. But elsewhere, in business especially, many managers seem to be impatient with the clumsiness and apparent wastefulness of such processes; their role, they believe, is to generate action, not debate.

But, apart from this misguided image of their job, the fundamental reason managers are frequently reluctant to think a problem through before making a decision is that they have no clear model of how to do it.

As everyone knows who suffered under an impatient teacher, it is no help to be told to 'Get with it', 'Wake up' or 'Think again' if one does not know *how* to think about the particular kind of question that is being considered. No amount of thinking, for example, will help the average fifteen-year-old solve a quadratic equation if he was not listening when the teacher explained the procedure for dealing with such problems. Ultimately the student will have to admit ignorance and ask the teacher to put matters right.

Many managers, like an ill-prepared student, lack a precise understanding of how to think their way through to the best decision. And, like many an inattentive student, they often try to disguise their ignorance by resorting to bluff: 'It is all a matter of judgment, intuition or experience,' they will tell you, 'and there is no way these things can be rationalized or explained.' But the truth is that, though it would be foolish to underrate the importance of these subjective factors, they are only valuable as tools to be used in the service of thinking, not as substitutes for it.

Thinking itself must be methodical. There is a procedure

to be followed whenever a decision of any importance is to be taken. With practice the four-stage decision-thinking process we are about to explore can become as automatic and instinctive a process as a pilot's pre-flight checklist. And it can be justified on very much the same grounds – at the very least it will serve as a control to ensure that nothing has been forgotten; and on occasion it may avert catastrophe.

★

Naturally the time devoted to the decision-thinking process and the completeness with which each stage is carried out will vary enormously. It would be ludicrous to suggest that the sort of decisions which have hitherto come easily and painlessly must, in future, be the subject of some complex rigmarole. There are enough genuinely complex and baffling problems in our lives without any of us having to turn a simple question, such as whether to travel to a meeting by train or plane, into the decision-making equivalent of a three-ring circus.

But a moment's reflection will reveal that, whether or not we are conscious of it, our minds do flip through an elementary version of the decision-thinking process even when they are coping with trivial or routine matters. For the process itself is a natural one; it is neither mysterious nor difficult to understand. On the contrary, in most cases we run through it so naturally and automatically that we never pause to analyze it. As a result, when we are faced with a really tough decision – Should we pledge our assets to buy a business? Should we take our company into a new market? How, as politicians or government officials, can we cope with terrorism or unemployment? – we often flounder or panic rather than tackle the thinking challenge methodically. What we lack in such instances is a precise theoretical model of the mental process we need to follow, consciously, in order to arrive at a well-considered and effective decision.

'Theory' is a word which is much abused. When we say, 'That is certainly fine in *theory*' or '*Theoretically*, of course, you are quite right', we are saying, in effect, that theory is one thing and practice is another – that theoreticians may deal with things as they ought to be, but that practitioners deal with them as they are.

Properly seen, however, theory is not the enemy of good practice; it is the very foundation upon which it is built. I doubt if any of us would relish the idea of working in an office block designed by an architect who had not mastered the theory of structural engineering. Why should we be any happier working for managers who make decisions without having any explicit theory of what they are doing or how they should set about it?

To look at another example of clear methodology, based upon sound theoretical foundations, let us consider what happens when we go to see our doctor. Having listened to our description of the symptoms, he will immediately embark upon a step-by-step process designed to lead to an accurate diagnosis. That mental process, inculcated by education and perfected by experience, is far more important to a doctor's professional performance than a stethoscope or a good bedside manner.

In decision-thinking, as in architecture or medicine, we must get the theory right before we can hope to improve what we do in practice. Only when the theory – and the rules for implementing it – are consciously understood, can we set about improving our performance. We must not only understand *what* to do, we must also understand *why* we do it. There is all the difference in the world between the amateur who proceeds by rule of thumb or trial and error and the professional who has mastered the theory as well as the practice.

The process which the doctor follows is directed towards a specific end: to diagnose the cause of the patient's problems. In decision-thinking the object of the exercise is equally clear: to determine a future course of action. The action may be one to be taken immediately – 'Fire him', 'Sell the division', 'Delay the offer' – or it may consist of a plan to be implemented over a period of several years.

In every case, however, the thinking can be divided into four main stages, which are combined in a single process, as is shown diagrammatically in the chart on p. 31. Each stage must be gone through, no matter whether the issue at stake is what to do about an immediate problem or the achievement of a medium- or long-term objective. The four stages are:

The Decision-Thinking Process

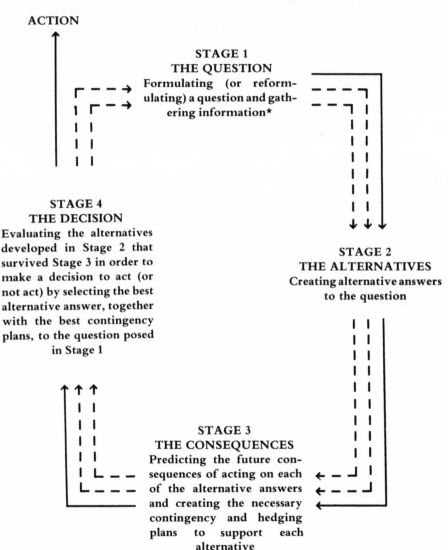

ACTION

STAGE 1
THE QUESTION
Formulating (or reformulating) a question and gathering information★

STAGE 4
THE DECISION
Evaluating the alternatives developed in Stage 2 that survived Stage 3 in order to make a decision to act (or not act) by selecting the best alternative answer, together with the best contingency plans, to the question posed in Stage 1

STAGE 2
THE ALTERNATIVES
Creating alternative answers to the question

STAGE 3
THE CONSEQUENCES
Predicting the future consequences of acting on each of the alternative answers and creating the necessary contingency and hedging plans to support each alternative

★ Until the final decision is taken, the possibility of altering the original question and/or returning to Stages 2 and 3 always remains – hence the dashed lines. The solid line represents the path leading to the final decision and action.

Stage 1   The Question. *Formulating* a question that addresses the issue in the clearest possible way, without sacrificing any of its subtlety or complexity, and then gathering the information relevant to answering that question.

Stage 2   The Alternatives. *Creating* the most effective range of alternative answers to the question posed in Stage 1.

Stage 3   The Consequences. Evaluating each of the alternatives that emerges from Stage 2 by thinking through its implications and *predicting* the likely, as well as the possible, consequences. This is not only to provide the basis for making a choice in the next stage, but also to allow for hedging and contingency plans to be created in case that choice proves to be wholly or partially wrong.

Stage 4   The Decision. Here, finally, we come to the 'traditional' decision-making skills of weighing up the probabilities of succeeding with each alternative, measuring the balance between risk and reward offered by each alternative – and then using our *judgment* to decide upon which alternative to act.

Certainly, if applied to a complex problem, this process is time-consuming and exhausting, demanding the use of a wide range of thinking techniques and skills, none of which is easy. But it is this mental process, and *only* this process, that gives us the chance to think our way wisely into the future.

Nor is the process different in principle when we have a less complex or more immediate decision to take. In such cases the time that can be devoted to each stage must necessarily be shorter, and the exploration of alternatives and consequences limited, but the sequence of the process still needs to be rigorously followed.

★

The next four chapters will analyze, in turn, each of the stages. Certain principles, however, apply to the process as a whole, and these, I think, are worth spelling out before we discuss each of the separate stages.

The *first* principle is that no one stage, not even the last, is more important or more worthy of the manager's attention than the others. Just as taking off, navigating a course to the correct destination and landing are all equally important parts of a flight, so each stage of the decision-thinking process is *equally* essential to its success. The manager who concentrates on the final decision-making stage at the expense of any one of the first three stages is as much a danger to his organization as a pilot who makes superb take-offs but has never learned to navigate or land would be to his passengers.

The *second* principle is that the decision-thinking process is not a linear process moving directly from the start of Stage 1 to the end of Stage 4. As indicated by the dashed lines in the diagram on p. 31, the entire process, or at least part of it, may have to be repeated several times before a satisfactory conclusion can be reached.

Perhaps the closest analogy is the design process, which has this same quality, known technically as 'iteration'. A designer's work can be divided into phases similar to the stages of decision-thinking. There is the initial drafting phase, followed by a phase in which the designer stands back to inspect his work, followed, normally, by a series of erasures and some redrafting. The whole process culminates in the specification of the dimensions, tolerances, etc., needed to complete a set of working drawings. Now obviously the sequence of drafting, inspection and redrafting may be repeated many times before the designer is satisfied. And while the stages certainly occur in a fixed order, the overall progress involves the cyclical iteration of a sequence of operations, not a simple progression from A to Z.

This non-linear aspect of decision-thinking means that the manager must stay in touch with the process at every stage, for it may be necessary at any point to go back to a prior stage. Unfortunately, many managers are tempted to concentrate on Stages 1 and 4. Having decided on the question that should be asked in Stage 1, they then delegate the thinking work involved in Stages 2 and 3 and get involved again only when it comes to selecting the best answer, at Stage 4.

This may appear, superficially, to be an attractive way of working. But what happens if, in the course of Stage 2 or Stage 3, it becomes clear that the wrong question has been asked; or if in the course of Stage 3 more alternatives are needed to provide more debate and choice?

The four stages cannot, therefore, be thought of as a set of stepping stones leading directly from the beginning of the decision-thinking process to its completion. They are, rather, bases, each of which may be touched – that is, reviewed and repeated – many times in the course of a single exercise. The process is therefore *cyclical*; it comes to an end only when the thinker or thinkers reach the decision-making stage, the home base as it were, for the last time.

This leads us to the *third* principle. Almost any serious piece of decision-thinking will demand the collective efforts of a number of individuals, and so, like any other organizational endeavor, it will have to be *managed*. I shall be examining the management of the decision-thinking process within organizations in detail in Part II. But it is important to bear in mind, as you read the next four chapters, that the decision-thinking process is envisaged primarily as taking place in the context of an organization.

Only in unusual circumstances will decision-thinking be done by a thinker sitting in solitude, like Rodin's famous statue. Usually it will take place in meetings, formal and informal; during encounters in corridors; over lunch or drinks; in the course of phone conversations; in planes, trains and cars; and on the hundred and one other occasions when colleagues find an opportunity to share an idea, to pick holes in one another's arguments or to discuss a company's problems and prospects.

Thus, when I say that managers must be – and be seen to be – professional thinkers, I am not only urging that they should learn how best consciously to manage each one of the four stages in their own thinking. I am also urging that they must become conscious of how to manage each one of those stages when stimulating and coordinating the thinking efforts of colleagues and subordinates.

The skills involved go far beyond those traditionally required of managers. Getting the best decision-thinking out of an organization demands patience, sensitivity, the ability to guide and inspire thinking and, crucially, the capacity to empathize with people whose approach to thinking is unfamiliar or even antipathetic. Decision-thinking is a living, dynamic process; it cannot be treated merely as another bureaucratic procedure.

Successful decision-thinking is a product of individual minds working together – minds that may be diverse in their approach to a problem and quirky in their reactions to each other. Getting the best out of people's minds means treating those people as human beings who, amongst their other physical, social and psychological needs, also have *thinking* needs. It also means recognizing that thinking abilities cannot be switched on when a meeting begins and switched off when it ends. If people are going to have a good idea, it is as likely to come to them in the bath or during a telephone conversation as in the conference room.

The *fourth* and final principle to be remembered is that throughout the four-stage decision-thinking process – and not only at Stage 1 – the participants in the process will *continually* be asking and answering questions. In other words, once we have defined the main question we begin to pose and answer such sub-questions as: 'What are the alternative answers to the question?' 'What are the future consequences of each of those alternatives?' 'What is the best alternative to achieve our objectives.' 'How could that alternative go wrong?' 'If that is so, what contingency and hedging plans need to be made?'

The question-and-answer formula is thus applicable to each stage of the decision-thinking process. It is asking the *best question* that starts that process in motion; and it is a supply of the *best sub-questions* that keeps it moving and on course.

★

The decision-thinking process which has been outlined above and which will now be discussed in detail, stage by stage, is intended to provide the theoretical structure we urgently need to apply openly to the management of our thinking. It is, therefore, essential that the manager, who must implement and manage the process, is able to see both the wood and the trees. He must become not only an expert in the rules that apply to each stage, but also have a firm grasp of the shape and purpose of the process as a whole.

Thus, the manager in charge of any important decision-thinking task needs to be continually aware: of what stage has been reached and of the management skills required by that stage; of how and when the process should be pushed forward or back; and of what has so far been accomplished and what still remains to be done.

Without a clear understanding and conscious application of the theoretical model of the decision-thinking process, it is fatally easy for a manager's thinking to lose its bearings and go off course. I would go farther, even, and argue that unless a manager can learn how deliberately to follow the model and to manage it consciously whenever he has an important decision to make, he will never become a professional decision-thinker.

Summary

The decision-thinker, like any other professional, must have a theoretical model of the unique thinking process that he manages.

The model of the decision-thinking process is built around four stages:

the question

the alternatives

the consequences

the decision.

All four stages are of equal importance.

The process is a cyclical and iterative one; at any point it may be necessary to go back and repeat one or more of the stages.

Throughout the four stages, the successful operation of the process is dependent upon the asking and answering of the best questions.

In the context of an organization, the process must be seen as a collective endeavor, involving the use of all available thinking resources – and that process, like all collective endeavors, needs always to be managed.

4

Stage 1: Defining the Rich Question and Gathering Relevant Information

A voyage of a thousand miles begins with a single step. Make sure that step is in the right direction.

Old Chinese saying with a modern amendment

The starting point for any decision-thinking effort is a question – a question beginning with a word like 'why', 'how', 'when', 'who', 'what', 'which', etc. The question may be immediately recognizable as such – 'Which job offer should I accept?', 'How can we fund the investment this subsidiary is recommending?' Or it may be a problem transformed into a question – 'My boss and I are obviously not getting on with each other – when should I look for a new job?', 'We are behind budget for the quarter – what can we do to recover the lost ground before the end of the year?'

It is, as you can easily verify for yourself, extremely difficult to think without posing questions. Questions come naturally to the thinking mind. The difficulty is not in finding questions to ask, but rather in finding good questions and discovering the right way of asking them.

Framing the right question in the right way is the first step in every decision-thinking process. The self-evident quality of this assertion ought not to mislead one into thinking that this stage of the decision-thinking process is easy, for, as the Chinese adage has it, 'A voyage of a thousand miles begins with a single step.' And if that step is taken in decision-thinking in the wrong direction, the journey will, at best, be longer and more arduous; at worst, it will be wasteful or even perhaps ruinous.

The crux of the matter is summed up in a saying familiar to every child: 'If you ask a silly question, you get a silly answer.' It is equally true to say that if you ask slanted, short-sighted or simplistic questions, you will get answers suffering from the same defects.

To those who object that this point is too obvious to need enlarging upon, I make no apology. In my experience at least half the problems in any organization can be traced back to decisions doomed from the start, simply because those responsible for making them were thinking about a question that was inappropriate, incomplete or just plain bad.

★

The executive who excels, like the general who wins, is the one who, by thinking ahead carefully and continuously, seizes and keeps the initiative. And the most important factor in this constant effort to keep ahead of events is the quality and range of the questions which are asked.

Thus the manager of a successful organization continually searches for questions needing to be asked; he does not wait for problems to reach a crisis point before considering them. One way of helping to ensure that this happens is to institute a 'thinking audit', rather along the lines of the legal audits which have now become a standard practice in several American corporations.

Those businesses have found that a regular check of a company's potential legal exposure, on every front, from environmental legislation to customer liability, by a competent team of professional lawyers, will often identify risks that would otherwise have gone unrecognized. In much the same way a periodic scanning of the key questions an organization's mind is being asked to answer can help ensure that the hazards ahead are spotted in good time, that potential problems are avoided, and that thinking energies are not being misdirected.

Many organizations do, of course, have people, or even whole departments, such as planning or economic forecasting, which are supposed to think about potential problems. All too often, however, they are relegated to a backwater where their musings will not distract front-line management. They are tolerated, they may even be humored, but they are rarely taken seriously.

What I am proposing is that managers use the device of a thinking audit to force themselves to consider whether or not they are asking their organization to answer the best questions.

In my own advisory business one of the first questions we ask a new client is: 'What are the most important questions you are currently asking your organization to answer?' The client's answer to our question will quickly tell us whether management takes its thinking responsibilities seriously. As with an individual, you can judge the quality of an organization's thinking by the questions it is asking itself – that is, requiring its managers to answer.

It follows that Stage 1 of the decision-thinking process demands the manager's full attention, because asking the wrong questions and obliging an organization to answer them is doubly dangerous. First, it means that, when problems reach a stage requiring action, the best answers will not be available. Secondly, it means that the organization is squandering its most valuable asset – its thinking resources. Requiring employees to spend time thinking about wrong issues or working on bad questions is as much of a loss as a breakdown on the factory floor.

Moreover, it is a loss for which the manager is directly responsible, for in the last resort it is his responsibility to see that the company's decision-thinking skills are being applied not just to the right priorities but, more precisely, to the right questions.

★

To be successful, managers must do more than ask the right questions. They must also ask them in the right way. What makes a question a good one? The most important test that I apply to any question in decision-thinking is: Is it rich enough?

A question must be rich as a sauce is rich. It must be a blend of ingredients, each of which contributes to the whole and yet retains its own identity; a sauce in which each element has its proper weight, no more and no less. Above all, a question, like a sauce, cannot be skimped. Too often questions are poor and thin because one or more of the ingredients is missing; instead of being subtle and matching the full flavor of the issue, the result is bland or inadequate.

I emphasize the need for richness because there is a prejudice, shared by many people, in favor of simple questions. This prejudice unfortunately leads to poor thinking, because simple questions cannot generate 'rich' thinking at the subsequent stages of the decision-thinking process. It is always tempting to suppose that a question can be simplified, especially since so much of our training leads us to admire brevity and succinctness. We are predisposed to believe that only lawyers and bureaucrats relish complications and qualifications.

Today no one would argue that where one word will suffice, two should be used. We can all do without the sort of verbal padding which so often serves as a substitute for thought. But it is a mistake to suppose that simplicity and clarity of language are ends in themselves. They are simply means which, properly used, will ensure that our ideas are expressed with precision and in language which reflects their richness, if they have it, or exposes their poverty, if they do not.

We should, by all means, eliminate complexity and confusion from our *language* when we are framing a question, but we must not try to remove complexity from the *question* itself. We must not gloss over important factors just because they are difficult to express concisely.

A question too tightly framed is like an ill-conceived blockade or an exclusionary tariff: it may have short-term advantages, but ultimately it will rebound on those who impose it. It will place an interdiction on the free flow of ideas, and almost certainly will deny entry to the right answer. If a question is framed too broadly, those working on the answer can narrow it down fairly easily, but if a question is framed too narrowly, the resulting handicaps are almost insuperable. We will never discover that something is gray if we ask the person who is looking at it to tell us only whether it is black or white. It takes a rich question to generate rich thinking and, at the final stage, to reach a decision with real value.

To illustrate the point with a simple example, take the sort of question any manager will often ask: 'How can we increase our profits?' In this, its most basic (and poorest) form, the question could be answered in hundreds of ways. It becomes more precise and richer if, for example, it is enlarged to read: 'How can we increase profits by at least 50 per cent over the next three years?'

Now those who are being asked to do the thinking at least have a specific (but not a limiting) target and a time frame within which it is to be achieved. This will help to focus their thinking, but it still leaves room for a great deal of wasted effort. If the manager wants his colleagues to think as effectively and efficiently as possible, he must further 'enrich' the question by stating not only what he wants to achieve, but also what he wants to avoid.

In its final form, therefore, the question might look something like this: 'How can we increase our profits by at least 50 per cent over the next three years, without,

demoralizing our employees?

offending or losing customers?

opening our market to new competitors?

destroying our long-term competitiveness?

weakening our reputation for soundness and reliability?

using accounting practices which could alarm our bankers?

laying ourselves open to attack by government agencies or share-
   holders?

This may look cumbersome and unattractive by comparison with the original question, but just consider how much
wasted thinking is eliminated by spelling out the question in
detail right from the start.

There is, as I have said, a tendency to resist this process of
enriching a question by qualifying it and adding conditions. In
part this is because much of our training encourages us to try
to simplify complex questions by reducing them to 'essentials'.
We should all be concentrating on essentials. But in my experience a question which has been boiled down until it is stark and
simple has, too often, become not just simple but simple-
minded.

To illustrate the way in which questions become impover-
ished, we need only to observe those people (every business has
them) who, when asked to consider a complex question in
which many factors are intricately related, insist that the whole
issue must be reduced to a single financial point: 'What's the
bottom line?'

Executives who think in this way will seize every opportunity to cut short 'wasteful' debate and zero in on this simple
question, thus demonstrating (to their own satisfaction) what
tough, incisive minds they have. It can be difficult to counter
this tactic, even when you intuitively sense that things are more
complicated than that. But in my opinion such arguments do
not get to the heart of the matter; rather, they avoid it. For the
question 'What's the bottom line?' nearly always begs the much
more fundamental ones: 'How many different important bottom
lines are there?' and 'Which ones do we now need to consider?'
When an issue of any complexity is involved, there will almost
always be several different ways of weighing up the vital factors
and, therefore, several different bottom lines.

In business, for example, an important decision will inevitably affect the different stakeholders in different ways. What is good for the shareholders may be bad for labor; what is good for customers may look terrible to the bankers. The bottom line that produces applause at this week's meeting of shareholders may produce a strike vote at next week's union meeting. The increased credit which wins fresh orders from customers may look rash to the bankers who control the credit line that will have to be tapped if the orders are to be met. The manager cannot afford the simple question 'What's the bottom line?'; he has the far more intricate problem of *always* figuring out how compromises between many different bottom lines will yield an overall benefit to many different stakeholders *and* to the business.

Lee Iacocca, in his autobiography,★ gives a good example of where simplified 'bottom-line' thinking leads – even at the most elevated level of management. By the mid-1970s, he suggests, motor industry executives were being offered such immense rewards for producing good quarterly profit figures, that they became preoccupied, at the expense of all else, with immediate short-term results. Their attention was, after all, being directed to one particular bottom line most forcefully. They persuaded themselves, for example, whenever they were confronted by labor unions, that the right question to ask was the short-term one, the one which, if correctly answered, would ensure next quarter's extra reward.

Iacocca admits that he was at fault along with the others: 'The executives at GM, Ford, and Chrysler have never been overly interested in long-range planning. They have been concerned about expediency, improving the profits for the next quarter – and earning a good bonus. . . . Our motivation was greed. The instinct was always to settle quickly, to go for the bottom line.'

As Iacocca's analysis suggests, one question that should be put to those who stress the importance of a single bottom line is: 'At what point in the future are we drawing the bottom line?' It does not take much imagination to see that practices delivering good results this quarter may cause bad results at the end of the

★ Lee Iacocca, *Iacocca, An Autobiography*, Bantam Books, 1984.

year and catastrophic results in three years' time. It is obvious that anyone can get quick results and mortgage the future of the business by asking a simple question like: 'How can I increase next year's profit by 30 per cent?' and then implementing the easy answers – slash R&D, reduce the advertising budget, cut back on repairs and maintenance, and so on.

But unfortunately far too many 'single-issue' executives continue to ask that sort of question and implement those sorts of answers. Frequently their 'wisdom', their 'realism' and their 'sense of urgency' win wide praise – but often, by the time the companies concerned come to pay the price of their folly, the executives will be elsewhere.

Politicians even more notoriously tend to find the lure of the short term and the quick fix irresistible. A classic example was the British prime minister, Harold Wilson. He was elected on the strength of his promises of radical reform and a program to forge a 'new Britain' in the 'white heat of the technological revolution'. But his behavior in office reflected not a determination to rebuild his country over the long term but a belief that, as he put it, 'A week is a long time in politics'. His political manoeuvring and manipulation may have seemed ingenious at the time, but can be seen in retrospect, I believe, to have only deepened the problems he had promised to solve.

Thus it turns out that the bottom line is by no means a simple concept and certainly offers no short cut to the heart of a question. Rather, it suggests a whole series of further questions: 'Whose bottom line?' 'Which bottom line?' 'When is the bottom line?' and 'How many bottom lines are there?' In business and government, as well as in private life, a rich question will take account of all the important bottom lines and will recognize the need for an answer giving due weight to each of them.

★

How should we, as individual managers, go about checking a question for richness? One technique is to backtrack and check on the question's hidden assumptions. If, for example, a client came to our company and said that he wanted to know what he must do in order to increase his firm's market share by 10 per cent over the next three years, our first priority would be to discover what assumptions underlay this apparently straightforward question.

By dragging out the unacknowledged assumptions, we first hope to find out if the question the client has asked focuses on the real problem he needs to deal with; second, we hope by this means further to enrich the question. In this hypothetical case it could be, for example, that the client's question arose because he really wants his business to grow more rapidly relative to its competitors. But it could also be that he finds his margins under pressure and has picked, rightly or wrongly, upon an increase in market share as the best way to ensure that his profits do not fall with them. If the latter is the real motive, then we will be better employed thinking about the real question, which is 'How can I maintain my profit growth?'

To illustrate the point further, let us consider another example, this time a real one that happened a few years ago. The company concerned held a dominant position in the market for certain food products, which had traditionally been packaged in glassware. The company had become aware that a new process would permit much cheaper packaging in plastic. As a consequence the company was in a position to offer its product at a lower price; this in turn would lead to a large increase in sales at the lower end of the market. The question: 'To expand our sales and profits, when should we launch some of our products in the new packaging?' seemed to be as obvious as the answer: 'As soon as possible.'

Fortunately, however, one executive stopped to ask an awkward but wise question: 'If there are any serious potential competitive risks, should we launch the new products at all?' Surprisingly, once that question had been asked it quickly became apparent that one of the implicit assumptions – i.e. that introducing new packaging would result in no new competitive threat – had been overlooked. Once that oversight was corrected, the answer to the new, and richer, question that the executive had posed was 'Clearly no'.

'How come?' one might ask. Here was what seemed like a wonderful opportunity which any company worth its salt would take. Why turn it down? The explanation was that, although it had a dominant position in its market, the company had never before competed in the market for goods in plastic packaging – overall a far larger one and one which was itself dominated by a few larger firms. To be sure, the company could steal a march on those firms and, because of its knowledge of a specialist market, enjoy success in the short run. But in the longer run the result would be that the food firms already well accustomed to using plastic packaging would realize as they so far showed no sign of doing, that they could easily create and market products priced to compete with those of the company.

Repackaging the product in the cheaper container, therefore, would spawn a very real danger that these *potential* competitors could enter a market where continuing predominance was vital to the company's survival. The decision not to create new competitors by launching the product amounted to a realization that, although you may grab a handful of honey, the consequence of sticking your hand into a bees' nest is likely to be painful. The question that was finally posed and answered was: 'Should we introduce plastic packaging into our market with its tradition of bottled packaging and run the risk of having firms larger and financially more powerful than ours follow our example, and thereby create new competition for our products?' Risk-reward considerations then dictated the answer.

Although the proposal came to nothing, it is worth emphasizing that the time spent in considering it was not wasted. For the company was able to create contingency and product development plans against the day when a major competitor might try to invade their market with a new form of packaging.

If I had to sum up the factors which lead to questions being insufficiently rich, I would say they fall into four categories, each of which results from trying to make the question 'simpler'. First, there is the mistaken idea that all questions are, at root, simple and that their underlying simplicity can be discovered if one reduces the number of words in which they are posed. Second, there is what I would call the 'greed factor', the belief that everything can be boiled down to one single, seductively simple dollar-and-cents bottom line. Third, there is the narrow time factor, caused by a short-term horizon, which leads people to imagine that they can win the war by coming out of the next skirmish on top. Finally, there are the facile assumptions, which can all too easily be taken for granted because they seem so obvious, but which can alter the question dramatically once they are spelled out.

A manager must check any important question on each of these four counts before accepting it as the basis for further thinking by himself or his organization. It is not difficult to avoid the traps of over-simplification, once you are aware of their existence, but it is all too easy to tumble into any of them if you are not aware of them or if you ignore them.

*

In most cases the first stage of decision-thinking is essentially concerned with checking and, where necessary, expanding and enriching a question which, in its original and most primitive form, was too loosely framed. Sometimes, however, the best solution to a problem comes not from question enrichment, but from a complete reformulation. Often such cases depend upon the kind of insight or the change of perspective which is achieved by 'lateral thinking'. The reformulation of the question may be far-reaching in its implications, even though the change is very simple.

For example, the wasteful flaring of unwanted natural gas by oil companies ended when, instead of asking 'How can we get rid of this stuff?', they saw that the gas was a valuable energy resource and asked 'How can we *use* this stuff?'

A rather more complicated example is provided by the planning of the Apollo moon missions. In its most straightforward form – how could a spaceship large enough to carry a human cargo be launched from the surface of the earth, make a soft landing on the moon and then be re-launched back to make a safe landing on earth? – the question posed to the engineers seemed impossible to resolve. But when the problem was re-defined and the engineers were asked to design a lunar module which could be launched from a spacecraft in orbit around the moon, make a soft landing and return to dock with the orbiting craft, it became possible to find the solution.

Another technique of lateral thinking, turning a question upon its head, shows how changing a question can lead to a fortunate outcome. The mail order industry came into existence when a few retailers stopped asking: 'How can I get more customers to come into my store to see my goods?' and substi-tuted the reverse question: 'How can I show my goods to customers in the comfort of their homes?'

More recently the example of the computer industry has shown that, given the right combination of circumstances, the trick can still yield a bonanza for those who do not accept that because a particular question was the right one to ask yesterday, it will necessarily be the right one to ask tomorrow.

In the fifties and sixties the word 'computer' was synony-mous with what we now call a 'mainframe', that is, a gigantic, centralized appliance capable of serving the needs of dozens, even hundreds, of users simultaneously. The marketing strategy of the computer industry was based upon the belief that com-puter hardware would always be expensive, and that there was, therefore, little prospect that small- or medium-sized businesses could acquire their own machines. The obvious way to grow was to build bigger, better and faster machines and to equip them to do a wider and wider range of tasks; that way, profits would come from the sale of a few, expensive, machines.

This idea, that the future lay with ever bigger machines capable of servicing the needs of more and more users simul-taneously, was so entrenched in the industry that when the silicon chip emerged in the 1960s and the cost of hardware began to fall dramatically, none of the existing companies stopped to ask the question that then needed to be asked: 'Should we, instead of making only big computers for many users, also make small computers, designed for just one user?' It was left to a couple of young men, working out of a garage, to ask that question. In answer, they founded a corporation called Apple.

By its very nature the sort of lateral, original thinking which allows one to see how a question can be put in a new way to produce a new answer is hard to define and difficult to teach. The key notion, I think, is to remove logical restraints surrounding the problem. We do not always arrive at the right question by keeping strictly to the logical paths that lead from A to B to C to D. Often it is useful, mentally, to toss all the elements of a problem into the air, as it were, in order to see into what sort of a pattern they might fall when orderly boundaries are removed.

To do this it is necessary to relax, to get out of our mind's way and leave it free to play with the elements of a problem. I shall be coming back, in chapter 16, to the question of how that playfulness can be productively encouraged and channeled.

Gathering and Distributing Information

Once the manager is satisfied with the question and the way in which it has been formulated, the next step before moving on to Stage 2 is to gather and distribute information relating to the question. Whether we are looking for one good answer or for twenty answers to test against each other, it would be, to say the least, imprudent to start searching until we are confident that the information we will require is available and understood.

Some questions require the accumulation and classification of large amounts of raw data. Before deciding, for example, whether to mount a takeover bid or to embark upon a merger, any corporation will want to review and analyze the facts and figures relating to the other company. The possibility of moving into a new market, either by extending a product range or by widening the distribution of an existing one, similarly is something to be determined only on the basis of good research.

In such cases the kind of information that is needed and the sources from which it can be secured are likely to be obvious. However, the actual process of information-gathering, as with all decision-thinking efforts, must be controlled and managed with care and judgment.

At this point two distinct hazards confront the manager. On the one hand, it is fatally easy to gather enough information to indicate that an urgent problem exists and then rush ahead without pausing to obtain the data that are vital if it is to be solved in the right way. But even more dangerous – in part because it is so attractive – is the temptation to prolong the research phase indefinitely.

The dangers are obvious: circumstances, and other people, will not wait for ever. The attractions are equally apparent. It is difficult to quarrel with someone who suggests that the accumulation of more information will result in a better decision. It is such a sensible, persuasive argument – but, if deployed with skill and subtlety, it can delay a decision almost endlessly. Bureaucracies well know that delay is one of the most effective forms of denial.

The crucial skill, if the aim is actually to make a decision rather than to delay it indefinitely, is to match the time allowed for gathering information to the time available for making a decision. Time there will always be, even if it is no more than ten minutes; and it must be used, if only to make one phone call to check one fact. But there is seldom enough time to find every fact that might be relevant. It is the job of the manager to ensure that whatever time is available is not wasted; he must decide which information is necessary and which, however desirable, he will have to forego.

★

When a decision is primarily concerned with the internal affairs of an organization rather than its relationship to the outside world, most of the needed information is readily available. The manager's task will be not to accumulate information, but rather to assemble the people who have the relevant information and experience and to make sure that each contributes to the decision-thinking process. The manager's major pitfall here will be omitting from his councils some person or department with important knowledge.

If, for example, a question has legal implications, it will be better to have a lawyer, the right lawyer with the right expertise, on the thinking team from the outset, rather than asking for a legal opinion when the matter is all but decided. The same consideration applies to any other professional or departmental inputs which may be useful. Involving people who have specialist information and experience at their fingertips in this way not only helps ensure that the information will be there, on tap, when it is needed; it also helps make certain that others, in their own deliberations, will take that information into account. Thus, it is as vital for the manager to distribute relevant information to those who will need it in the course of their thinking as it is to organize the collection of information in the first place.

This point was brought home to me recently by a lawyer friend who pointed out the inefficiency of the system many large companies adopt when seeking outside advice on a problem. As he put it, 'Those inside the company retain a near monopoly of the *facts*, and the external advisers a near monopoly of the *expertise*.' The result of such an arrangement is that the expertise is applied only to those facts which non-experts feel to be relevant. This can be a serious source of trouble because, in many instances, the expert's true value lies in his ability to recognize the relevance of facts which, to others, seem insignificant.

It is both unintelligent and wasteful to ask people to think about a problem and, at the same time, to withhold information that may be relevant to a solution. Yet, this temptation is always present in any organization, and it is one managers frequently succumb to, not because of any real need to preserve secrecy, but because knowledge represents hierarchical power and 'the fortress' must be protected.

In Part II, I will explore how the manager should cope with the mentally destructive forces of internal politics. At this stage I simply want to make the point that a manager who will not share information with his colleagues demonstrates that he lacks confidence either in them or in himself. In neither case will the results be beneficial. Few things are more discouraging than to produce what seems, on the basis of the available facts, to be a worthwhile suggestion, only to be told that some hitherto unrevealed factor makes a nonsense of the idea. If an organization expects people to think seriously about their problems, then it has to be prepared to be frank and open with them.

The task of gathering and distributing information, then, is one in which classic management skills must be used. Judgment must be exercised to determine what information should be gathered and how much time can be spared for the task; control must be exercised to ensure that the available time is well used and that information-gathering does not continue too long or, worse, become an end in itself.

The initial phase of gathering and distributing information is a vital bridge between Stage 1 and Stage 2. But that does not mean that further information may not have to be sought as the thinking progresses.

For example, a new alternative solution emerging during Stage 2, may well necessitate further fact-gathering. This additional inquiry might take the form, for instance, of adding people with unusual expertise to the thinking team or, more simply, going to the computer records to check some facts. The essential point here is that no one, least of all the manager, should assume at any point that *all* the necessary information has been accumulated. Facts which seemed irrelevant at first may well become critical as Stage 2 or Stage 3 progress, at which time the process must revert, temporarily, to Stage 1, so that more information can be assembled and distributed.

There is one further category of 'information' which plays a large part in all three subsequent stages – the 'facts' that are not really facts at all, the 'facts' that we often rely upon without even being aware that we are doing so. It is inevitable that when we consider some aspect of the future that is of particular interest to us – and decision-thinking is, by definition, always concerned with the future – we will make use of a whole range of assumptions about the wider world, many of which may seem so obvious that we simply take them as read.

In some cases we are justified in doing so; there would, for example, be little point in prefacing every business plan with the statement that it was based on the assumption that a third world war would not break out within the next five years. But there are also many such assumptions which, while being widely shared, may nevertheless be highly questionable.

Before concluding that Stage 1 has been completed, therefore, the manager should always review all the factors that might be relevant to the question and ask himself if there are any which have too easily been taken for granted. All too often, *after* a crisis has arisen or a plan has misfired, one hears laments beginning with: 'It had never crossed our minds that . . .' or 'We never imagined that . . .' or 'I guess we simply assumed that . . .'. If you do not want to find yourself in this sort of situation, then you must make a deliberate and careful effort to sort through the mental baggage which you and your colleagues have brought to the thinking effort and make sure that all the relevant assumptions have been *explicitly* examined and understood.

If you doubt the necessity for this sort of exercise, you do not have to go very far back in history to remind yourself what can happen if it is neglected. Remember the 1950s, when it was an accepted 'fact' of business life that Japanese goods would always be inferior copies of Western products? Remember the 1960s, when it was a 'fact' that oil prices would always be low? Remember the late 1970s and early 1980s, when it was a 'fact' that oil prices would always be high? Remember when the personal computer was such a crazy idea that none of the big electronics companies was even interested in it?

I am not saying that we can necessarily foresee which of today's 'facts' will be shown to be illusory tomorrow. What I am suggesting is that any scenario of the future will always incorporate a wide range of assumptions and those assumptions should not remain unprobed. The future has always got plenty of unexpected cards up its sleeve. There is nothing we can do about that. But the assumptions we make about the future are cards that we hold in our own hands: we should make sure we put them on the table before we start or we ask others to start thinking about the remaining three stages of the decision-thinking process.

★

In conclusion, it is worth re-emphasizing that the four stages of the decision-thinking process should be regarded not as a rigid sequence but as a *cycle* which may have to be repeated several times. Just because you feel ready to move on to Stage 2 and beyond, you should not choke off further thinking about the question formulated in Stage 1. You need to keep your mind open to the possibility that the question will have to be reconsidered, refined or even completely recast. It is obviously wasteful and damaging to take the first step of your journey in the wrong direction, but it is hardly wise to continue in that direction after a mistake has been discovered.

Obstinacy is, however, a widespread human weakness, and organizations as well as individuals are often reluctant to admit that they have been thinking about the wrong question. Once a group of people have committed themselves to the task of answering one question, it can be very difficult for them to stop, stand back and recognize that they must start on the problem afresh.

Indeed, it may be very much easier for the individual, doing his decision-thinking alone and unaided, to cope with this difficulty. For he can change the question, or admit that it needs to be reconsidered, without any risk of public embarrassment or a sense that he has been wasting other people's time. To adopt a 'back to Stage 1' strategy in an organizational context, on the other hand, once the process has moved on to Stage 2 or Stage 3, may require considerable courage; and to implement it the manager will have to show great determination.

We must also face the fact that the further the decision-thinking process has gone, the more difficult it is likely to be for the manager, or anyone else, to see that the wrong question has been asked. For once alternative courses of action have been projected and the consequences have been explored in detail, it becomes difficult for those involved to stand back and again re-examine the whole issue. People will have become absorbed in the minutiae: the pros and cons of one particular alternative, a set of contingencies that have been identified, the facts or statistics which have been accumulated. They will, in other words, have become committed, whether they are aware of it or not, to answering one particular question. Yet it is always possible that the real effect of their thinking has been to invalidate the original question or to reveal it as inadequate.

In managing our own mind or that of an organization we need to be on the alert for just this danger. It is as wasteful for managers to be thinking about the wrong question as it is for the workforce to be making an unsaleable product – in both cases resources are being misused and money is being wasted. In both cases, too, management has only itself to blame. It is as much a part of the professional manager's duty to ensure that the right questions are being asked of his organization, as it is to ensure that the right goods are coming off the production line.

Summary

It is a manager's first thinking responsibility to make certain that his organization is asking and seeking to answer the right questions.

If you ask the wrong question, or the right question in an incomplete way, you will inevitably arrive at the wrong answer and therefore the wrong plan for action.

Wherever possible, do not wait for questions to come to you demanding an answer; instead seek out the questions that you should be asking of yourself and your organization.

When considering a complex issue, remember there will always be many 'bottom lines' that have to be calculated.

To ensure that the richness of the question matches the complexity of the issue, check that:

you have not oversimplified;

the 'greed factor' has not led you to concentrate on just one bottom line;

short-term priorities have not obscured or created medium- and long-term problems;

assumptions are spelled out, not left implicit;

you are not trapped into looking at a problem from only one perspective before formulating a question – give lateral thinking a chance.

In decision-thinking, creating the best question in Stage 1 is as creative an act as creating the best alternatives in Stage 2.

Never be afraid to go back to reconsider and, if need be, to reformulate the question.

★

Always have a healthy respect for factual information and the information derived from other people's experience. But never let the gathering of such information become an end in itself.

Balance the time allowed for gathering information to the time available for the entire decision-thinking process.

Remember that gathering together the right people is often as important as collecting the right information.

The expertise and experience in people's heads can be more valuable than facts on paper.

Information that has been gathered will be useless, unless it is distributed, in advance, to those who need it to think with.

5

Stage 2: Creating Alternatives and Tolerating Waste

The understanding that underlies the right decision grows out of the clash and conflict of divergent opinions and out of the serious consideration of competing alternatives.

Peter Drucker

According to Charles Darwin's own account, the first glimmerings of the idea that was to develop into the theory of evolution came to him while reading Malthus's essay on population, when he suddenly saw how a mechanism such as natural selection would make sense of what was otherwise senseless – nature's vast prodigality. Only if a struggle for survival between individuals in each generation somehow advanced the interests of the species as a whole could there be any logic in a system which over-produced on such a universal and apparently wasteful scale. Darwin's contemporaries, who had grown up with a picture of nature as the creation of a divinity whose plans for the world were orderly and reasonable, found it hard to switch to the idea that life was governed by forces which relied for their effectiveness upon continual, colossal waste.

In very much the same way, and for rather similar reasons, managers frequently find it difficult to come to terms with the fact that waste is an indispensable element in decision-thinking. Most managers, after all, cherish efficiency and economy as cardinal virtues, and the suggestion that they should deliberately set about creating waste is bound to be startling, if not offensive, to them. But the fact is that the success of an organization, no less than that of a species, depends crucially upon its capacity to create and exploit waste. The difference is, of course, that in the case of an organization it is ideas which must be overproduced and then eliminated, one by one, until only the fittest survive.

Before ideas can be subjected to the testing process of debate which will eliminate the weak and the unworkable – the function of the third and fourth stages of decision-thinking – they must *first* be created in the necessary profusion and variety. For just as natural selection can only be effective as an agent of evolution if it has a large surplus population upon which to operate, so decision-thinking will only be effective if, at Stage 2, as many feasible answers as possible are created in response to the question framed in Stage 1.

Managers who are responsible for organizing and orchestrating their organizations' decision-thinking efforts must, therefore, not just tolerate but positively encourage the 'wasteful' creation of surplus answers, even though they are aware that only one of them, however modified, will ultimately be adopted.

★

I have begun by stressing the importance of waste not only because it is one of the two most vital factors in the second stage of the decision-thinking process, but also because it is, in my experience, the one most managers find hardest to accept. The second factor is the need for the manager not just to tolerate, but to create this indispensable kind of waste by stimulating and encouraging the thinking efforts of his colleagues and advisers to produce as many practicable answers to the question posed in Stage 1 as imagination, ingenuity and inspiration can contrive.

Thus tolerance of waste and the ability to persuade people

to create their best thoughts are the two key management requirements for successful performance at Stage 2 of our decision-thinking process.

★

It is not surprising that many managers and leaders find Stage 2 to be one of the two most difficult and unnatural phases of decision-thinking – the other, as we shall see in the next chapter, being Stage 3. All their training and instincts suggest that they should concentrate on finding the one right answer and not waste time dreaming of other, alternative answers. For the person who feels comfortable only when moving forward with a clear goal in mind, the business of letting one's thinking or that of one's colleagues drift in an apparently vague and undisciplined fashion can be distinctly disturbing. Yet it is essential to accept that ideas – possible, probable and, yes, even remotely conceivable answers to the question created in Stage 1 – must be over-produced at this stage. The more alternatives that are generated and the greater their variety, the more chance there is of finding one that will be appropriate.

'Robert McNamara taught me never to make a major decision without having a choice of at least vanilla or chocolate. And if more than a hundred million dollars were at stake, it was a good idea to have strawberry too.' Thus, in a couple of sentences, Lee Iacocca sets out the crux of the matter. But producing choices is a far more demanding task than Iacocca's statement would suggest; and the time and skill needed to generate them must be invested, even when the stakes are lower than 100 million dollars.

The keynote of Stage 2, then, is choice – and the necessary waste of time, thought and effort which inevitably goes with it.

To every complex question about possible courses of future action there are likely to be a wide variety of answers, none of which can be judged on the basis of the available information to be clearly right or wrong. What is being sought is not some final, definitive answer which is flawless and foolproof; such solutions are seldom available in the world of practical decision-thinking. The aim must be to generate the widest range of possible answers, each of which will have its own particular advantages and drawbacks. Once that has been done, the field can be narrowed down to find the answer that has the most advantages and the fewest drawbacks – the answer that will prove to be less imperfect than all the other answers proposed.

In the quest for the most effective answer the professional manager must see to it that everyone gives their best. Above all, diversity and variety of opinion, rather than consensus, must be encouraged. There is always a dangerous tendency for opinions to converge on what seems to be an obvious answer, acceptable to all and painful to none. This has to be resisted, for such answers, if accepted too quickly or too readily, almost automatically preclude the discovery of the most elusive, yet often the most valuable kind of answer – that which is unorthodox, original and, yes, most effective.

★

As Peter Drucker points out in the quotation cited at the beginning of this chapter, real debate between people with conflicting views is not just unavoidable, it is absolutely essential. The best answers are unlikely to be the ones that raise the fewest objections; on the contrary, the chances are that they will be those that arouse the most controversy.

Anyone who embarks on Stage 2 requiring that all discussions and meetings will be cool, calm and rational, and that no one will be allowed to let his feelings to become involved, is, in effect, foredooming it to failure. The manager's task at this stage is not to smooth over divergencies of opinion or to find acceptable compromises between opposing views. Nor is the aim to find one answer which no one really dislikes – even if no one really likes it very much either – but rather to find a whole range of answers each of which will, if they are good ones, attract passionate support and, perhaps, equally strong opposition.

The idea, after all, is not just to find answers that look good on the surface, but to probe them for possible weaknesses and to establish that they have staying power. The answers, in other words, should be tested, if necessary to destruction. It is one of the most difficult tasks of the manager to make sure that this happens without egos becoming bruised or anyone being left with the feeling that he has not had a fair hearing.

Another, less obvious, danger is that if and when some innovative and attractive proposal does emerge, everyone will become so excited by it that they will cease to search in their minds for other possibilities or for ways in which the proposal might be improved and refined. I witnessed a good example of this just a few months ago.

Together with some friends, I had been informally advising a restaurateur who had built up a highly successful business in London and was seeking to expand his operations by attacking the American market. After a good deal of discussion of the financial and management issues that would arise, someone proposed that the best solution might be to offer franchises.

The proposal, once made, seemed so attractive that most of the group were eager to rush ahead without further debate and became very impatient with those of us who hesitated. Since the restaurateur himself was among the most enthusiastic, the decision finally went in favor of going ahead without delay.

Those of us who were opposed remained convinced that, although the franchising idea might be the right one, there would have been little to be lost and much to be gained if everyone had paused a little longer to think about when and how it should be implemented. For although the London side of the business had grown rapidly, it had not yet reached the point at which its fame had spread across the Atlantic; initially at least, it would be necessary to offer very advantageous terms to would be franchisees in the States. A year's delay, during which time the name and reputation of the restaurant could be further built up and plans for the American launch carefully laid, would, we felt, be a small price to pay for the gains that might be expected in terms of a better deal for the franchisor and a more concerted and more carefully considered assault on one of the toughest restaurant markets in the world.

Only time will tell whether or not we were right. But the way in which a good idea, once articulated, grabbed a leader's imagination and virtually suppressed further thinking was a classic illustration of that dangerous urge, felt by far too many managers, to switch off the collective thinking effort as soon as an attractive idea offers itself. Most people (including managers) prefer to be perceived as brilliant; it is the manager's job to insist that it is necessary to be thorough and methodical as well.

Getting too excited too soon is, however, a secondary problem in that it only arises if at least one good answer to the question is found. It is certainly one which all managers should be aware of and should guard against, but *the* major problem of Stage 2, once the concept of waste has been accepted, is to ensure that those good answers are forthcoming.

★

There is a certain amount of mystery about the way in which our minds work at Stage 2 of the decision-thinking process. How do we create alternatives? Where do the ideas come from? These are questions I shall return to in Part II. But let us now at least dispose of one rather hoary idea, the notion that all such thinking must be either analytical *or* imaginative.

Analytical thinkers are generally supposed to operate by breaking a problem down into its component parts and reasoning their way through to the answer. Imaginative thinkers, on the other hand, are believed to conjure new ideas out of some mysterious region of their mind called 'the imagination'. In my opinion this distinction is both false and misleading. Without imagination we would not have much that was worthy of analysis; without our analytical powers our imaginations would leap to wild and reckless conclusions.

Nor is it the case that some people are wholly analytical and others wholly imaginative; most of us have some share of both faculties, and it is the cross-fertilization of the two that will prove most fruitful. Thus we can see the creative writer being logical in words and the analytical engineer imaginative in drawings. A combination of both types of thinking is needed in the creation of any practical alternative.

It may well be, for example, that a company might generate some alternative answers to a particular question by analyzing what its competitors are doing, or by looking at the strategies that have been adopted by similar businesses facing similar problems in other countries. Indeed, such an analysis ought to be an automatic and routine response whenever a major matter of strategy is at issue. There is never anything to be lost by looking at what the competition is up to; more often than not, the exercise will both provide ideas and stimulate new thinking.

But analytic thinking of this kind will only realize its full potential if it is harnessed to the imagination, so that both work together. The genuinely original and exciting idea is far more likely to be a product of some fusion of the two, than the result of either working in isolation.

The subject of creativity and the roles of both imagination and rational analysis bring me back to the metaphor with which I began the chapter. It is fair to say that the real breakthroughs in decision-thinking often arise out of creative, even wild thinking, just as the progress of evolution has depended upon mutations.

The biologist Richard Goldschmidt has, indeed, suggested that the really dramatic evolutionary developments must have started with the birth of what he calls 'hopeful monsters', creatures which differed drastically from their parents but were 'hopeful' because, fortuitously, they were equipped for survival. All my experience suggests that the organization which hopes to cope with intractable problems or to leapfrog into the future ahead of its competitors must foster the creation of strange or radical ideas – ideas which, though they may indeed seem monstrous, and therefore distasteful to those whose minds run along orthodox ruts, are also 'hopeful'.

For every 'hopeful monster' that emerges, there will nevertheless be a score of hopeless ones – the price to be paid for finding one brilliant idea is the need to tolerate ten or more that turn out to be futile. And the professional manager must not just learn to tolerate those wasted ideas; it is his responsibility to see to it that his people produce them. Managing the second stage of decision-thinking is in a way like running a gold mine: you are paying people to bring vast quantities of dross to the surface, all for the sake of the small percentage of ore which it may contain.

This process can tax even the best manager's resources of tact and patience, but the investment must be made. Not merely for the sake of the present task but for the future as well. Most participants in a decision-thinking effort can learn to live with their ideas being considered and rejected in favor of others', provided that the person in charge handles those ideas with care and consideration. But the individual whose thinking is treated with contempt or indifference because, this time, it is too wild or extravagant – 'Don't be absurd!', 'What rubbish!', 'How dumb can you get?' – will quickly come to the conclusion that, next time, there is no point in making the effort to be imaginative.

I try to put this point over to our clients by reminding them that they need – year in, year out – the very best ideas that their colleagues and subordinates can produce. They may think that those ideas, the bad ones as well as the good ones, are their property, to treat as they like. They have, after all, paid for them. But to the person who gives birth to it, an idea is not something to be treated carelessly or cruelly – even if it seems to deserve it. It is, literally, that person's brainchild. And if a manager wants to ensure that people continue to produce brainchildren and to offer them to the organization, he will have to treat those ideas and those who produce them with some of the gentleness and respect he would show to a real child.

Managers, then, must learn to hold their fire when tempted to shoot down the flights of fancy launched by imaginative thinkers. But, the manager who wants to ensure that his organization will produce a steady flow of original and creative thinking must also seek ways of encouraging the more reluctant and conservative members of his organization to leave the ground and take to 'blue-skying' and lateral thinking.

Often those whose thinking remains earthbound are suffering from nothing more complicated than a fear that to give voice to their ideas will be to expose themselves to criticism or ridicule. For, to be frank about it, the attractions of sitting quietly through a meeting and keeping one's head down can weigh heavily when set against the risks of speaking up and, perhaps, being forced to defend one's ideas against the attacks of colleagues or the boss.

Furthermore, in any large organization people will feel that their primary concern should be their own survival, and that this will best be guaranteed by gaining a reputation for soundness and orthodoxy. 'If,' a person may well ask himself, 'I can keep my job, and be reasonably confident of regular promotions in the course of time by running my department competently and establishing a reputation as a safe and loyal fellow, why should I stick my neck out and give the boss the benefit of my real opinions about the way the organization should be heading? If he disagrees with me, I will have put a question mark against my next promotion; if he agrees with me, then the chances are that he will make sure that he gets the lion's share of the credit and my contribution will be quickly forgotten. Why should I put myself in a can't win situation?'

Any organization in which people come to believe that innovative thinking is a thankless or, what is worse, a dangerous task is in serious trouble. And any manager who senses that his subordinates are starting to think that way should take a long hard look at the way he manages the entire decision-thinking process. Otherwise his thinking team will quickly disintegrate into little more than a group of fence-sitters and second-guessing Monday-morning quarterbacks.

The people around the conference table will defer to his experience and judgment, but, if things start to go wrong, they will soon be telling each other (and any one else they can get to listen) that the mistakes need never have happened, if only the boss had been willing to listen to their opinions. And they will be right to blame their boss, not because he is in reality overbearing or indifferent to other views, but because he has not faced up to his most fundamental responsibility –

to get the very best thinking out of those who work for him.

In Stage 2, the professional manager's aim must be to create an atmosphere in which people feel positively encouraged to think out loud, and in which the thoughts they express are welcomed, respected and taken seriously, even if some of them are badly articulated, half-formed or even half-baked. Such thoughts may, ultimately, be rejected – with, if my advice is followed, care and courtesy. But even if that rejection turns out to have been a misjudgment, it will be much better in the long term that people should say 'I told you so' rather than 'I could have told you so, but I saw too many risks ahead if I opened my mouth.'

★

Thus, from the point of view of the person who puts it forward, any new idea, especially one that seems far-fetched or outlandish, will *always* involve an element of risk – the risk that it will be laughed out of court; the risk that, upon further consideration, it will turn out to be impractical; the risk that, by trespassing upon someone else's corporate territory, the proposer will be making enemies for himself; even the risk that it will be adopted and fail, leaving its creator open, ultimately, to attack and blame.

It follows, then, that in any organization there will always be a strong incentive for people to stick to the safe ways of orthodoxy and, even if they privately disagree, to go along with the majority opinion. People at the top, who are generally forceful personalities, used to expressing their opinions strongly and having them listened to respectfully, can easily forget that it may take considerable courage for others down the line to make what, at first, may seem an incomplete proposal or to give voice to a heretical idea.

As always it is the manager's role to get the best out of colleagues by the exercise of leadership, tact and skill. The natural reaction, when presented with a piece of thinking which is incomplete, unoriginal or second hand, is either to file and forget it or reject it as unwanted rubbish. In neither case will the individual concerned be encouraged or stimulated to do better or try harder. But, put in the right way to suit each individual case, the message that 'This is not quite good enough, please try again' will generate further and more valuable ideas.

No one, and certainly not the manager, should ever delude himself into believing that decision-thinking is not hard work. People who put a premium on action, and who find thinking tedious and unexciting, often excuse their attitude by arguing that thinking is a pretty soft option. But thinking – pushing yourself to pursue an idea to its logical conclusion, however unpleasant, urging your imagination to 'give, give and give again', looking for the hidden flaws in an argument – is hard work, damned hard work, and anyone who thinks differently has never really thought at all.

Thinking, like most hard work, is something that people will only do willingly, even eagerly and enthusiastically, if they understand why they are doing it, get a kick out of doing it well and are confident of being fairly rewarded for their efforts. The trick of fostering the sort of team spirit that leads to really inspired thinking is not easily defined; some managers do it almost instinctively, others find it extremely difficult.

Although, on the face of it, the tasks of persuading others to think creatively and of managing one's own creativity may seem very different, I think that there are several basic similarities. In both cases it must be accepted that once a mind – be it your own individual mind or the collective mind of your organization – has been directed to find the solution of a particular question, it must be allowed free rein. There must be no prior censorship, no thoughts that are declared in advance 'unthinkable'.

The creative imagination of a human being is an utterly indiscriminate, totally amoral mechanism. Left to itself it will churn out ideas in undifferentiated profusion – the brilliant along with the banal, the silly along with the subtle, the outrageous along with the orthodox.

If you try *in advance* to tell yourself or others that some thoughts are permissible while others are prohibited, you will not succeed in concentrating thought upon the valid ideas and eliminating the unwanted ones; you will simply cut off the flow of ideas altogether.

When dealing with other people's ideas you can normally rely upon the people concerned to operate some sort of preliminary sorting procedure which will eliminate the real dross; but when the choice is between having too many ideas on the table and too few, you have, obviously, to opt for the former. It is comparatively easy to eliminate the suggestion that turns out to be useless, and with a little extra care no offence need be given. But the idea that is withheld because it seems to its parent too peculiar, sensitive or delicate a brainchild to be exposed to possible ridicule is lost for ever.

★

There is, of course, no single prescription for creating alternative answers in the necessary quantity and variety; no one organizational structure or managerial policy which will ensure a steady supply of inventive thinking. There are, however, three rules which can help us to create an atmosphere in which such thinking will flourish. (How these rules should be consciously applied by professional managers will be explained in Part II.)

The *first* rule is to be, or stay, young. It is almost axiomatic that organizations which are themselves relatively new are also likely to be good at producing new ideas. Anyone who has had the good fortune to work for a successful company during that initial phase, when everything and anything seemed to be possible, will probably remember the excitement of working in an informal, urgent, positive atmosphere and the way in which, under such circumstances, sparks sometimes seemed to be struck from even the dullest minds.

If they have stayed on with the company into its maturity, these same people will probably have become aware that somewhere, somehow, the fun has gone out of the business; that there is no longer the same sense of adventure or the *esprit de corps* which went with it. It is probably impossible to pin down one single cause for this change – it goes along with a hardening of the corporate arteries, a solidifying of management hierarchies, a formalizing of communications between and within departments.

It is not easy to restore the lost youth of an organization, and with it the natural exuberance of the thinking which it displayed during its adolescence. But even if we cannot easily make our businesses and institutions young again, we can at least protect their thinking from the more obvious problems of middle age and senility.

Chief among these, and this applies as much to people as to organizations, are the complacency and arrogance which success tends to encourage. All too frequently a company, which owes its present success to good thinking in the past, allows itself to be lulled into the assumption that it no longer needs to think, because it knows all the answers.

Time and again we have all seen companies, governments and individuals suffer because of this kind of overconfidence. It usually takes the form of what might be called corporate conservatism, a belief that things should be done now and in the future as they were in the past; that change is to be feared and discouraged; and, most dangerously, that every problem can be solved by reference to precedents in the past.

Businesses which have fallen into the trap of this complacent conservatism may continue to prosper for some time; but when the end comes, it often comes quickly and dramatically. Faced with the need to react to new circumstances or to meet an unlooked-for crisis, the company simply falls apart, for the façade of success conceals a corporate mind which has become fossilized and inflexible. Fossilization can only be prevented, even if sometimes at the cost of broken bones, by deliberate management action to encourage and reward imagination and inspired mental risk-taking. If necessary, new thinking will need to be injected into the organization to revitalize it. For while it is inevitable that individuals grow old, organizations need not grow old with them.

The *second* rule is to resist the temptation to force the pace. It needs to be clearly recognized that the thinking talents which are required at the second stage of the decision-thinking process are not necessarily those which come most naturally to a manager or a leader. The 'decisive' person who is likely to excel at the final stage, when choices have to be made and decisions have to be taken, may, as I have said, have little patience or talent for the sort of speculative thinking which produces a fruitful range of alternatives. But, if he wants to excel, he cannot afford to short-circuit the process or be intolerant or impatient with those who do excel at it.

However wasteful and, on occasion, pointless the thinking that takes place at Stage 2 may seem, it has to be remembered that it is here, and only here, that the *raw material* is produced for Stage 4. An answer which has been overlooked or too quickly dismissed at Stage 2 is simply not available to the manager who must take the ultimate decision at Stage 4. In the last resort the outcome of the whole process can only be as good as the alternatives generated at Stage 2.

The *third* rule is that debate must be encouraged rather than avoided. It is critical for the manager to realize that it is the dynamic process of debate itself which will often generate new answers or result in a form of mental crossbreeding which combines elements of several different alternative answers. There is a chemistry which works when people think together, even if they seem at times to be at one another's throats or to be each pursuing his own hobby horse. Weaknesses and potential problems are exposed more rapidly and more clearly when ideas are put on the table even in the formative stage. And it also sometimes happens that the strength of an alternative which one person proffers only tentatively will be more immediately obvious to someone else.

Stage 2 thinking, therefore, must, to be fully creative, also take the form of a debate in which people strike sparks off one another. It is often surprising how the very best idea comes as a surprise even to its creator.

One of my favorite anecdotes concerns the writer V. S. Pritchett, who once observed to a friend of mine, when asked why he wrote, 'I write to find out what I think.' Those of us who lack Pritchett's disposition to write may find that we discover our best and most useful thoughts when we get them 'outside' ourselves and debate them verbally with others.

★

I will have more to say in Chapter 15 about the way in which open debates and thinking meetings of all kinds should be managed. But obviously, as already indicated, the going should never be allowed to become so rough that the more sensitive participants withdraw into their shells. The thoughtful and the reticent must be encouraged to speak out. The fence-sitters must be pushed off their fences. And the naturally bumptious and abrasive must be controlled.

Let me stress again, in conclusion, that the commonest cause of failure on the part of otherwise effective managers is that they are neither patient nor stimulating enough at the second stage of the decision-thinking process. The very qualities which help them in other respects – drive, efficiency, single-mindedness – work against them here. Successful managers often have to be able, in effect, to change gears – even personalities – at Stage 2 in order to tolerate wasted thoughts, so that the imaginative and speculative thinking efforts of their organization can flourish.

It is all the more important, therefore, that all of us – both as managers and as individuals – should be on our guard against impatience and intolerance at this stage. We should remember, above all, the following rule: apparent waste in the form of too many alternatives is not just unavoidable, it is essential. Somewhere among the wildest ideas and the silliest suggestions there may lurk a 'hopeful monster', a valid solution which came out of the blue with all the marks of real inspiration, or a half-formed idea which will, after debate, spark off an alternative answer that proves to be the most effective one.

If we are to make the best decision, we must be able to choose. And we can only choose if we are presented with a fertile range of alternative answers to our question – most of which are going to have to be, as in Darwin's perception, rejected. Thus we need to ensure that more alternatives are created than we will ultimately use. Such is the prodigal, but unavoidable, arithmetic of Stage 2 of our decision-thinking process.

Summary

Alternatives are the raw material of decisions.

Waste in decision-thinking is inevitable. To make a wise decision at Stage 4, more alternatives have to be created at Stage 2 than will be used. Alternatives that are never created can represent decision opportunities that are never seized.

Insufficient patience, courtesy and tolerance at Stage 2 are serious management failings.

People need to be highly motivated to create and be willing to put forward their ideas – their brainchildren – no matter how wild or unorthodox. This is a fundamental thinking responsibility of management.

Creating and defending alternative ideas which may ultimately be rejected is not worth the personal risk for their authors *unless* the manager makes it so. Never put your decision-thinkers in a 'can't win' situation.

There will always be a tendency for people within an organization to favor orthodox ideas or to seek consensus too quickly; these stifling forces must be firmly and continually resisted.

It is also wrong to force the pace; good alternatives can only emerge where diversity of thought, free debate, a lot of thinking out loud and lateral thinking are *all* encouraged.

Individuals who are best at deciding are not always the best at creating alternative solutions, and vice versa. In decision-thinking, deciders and innovators are often dependent on each other.

6

Stage 3: Predicting the Future Consequences and Planning for Contingencies

Gouverner, c'est prévoir. (To govern is to foresee.)

Attributed to Emile de Girardin

We Americans have enormous confidence in our ability, individually and as a nation, to confront and solve problems as and when they arise. This 'can-do' attitude is a great national virtue and one, I might add, that you appreciate all the more if you have lived and worked in places where it is not generally shared.

But confidence in your capacity to cope with the problems of the present ceases to be a virtue and becomes a vice, if it blinds you to the need to try to foresee and avert the problems of the future. Unfortunately, America and we, its citizens, have been suffering during the last twenty-five years from just this thinking vice. The result is that we have been, as James Reston has observed, 'usually surprised'.

If we doubt this, then let us remind ourselves of a few examples which illustrate both our lack of foresight and the price we are now paying for allowing events to take us by surprise. If we had thought more carefully about the implications of our dependence upon Middle East oil in the 1960s, would we have adopted an energy policy which could be destroyed, almost overnight, as happened in 1973? If we had looked seriously at some of our most vital priorities in our own hemisphere, would we have tragically embroiled ourselves for almost a decade in a futile effort to resist the tide of Vietnamese nationalism? And if our industrialists and those who regulate their activities had fully considered the problems of competing with nations which pay lipservice to the ideas of free trade and ignore its spirit, would we have allowed so much of our industrial strength to have been sapped? In short, if, as a nation, we had made greater efforts to foresee the future and plan more intelligently for it, might we not have been less frequently and less unpleasantly surprised by it?

Unless we move swiftly to redress the imbalance between our proven skill at solving problems and our often lackluster record in foreseeing them, then I fear that the surprises will come upon us even faster and more furiously and will prove even more costly. Already, indeed, it is possible to foresee some of them.

Our banks, for example, extended billions of dollars of credit to the oil industry on the supposition that oil prices would remain at a high level. It would be both ironic and painful if, having allowed an oil price rise to surprise us in the 1970s, we find our financial system equally surprised by, and equally unprepared for, a dramatic and durable oil price collapse, which might last for at least another ten years.

And what is going to happen to public confidence in our banking system, if we continue to travel blindly down the naive path of 'deregulation', when the future of banking profits and, in turn, provisions are both suspect?

We are also awakening, belatedly, to the realization that a time bomb has been ticking away, almost unnoticed, on our southern border and that an explosion may now occur at any time. Mexico, with its unmanageable debts (primarily to our own banks), a population already standing at over 75 million, rising by some 2 per cent a year and suffering from ever deepening poverty is, in effect, a crisis just waiting to happen, right on our doorstep.

Unless we start thinking hard and planning how this problem can be defused, we could find ourselves mounting a new military operation to defend ourselves – along a 2000-mile, easy-to-cross, border – against a neighboring country with a strong anti-'gringo' mentality and with millions of its own citizens working, legally and illegally, in our country. If we are not careful *and* thoughtful, Mexico could become as big a problem for the US as Afghanistan has become for the Soviet Union.

The need for more foresight is also made urgent by the success of our competitors who, in some respects at least, have demonstrated an impressive capacity for foreseeing the future and a startling skill in planning what to do about it.

In the economic sphere it is obvious that Japan has consistently remained at least one thinking step ahead of the US (and her other competitors for that matter) over most of the past two decades. And while the Soviet economy, admittedly, is no monument to farsightedness, on the military and espionage front over the last forty years the Russians have certainly reaped vast strategic rewards for their foresight.

In these and other cases it seems clear that the key to success has been the ability to make predictions about the way in which the future could be made to unfold. Predictive thinking of this kind will become, if anything, even more indispensable in the years ahead.

The world becomes more complex every day and as it does, so the problems it poses become less and less susceptible to off-the-cuff solutions, simplistic bottom-line calculations and quickfire decision making. It may still just be possible for small businesses to survive, living from day to day and taking each day's problems as they come. But neither a large business nor an organization of any size (let alone the government of a superpower) can hope to flourish unless it is prepared to make a well-managed, imaginative and consistent effort to *think* its way into the future. We would be foolish if we pretended that making such predictions could ever be an exact science; we would be even more foolish if we imagined that it was not a necessary one.

Given that managers' decisions are the basis for action (or inaction), almost any decision you care to consider can be seen to involve an element of prediction. If, for example, you decide to hire someone from outside your organization to head one of its most troubled divisions, it is presumably because you have calculated that the people in that division will respond positively to the shock of an outsider taking charge – or that even if they do not, he will still be able to put things right. If you decide to sell your holdings of ten stocks and invest the proceeds in just two stocks, it is, one must assume, because you predict that a rifle-shot approach to investment is more likely to pay off than a shotgun one.

The company which decides to launch a billion-dollar takeover bid is backing a prediction about the future; so is the fellow who puts $5 on a horse to win or the economist who tells us that supply-side economics will never damage our fiscal equilibrium. The scale of their gambles may be vastly different, but they have one thing in common – in no case can success be guaranteed.

Professional decision-thinkers, unlike fortune tellers, cannot pretend that they can predict the future infallibly. Rather, what they have to aim for is the best rate of success that can be achieved with the imperfect instruments at their disposal. Knowledge of the present, experience of the past and imagination to help us predict and construct what the future might be like – these are the mental instruments which we will require in Stage 3, as we set about the task of creating pictures of the future consequences of the alternatives created in Stage 2.

★

When the curtain rises on the third stage, it finds us standing, as it were, at a crossroads, contemplating a number of alternative routes that radiate outward into the future. Each of those routes represents one of the possible answers which were created in Stage 2 in response to the question which we set ourselves in Stage 1. Each alternative route will lead through different territory and, dividing and sub-dividing as it goes, could lead to many different destinations – that is, many different versions of the future.

Rooted as we are to our position in the present, we cannot see into the future with any certainty; in the case of most of the roads, barely beyond the first bend. Nor, of course, are there reliable maps of the future to which we can refer – if such things were available we would obviously have to consider only one version of the future, the one that was going to happen.

Yet if we are to make the best decision and choose the best road, we must try to determine the answers to two sorts of questions. First, how safe is the terrain through which each route passes and what are our chances of traversing it successfully? Secondly, which of the alternative routes leads to the version of the future that is, from our point of view, the most credible and desirable?

The difficulties and complexities of trying to answer these questions are undeniable, and many managers will go to great lengths to avoid them. Some, for example, refuse even to contemplate the need for a decision, hoping that if they stand still, time will do likewise and the problem will disappear or solve itself. Others pick a road with little forethought and set out along it, boasting of their decisiveness. Yet others convince themselves that, common sense notwithstanding, it is possible to snatch a glimpse of some hidden map of the future. In the past such people turned to oracles or studied the entrails of sacrificial sheep; today they put their faith in the stars, Wall Street pundits or computer programs.

In every case such substitutes for thinking are an admission of defeat. Those who adopt them are saying, in effect, that since thinking about the future is a testing, painstaking and, ultimately, inexact business, they will not even try to find a reasonable, thoughtful basis for their decisions. Rather, they seem to believe that *reactive* thinking will save them when the time comes. Or, more cynically, they will plan to be out of office or in a different job by the time the consequences of their decisions have to be dealt with.

But when the decision we face is an important one, however tough the mental going and however imperfect the results, we are obliged, if we are to become professional decision-thinkers, to make a serious attempt to predict both the future and the consequences of our decisions in that future. Otherwise, when we come to the fourth and final stage of decision-thinking, our decision will be based on little more than guesswork.

Since we cannot foresee the one version of the future which will come about, it follows that we must try to think about all the possible versions which might be realized or which we have the power to realize. We must, in other words, explore each of the routes into the future by simulating a journey along it.

★

Richard Dawkins, in his book *The Selfish Gene*, puts the case well:

> When you yourself have a difficult decision to make involving unknown quantities in the future, you do go in for a form of simulation. You imagine what would happen if you did each of the alternatives open to you. You set up a model in your head, not of everything in the world, but of the restricted set of entities which you may think may be relevant. You may see them vividly in your mind's eye, or you may see and manipulate stylized abstractions of them. In either case it is unlikely that somewhere laid out in your brain is an actual spatial model of the events you are imagining. But, just as in the computer, the details of how your brain represents its model of the world are less important than the fact that it is able to use it to predict possible events.
>
> Survival machines which can simulate the future are one jump ahead of survival machines who can only learn on the basis of overt trial and error. The trouble with overt trial is that it takes time and energy. The trouble with overt error is that it is often fatal. Simulation is both safer and faster.★

★ Richard Dawkins, *The Selfish Gene*, Oxford University Press, 1976.

If we intend that our organizations (and indeed ourselves as individuals) are to become more effective 'survival machines', then we are going to have to become more effective in the art of simulating the future.

Simulations will only generate accurate predictions about the future if they start from realistic assumptions about the present. But that does not mean that it is safe to assume that everything that has been true of the past and remains true of the present, will necessarily hold good in the future. I stress this point because there is a strong temptation to try to short-circuit the complexities of the decision-thinking process, either by simplistically supposing that the future will repeat the past or by merely extrapolating existing trends into the future.

Trends can, of course, be significant. Many an entrepreneur, for example, who detected a financial or market trend at an early stage and rode it while it lasted has prospered. But simple extrapolation is not enough. If it were, all the chartists employed by stockbrokers and investment managers would be millionaires. Trends have an awkward habit of petering out or going into reverse, often at the very point when the slower-moving individuals and organizations have finally geared themselves up to exploit them.

There is, superficially, something solid and comforting about a simulation which simply takes past trends and extrapolates them into the future. It is, after all, based on firm factual foundations, and experience suggests that the future is often like the past. Unfortunately it is also invariably different in some significant respects. It may be that there is truth in the maxim that those who ignore history are doomed to relive it, but it is also certain that those who expect history to repeat itself are doomed to disappointment.

This is, of course, bad news for those who have become accustomed to the idea that a business forecast is best calculated by taking last year's figures and adding 5 or 10 per cent to everything – if that were indeed so, decision-thinking would be child's play. My own experience has taught me to take forecasts that begin with the words, 'On present trends we will . . .' only slightly more seriously than I would take stories that begin, 'Once upon a time . . .'.

★

As we explore the map of possible futures that we have created in Stage 2 of our decision-thinking, simulating a journey down first one route and then another, we begin to see a structure emerging. The roads – that is, the alternatives – that lead away from the present divide, sub-divide and sub-divide again, so that the further we look into the future the more variations of it we must consider. A structure of this kind is called a decision tree, and each node or junction in the structure represents either a decision which we must take or a decision which may be taken for us by circumstance.

In theory at least a decision tree can embrace all the future consequences which could flow from a single decision in the present. And it is indeed possible to design programs which will allow computers to become unbeatable at simple games like tic-tac-toe merely by looking ahead along every single branch and sub-branch of a decision tree.

But those who have tried to apply the same principles to more complex games like chess have found that, while they can certainly program a machine to achieve a high standard of play, they cannot make it infallible, for the number of different combinations of moves and counter-moves which must be considered soon grows to the point at which even the largest computer cannot cope. Once we leave the restricted and comparatively simple world of the chessboard, things get even worse, for most important decisions involve human actions and reactions. Once you inject human behavior into your calculations, then the complexities ramify beyond the scope of any conceivable computer program and we must fall back upon our own mental resources – our experience, reason, imagination and intuition.

The real-life problems with which decision-thinking is concerned (should we hire this executive? buy this company?

launch this product? resist this pay claim and let the union go
out on strike?, etc.) are almost always extremely complicated.
Rarely, to start with, does a business or a political 'game' involve
only two players. Moreover, rather than being totally logical,
the issues are often ill-defined. The moves made by competing
companies in the marketplace, for instance, cannot be described
by the sort of simple rules which govern the movement of
chessmen.

But there are some lessons which can be learned from
the theorists of game-playing and the techniques they have
developed for constructing decision trees and searching them
for solutions. The most important of these is the use of the
strategy known as 'minimaxing'. A minimax program is, essentially, a formal system for coping with the implications of
Murphy's Law, that awkward law of everyday life which states
that 'What can go wrong, will go wrong.'

A decision-thinker following the minimax rules must
assume that, while he himself will always make the move which
maximizes his own chances of winning, his opponents will
always make the moves which *minimize* those chances. Applied
to the sort of problems which a decision-thinker faces, the basic
idea can be expressed as follows: 'By all means assume that you
will always be clever, but never assume that you will be lucky;
that is, never assume that the other fellow will lack either skill
or luck. On the contrary, the only safe assumption is that if a
competitor (or fate) can put a spoke in your wheel, he will.'

It is necessary to keep this basic rule in the forefront of our
mind throughout Stage 3, especially as there seems to be an
almost universal temptation to ignore its implications. All too
frequently people are prepared to give themselves the benefit of
the doubt at some crucial point in the future by assuming that
the dice will fall in the way that is required if their nice,
neat, smooth-running simulation is to work out. A classic, if
somewhat blatant, example of the sort of thing I am talking
about recently caused serious problems for a Swiss company.

A senior executive of the firm in question had been asked
to prepare financial forecasts and a business plan for the coming
year, 1985. The figures which he eventually produced seemed

attractive and, in the general euphoria which greeted the prospect of a very good year, little attention was paid to one of the basic assumptions appearing in the middle of the plan.

For reasons that were either cynical or naive, the executive had chosen to assume that the price of gold (a crucial factor in the company's business) would average around $450 per ounce throughout 1985. No justification was offered for this cavalier prediction. At the time it was made gold stood around $350 and there were no strong reasons for expecting a substantial rise. Indeed, the executive seemed to make this prediction simply because it was the *only* way in which one aspect of his simulation – the profit forecast – upon which his entire plan depended, could be realized. It was, unfortunately for him, a fantasy. During 1985 the price of an ounce of gold actually fell below $300, the forecast profits of the Company for 1985 were never approached and the executive concerned found himself in serious trouble.

This was perhaps a rather obvious example of the dangers that arise from applying what might perversely be called 'maximax' rules. But there are plenty of cases in which the deadly little seed of optimism in a plan, though perhaps more carefully concealed, is no less insidious.

Another example of the way in which over-optimism or lack of realism in a plan can betray a management into folly was provided by the world famous travel and travelers checks group, Thomas Cook. Early in the 1970s the Thomas Cook board, having committed itself to a policy of aggressive expansion to get the business out of a loss-making situation, was presented with a plan which showed the projected growth in sales over a five-year period. The graph describing this increase rose evenly throughout the period, except for a dramatic spurt in year three.

If there had been, as there was not, any sound basis for assuming that sales would suddenly leap in this fashion, all might have been well. But the truth was that the plan only predicted the jump because it was necessary. If the spurt had not been assumed, then the plan would have shown that insufficient earnings would have been available to fund the costs of the planned expansion. Fortunately the weakness of thinking in such a plan was soon exposed and the management situation remedied. Two years later Thomas Cook, after years of making a loss, once again became a profitable enterprise.

One of the quickest ways to find out if a business takes its planning, and in turn its decision-thinking responsibilities, seriously is to examine its plans to see how management forecasts future turnover and profits. If the figures merely reflect 10-per-cent-a-year extrapolations, you know that little thinking has gone into the plan and that it is basically designed to please, at least for a while, the owners of the business or the board of directors.

If, on the other hand, as with the Thomas Cook plan, sudden, arbitrary fluctuations are required to make the numbers look right in future years, then you can be assured it is based on either half-hearted or wishful thinking. Looking into the future is a complex business, and if that complexity is not reflected in the plans, then we have to be worried about the quality of management. Sooner or later its thinking incompetence will be exposed.

All plans need therefore to be examined carefully to make sure that no wishful or political thinking distorts their conclusion. For it is in our plans that we make our most important forecasts about the future and the future consequences of our proposed actions.

★

Like most people, I find the company of optimists stimulating and enjoyable. But their natural buoyancy and willingness to look on the bright side can be a severe liability during the third stage of the decision-thinking process. The personality which often has most to contribute here is what I call 'the conscientious worrier' – the character who asks the awkward questions, looks the gift horse in the mouth and assumes that all will not, necessarily, come right on the day. So vital is the contribution that such individuals make at this stage of the decision-thinking process, that it could be called the stage of the worrier, just as Stage 2 might be called the stage of the creator.

By asking inconvenient questions – Can we really expect to get that share of the market without increasing our advertising and reducing our profits? Can we be sure that the competition will be that stupid? What would happen if X or Y came to pass? – conscientious worriers (alias devil's advocates) force us to do two things. First, they force us to check our simulation of the future to make sure that it is not turning into fantasy. Secondly, they ensure that we have, at a minimum, considered those risks which can be foreseen, as well as the contingency steps that can be taken to guard against them.

Worriers do, of course, tend to take a lot of the fun out of simulation – who wants to be brought back to earth with a bump every time their favorite flight of fancy gets off the ground? But in our complex times any organization which chooses to ignore them or casually dismisses their doubts will, sooner or later, pay the price. Twenty simulated problems, even if in the event they turn out not to be problems at all, cause far less trouble and expense than one real problem that was not foreseen.

★

So how should we set about managing Stage 3 of the decision-thinking process? Managers who find themselves irked and impatient with the demands it makes on their tolerance, should remember a maxim much favored by boxers and their managers: train hard, fight easy. It is always possible that the time and energy a boxer puts into preparing himself for a big fight will turn out to have been wasted. His opponent may be less dangerous than expected or the fight may not go the full distance. But the man who has trained hard goes into the ring confident that he can cope with all eventualities. And, as far as he and his manager are concerned, the hours spent with the punchbag and the sparring partner will not have been wasted, even if victory comes easily in an early round.

Another parallel which may help to illustrate the necessity

for over-preparation was suggested by a lawyer friend, after he had read a draft of this chapter. The manager's thinking responsibilities, as I have outlined them, were, he pointed out, also very similar to those of a trial lawyer who must go into court not only fully equipped to put the case which he and his client have prepared, but also armed to defend his client against the opposing attorney and, if the opportunity offers itself, to counter-attack. In order to do this effectively the lawyer will have to try to foresee all the possible strategies which the opposition might adopt and make plans to counter them. Since he cannot know what the other side will do, he must be prepared for all eventualities.

It may be frustrating to have to think about ten versions of the future when you know that only one will actually happen. It may seem wasteful to invent things to worry about when there are real worries enough to be faced; or unnecessary to prepare for surprises that may never come. But unless you have made sure that this type of predictive thinking has been done as well and as thoroughly as possible, accepting again wisely the 'waste' of time and energy it involves, you will, in effect, send your organization into the ring unfit and unprepared for the coming contest.

A manager in business or government who has ensured that all foreseeable consequences and contingencies have been covered can be confident that the time and energy involved have not been wasted. *Such so-called waste is as necessary and unavoidable at Stage 3 as it was at Stage 2.*

The strong personality who often makes a good manager in other respects is, in my experience, frequently tempted to cut short Stage 3 of the decision-thinking process. The apparent waste and uncertainty involved, as well as the often airy fairy nature of the predictive process, are all anathema to a manager's traditional down-to-earth, feet-on-the-ground instincts. The manager who is naturally forceful may also find it difficult to wait while colleagues speculate about versions of the future which, from his point of view, appear unrealistic.

But the professional manager must learn to temper impatience and disguise irritation. This is a psychological barrier which he can only overcome by deliberately injecting massive amounts of patience into both his own thinking approach and that of his organization. And, however great the effort required, it must be made, for laziness or impatience at the third stage will lead, ultimately, to failure or worse.

People who excel at Stage 3 may be very different from those who are good at the other three stages of decision-thinking. Often they are not decisive enough to be good decision-makers or strong leaders at Stages 1 and 4. It is also rare to find individuals who perform brilliantly at both Stage 2 and Stage 3. As we saw in the previous chapter, Stage 2 places a high premium on creativity and originality. But the person who is capable, in a moment of inspiration, of seeing a new and inventive answer to a question is not necessarily the one best qualified to think through the consequences and imagine all the possible implications that may arise. This task, to be sure, also requires imagination, but it is of a different kind.

In order to produce a useful simulation of the future our imagination must be harnessed to patience, experience and wisdom. To patience, because this is not an area in which there are simple answers, some right and some wrong, but a whole range of *possible* answers, all of which must be weighed up and have their consequences forecast. To experience, because experience gives people a feel for what is realistic and what is not, an intuition that enables them to put their finger on a possible problem, an insight into the way in which others are likely to react to a decision, which no intellectual brilliance or book-learning can replace. And finally to wisdom, because it represents the distillation and application of experience. The more experience we have (and surround ourselves with), the more chance we have of making wise predictions, decisions and plans.

★

For the professional manager a major difficulty with Stage 3, as with Stage 2, is that those who contribute most to it can often be left with the feeling that theirs has been a thankless task.

It is all too easy for the legitimate thoughts of the conscientious worrier or devil's advocate to appear to his or her colleagues and, perhaps, even to the boss, as merely the fussy point-scoring of a pedant or the hand-wringing of a coward.

In organizational life to criticize can demand as much courage as to originate. The person who has come up with a really innovative idea at Stage 2 may, in a couple of weeks' time, get around to forgiving the colleague who picked it as full of holes as a colander during Stage 3. But feelings may well run high in the meantime.

I have already suggested that the manager will do well to go out of his way to thank the person who had the original idea. He should not withdraw those thanks; the guy who had it could not perhaps know that it was going to be a bum steer. But the fellow who performed the demolition job will also need a word of thanks and encouragement if he is to think equally effectively about the next proposal.

Many managers find it particularly difficult to express proper appreciation for thinking that may seem to be 'negative', however fully they recognize the need, in principle, for all alternative proposals to be treated with caution and scepticism. It is not easy to feel gratitude toward the person who is always looking at the downside rather than the upside, or who seems to be more concerned with the dangers than with the potential benefits of implementing a plan.

When I find some of my own clients becoming impatient with this kind of thinking, I remind them that there was, almost certainly, someone in Union Carbide who suggested that maybe the safety equipment at the Bhopal plant should be checked, and someone at Continental Illinois who said that maybe it was not such a great idea to lend yet more money on deals coming out of a bank in Oklahoma. 'What,' I ask, 'do you suppose happened to those people? Do you think that their farsightedness won them any gratitude? Maybe, just maybe, this fellow who is irritating you with his hyper-cautious attitude could prevent disaster striking your company in the future; and maybe, if you do not show your appreciation for his concern by taking his worries seriously, next time he just will not bother.'

Even as I write this chapter, what looks very much like yet another example of this phenomenon is beginning to emerge in the press. If the stories which have appeared so far are confirmed, then it will be clear that the loss of the space shuttle Challenger, together with the seven members of its crew, was a tragedy which need never have happened. For there were, it seems, some conscientious worriers within the NASA decision-thinking process who tried to draw attention to possible faults under lower temperatures in the booster rockets and who were roundly snubbed by their superiors. It will be interesting to see, as the investigation proceeds, whether anyone ever commends *them*.

Of course, we also need visionaries at Stage 3, people who can see how a decision can be made to work successfully in the future. If we, as managers, surround ourselves only with negative people, nothing will ever get done. There is an equal need for vision as well as caution; a need for people who will ask, 'Why shouldn't we do it?' as well as for those who ask, 'But what happens if . . . ?'

It is the need to combine the talents of both visionaries and worriers, 'upsiders' and 'downsiders', which makes the management of Stage 3 especially challenging. For the two groups are certain to be at loggerheads with one another, both intellectually and temperamentally. Yet success depends upon each recognizing and respecting the *dialectic* value of the other's contributions – and upon the manager's ability to stimulate both kinds of thinking.

It is also vital for a manager to recognize that a person who is asked to predict the future consequences of an alternative is often being placed in a 'can't win' position which may potentially expose him to much criticism. If he warns of dangers to come and proves to have been correct, he may well be resented. If his warnings turn out to have been unnecessary, there will be those who are eager to rub salt in the wound. And if he takes an optimistic view, for which he fights, then he will always be uncomfortably aware that, if things go wrong, he will have laid himself open to blame.

If these sorts of fears are allowed to dominate Stage 3

thinking, then the entire exercise will have been futile. People will simply cease to produce simulations and scenarios which are as honestly conceived as possible, and will instead concentrate on making sure that they never commit themselves to an opinion about the future which might subsequently be held against them.

The most intelligent managers I have been fortunate enough to work with have had an uncanny knack for: (i) surrounding themselves with people who are disposed to look – *both* with vision and with worry – into the future; and (ii) then listening carefully to the thoughts of these people. These managers have created an environment which encourages such people to indulge in predictive thinking. They have made sure that individuals are recognized and rewarded for their contributions, and are not exposed to ridicule from their colleagues when it seems that some of their thinking about the future is either over-cautious or far-fetched.

Such managers are, needless to say, the exception. And yet if we are to have professional managers who are more proficient in managing their decision-thinking responsibilities, we are going to have to ensure that they become particularly skilled at managing Stage 3 of the decision-thinking process.

★

How far you try to look into the future in any particular case, and how much time and effort you devote to exploring the alternative routes which open out before you as the decision tree ramifies will depend upon the importance, complexity and urgency of the question you are considering.

A sudden crisis may leave you time to paint the future with only the broadest of brush strokes. An important piece of corporate planning may demand that every contingency be delineated with a miniaturist's precision. In the case of a minor decision with minor consequences, it would be absurd to become involved in a full-scale predictive effort. In the case of a major decision, it would be equally absurd to rush ahead without doing everything possible to foresee the consequences, probable, possible and even improbable, which could flow from it, so that the best plans for action *and* contingency action can be prepared.

We need, all of us, in both our public and private lives, to try deliberately to reduce the number of times we leave ourselves open to the risk of being taken by surprise. Serious planning and contingency planning based upon the effective and patient management of Stage 3 of the decision-thinking process is the *only* way open to us to achieve this, now urgent, thinking goal. Let us hope that by the 1990s James Reston's laconic observation about our capacity for being surprised will no longer so accurately apply to our country and many of its decision makers.

Summary

We have a proven ability to solve problems. But because of the increasing amount of time it takes for us to correct our decision-thinking mistakes, we must now learn how better to foresee them and how better to plan to avoid them before they happen. To do this, we have to become more professional in the way we manage Stage 3 of the decision-thinking process.

Stage 3 is the most neglected stage in the decision-thinking process, because it is the most difficult, imprecise, uncertain, unrewarding and mentally exhausting. It is, therefore, all the more critical that it is neither skimped nor cut short.

We cannot foresee, because that is the human condition, everything that *will* happen, but we can simulate what *might* happen. Our simulations must be based upon:

a clear appraisal of the present situation;

a fully imagined picture of the future;

a recognition that present trends are not infallible guides to the future; and

a strategy that never depends on good luck or a mistake on our opponent's part in order to succeed.

Simulation not only allows us to evaluate the alternatives, one against the other, it also allows us to identify possible dangers and gives us the opportunity to devise hedging and contingency plans.

Attempts to foresee the future consequences of an alternative, like creating alternative answers, are often a thankless – can't win – thinking task. It is the manager's responsibility to make sure that the mental efforts of those who perform this type of anticipative, simulating thinking are encouraged, respected and truly appreciated.

Negative thinking is as valuable as positive thinking; never, therefore, underestimate the value of having conscientious worriers, as well as visionaries, on your thinking team and giving them specific assignments to act as devil's advocates.

People who are good at Stage 3 thinking, as at Stage 2 thinking, are not always good at making decisions. Forecasters, visionaries and worriers are also dependent on decisive people, and vice versa.

7

Stage 4: The Decision – Deciding on Probabilities, Risks and Rewards

*Our business is much more down to earth than one might think.
I therefore have no use for narcissistic intellectuals. What I need
are people who are willing to roll up their sleeves and take risks.*

Helmut Maucher, managing director of Nestlé

We now come to the point of the whole exercise: making
the best possible decision.

Taken in isolation, the fourth stage of decision-thinking is
relatively familiar and well-explored territory. The business of
actually making decisions is, after all, generally agreed to be the
manager's quintessential role in life.

Once we have completed the first three stages of the
decision-thinking process, all that remains, it would appear, is
to evaluate the alternatives, apply a 'yes', 'no', 'not yet', 'with
changes' or 'let's test it' score to each, and then select the
alternative which appears to answer the chosen question most
satisfactorily.

Actually this selection process is far from simple and defeats
many people. There are those who can complete the first three
stages quite satisfactorily but freeze when it comes to making a
decision. Just as there are others who love to ask questions and
make decisions, but loathe the essential though often thankless,

untidy and time-consuming thinking tasks involved in the second and third stages. Nevertheless, the key point, which underlies the theory of this book, is that all four stages are *equally* important, and if we fail to be effective in any single stage, our ultimate decision will also fail.

Golf provides a useful analogy. No golfer would expect to reach the highest professional level unless he is capable of sinking a 4-foot putt seven times out of ten. But however great his virtuosity with the putter, it will not help him very much unless he can get on to the green. He must also develop the skills needed to drive the ball straight down the fairway, drop a 30-yard chip within a few feet of the pin or, when necessary, blast his way accurately out of a sand trap. And so it is with professional management. Managers who concentrate on managing the decision-thinking stages which they find easy and ignore those which are difficult or uncongenial will be no more likely to excel than those golfers who can handle only one or two kinds of club.

The danger of laying too much stress upon the fourth stage of decision-thinking at the expense of the preceding three is increased by the tendency for the popular macho image of the manager – and too often the manager's own self image – to highlight the excitement and glamor associated with decision making.

The last stage is, it is true, the one where qualities like judgment and courage come into their own. Judgment is needed to choose between alternative courses of action when the balance of advantage may be finely poised; courage will be called for if the choice is a difficult one to make or a tough one to stick to. No one would dispute that these two qualities are admirable. But they will be *wasted* at this fourth stage of decision-thinking if the preparatory mental work has not been carefully carried out during the first three stages.

Again, sport can illustrate the point. The outstanding sportsman, the champion racing driver, say, or the leading jockey, will sometimes seem to take risks that, if taken by lesser mortals, would have been considered foolhardy or even dangerous. But if you watch such men going about the business of preparing for an event, you will notice that their capacity to act bravely and decisively when the chips are down is matched only by the obsessive care they take over their preparations. Every detail will be checked, rechecked and checked again.

Something of the same combination of apparently contrasting traits is often seen in managers of exceptional calibre. The meticulous care and attention to detail which they devote to their preparations for a major decision sometimes seem, to their colleagues, to be little more than excessive hand-wringing. You might almost suppose, if you did not know better, that they were afraid of facing up to the problem. But then, when the decision does come, it can sometimes have a boldness and clarity which takes the breath away.

The point is that the professional manager, like the professional racing driver and the professional jockey, has confidence not only in his own abilities, but also in the quality of his preparations. Thus, when the time comes to make a decision, he can move swiftly and surely, secure in the knowledge that whatever can be done to minimize the risk has already been done.

I have known several managers who are courageous and whose judgment has also been sound, but who have at the same time been hopeless when it came to stimulating their colleagues to produce useful thinking, let alone the best thoughts of which they were capable. Their organizations stumble from problem to problem and crisis to crisis – relying upon reactive thinking to see them through somehow. If they could professionally prepare for and manage their decision-thinking responsibilities, their courage and their judgment could then be put to better use for themselves, for their organizations, and ultimately for all of us. As has been said earlier, but it bears repeating as a warning to all managers – just as the Peter Principle and Murphy's Law are warnings – *a manager gets the thinking he deserves.*

★

Stage 4 begins, as it ends, with a decision – the decision to stop circling round the question and head for the finishing line. Determining when the right moment for this step has arrived is something which in itself calls for skilled judgment on the manager's part. For it is also the manager's responsibility to set the pace throughout the entire process, and the bell which signals the last lap must sound first in his own mind.

In a crisis, where speed is the essence of decision making, that bell may ring even though it is clear that the thinking has been rushed and that ends which should have been tied up have had to be left loose. That is unavoidable.

But a realistic manager will understand that a decision-thinking exercise will seldom be carried through to absolute perfection. What can, and must, be striven for in every instance is the best performance that the manager and his colleagues can achieve in a particular case, under particular conditions, within the time available and with the resources at hand.

Whether the time available for decision making can be counted in hours or days, weeks or months, the following four points may serve as a checklist of what should, as far as possible, have been established during the first three stages:

1. Is the question that is being addressed the right one? Is it, that is to say, one the organization needs to answer and has it been framed in the most rich and complete form?

2. Has the widest conceivable range of answers to that question been created and do the choices that now confront the decision-maker include all the options that are realistically available?

3. Have all the consequences and implications of each alternative answer been thought through and debated as carefully and comprehensively as possible?

4. Has a serious attempt been made to try to bring all the foreseeable contingencies that might arise to light? And in so far as it is possible to plan against them, has that planning been done?

Having prefaced this chapter by words of caution, let me now balance them by warning of the dangers of too much caution. Above all, it is fatal to be intimidated and paralyzed by the fear of making the wrong decision, to succumb to the temptation to procrastinate in the hope that, somehow, it will be possible to prove that one choice is better than another.

In the last resort decision-thinking is an art, not a science. There are no equivalents, in this field, of the laws of nature which guarantee that similar experiments under similar circumstances will produce repeatable results. Simply because a strategy worked for one company last year does not mean that it will work for a different one this year. The course of action that leads to triumph in one organization may be a recipe for disaster in another.

Just as the professional gambler knows that he cannot back a winning horse every time and that there always will be occasions when the 50:1 outsider will defy form and come home a winner, so the professional manager must be reconciled to mixed results. Decision-thinking, however well it is practiced, does not guarantee infallibility; but, if professionally executed, it can tip the odds in favor of making a good decision and against making a bad one. And those odds are what our practical life is now all about.

★

What, then, are the factors which will help us to decide that one course of action is likely to be more advantageous than the other alternatives? There are, in reality, two fundamental calculations to be made: the *probability of success* and the balance of *risk versus reward*. These calculations, judgmental and intuitive rather than mathematical, underlie *any* decision, whether they are formally recognized to do so or not. They are also the two calculations which clearly distinguish decision-thinking from all other human thinking efforts.

To deal with the question of probability first: no matter how great the benefits which one particular alternative seems to offer on paper, some attempt must be made to estimate how probable it is that those benefits will be realized in practice.

I have already made the point that it is all too easy to construct a chain of reasoning which demonstrates how one good thing after another will flow from a decision if it is assumed that all the breaks go our way. In any organization there will always be those who are ready and eager to make such happy assumptions, because it is in their nature to be optimistic about life in general or because it is in their interest to be optimistic on this particular score. That is why *every* thinking/deciding team must include devil's advocates responsible for challenging those who take good luck for granted with the awkward but critical questions beginning with those unsettling words: 'But what if . . . ?'

In the last resort, however, it is often impossible for the optimists to show that the worriers are wrong, or vice versa. It is then the business of the decision maker to weigh the probability of any particular alternative succeeding.

To some managers, if not most, 'probability' is a dirty word. They are, not unnaturally, looking for certainties upon which to plan their company's future and their own careers. But in decision making there are no certainties; there are only probabilities. No decision-thinker should ever surrender to the pressures and importunings of those who may try to bully or persuade him otherwise. He must never embark, even within his own mind, upon that slippery slope which leads from 'probably' to 'very likely' to 'almost certainly' to 'inevitably'.

The pressures to do so, especially from impatient leaders or those who wish to pass some part of the decision-making buck, can often be heavy. When the boss says, 'So you think that so and so will happen?', it is fatally easy to take a deep breath and say, 'Yes, I do', but difficult, and yet responsible, to say, 'No, what I said was that so and so will probably happen. I am willing to say that I think there is a 70 per cent chance of it happening, but that also means that there is a 30 per cent chance of it not happening.'

A probability, then, is exactly that. It is never a certainty. What is, however, more certain is that you can hedge against the probability that things will go wrong. That is what contingency planning is all about. If something is 80 per cent certain to work out, there is also a 20 per cent chance of it failing to do so. If you can foresee how, when and where that 20 per cent chance arises and take steps in advance to cover – that is, insure – yourself against the consequences, then you have in effect achieved a position in which there is still only an 80 per cent chance of things going right but, as far as can be foreseen, there is now *less* than a 20 per cent chance of them going really wrong.

When the bookmaker lays off his bets or the householder pays his insurance premium, he too is carrying out contingency planning, but it costs him money. When you plan against the risk of a decision going wrong, all you may need is some additional thought. But if you do not do such planning, the oversight may eventually cost a great deal of money.

★

But probability and contingency thinking, no matter how thorough, cannot eliminate risk. They can only diminish it. Thus, once you have assessed the probability of success, identified the damage that will be incurred in the event of failure and considered what can be done to reduce or avoid such damage, you will still be left with a basic, irreducible element of risk. The next step is to weigh that risk, the cost of failure, against the rewards that might come with success.

It is vital to recognize that assessing the probability of success and balancing the rewards of success against the risks of failure are two quite separate and distinct calculations. The chances of a new product succeeding in the marketplace, for example, might be rated at 85 per cent. If the company stands to increase its profits by 20 per cent in two years' time if that chance comes off, but risks losing only 5 per cent of profits if it does not, then it may be considered that the balance between risk and reward is a fair one. But what if the cost of failure is put at 50 per cent of annual profits? Obviously in that case it would be rash, all other things being equal, to take the gamble even though there is only a 15 per cent chance of failure.

Ultimately the factors involved in any decision can be expressed as a set of equations in which risk is balanced against reward – but, again, the choice will not be made on a coldly mathematical basis; it will depend rather on how urgently you desire the reward and your judgment as to how much you can afford to risk.

A decision to enter a new market, for example, which involves running a high risk in return for a high reward, might be acceptable to a small business which is in a position where it has either to increase the stakes or to put up the shutters. It might also be acceptable for a very large business which stands to lose little more than some 'fun money' if things go wrong. But the same decision, as indicated above, would be quite unacceptable to a medium-sized firm which could survive comfortably without the reward, but would be crippled if the risk went the wrong way.

It is, therefore, a misconception to imagine that each alternative can be evaluated in some mechanical fashion – by computer, say – and awarded so many points for its potential reward, with so many others being deducted to take account of the risk. If this were so, then arriving at a good decision would be a simple matter of addition and subtraction. The truth, of course, is that each of the choices available is likely to be a *unique* package, a particular blend of probability calculations and the risk/reward balance, and one can be compared with another only indirectly.

I have found that many managers are profoundly reluctant to face up to the fact that, in the last resort, the calculus of decision-thinking involves a balance of uncertainty. No decision can be reduced to a set of black and white issues; there will always be a need to choose between a number of murky shades of gray. It is understandable that managers should dislike the gray uncertainties of the future – don't we all? – but it is unforgivable if they pretend that they do not exist.

Yet in many cases this is precisely what managers attempt to do. Instead of recognizing risks and devising contingency plans to guard against their worst effects, they pooh-pooh them and imagine they are so remote as to be negligible. They persuade themselves that if they want a decision to succeed badly enough then it will do so, and they accuse anyone who disagrees with them of cowardice or lack of determination. They gloat over the crock of gold that weighs down the reward side of the equation and they refuse to look at the crock of – well, something else, which counterbalances it on the risk side.

The only way of making yourself or other people think clearly about the problems of coping with uncertainty is to subject your thinking to the discipline of numbers. If you rate the probability of success highly, then put a figure on it. Ninety per cent? Eighty per cent? Only sixty per cent perhaps? If the reward looks so glittering, then perhaps it is worth trying to work out, in terms of dollars and cents or other values, just how expensive the risk could turn out to be in terms of profits or corporate morale if, say, the new factory has to be closed and the staff paid off or if the advertising campaign misfires. Words like 'almost certain', 'enormous potential' and 'negligible risk' are cheap and dangerously intoxicating – there is nothing like a few specific figures on risk/reward estimates to sober one up and concentrate the mind.

★

In order to illustrate some of the points I have been making in this chapter, let us look at a hypothetical decision that might be faced by a company in a number of different contexts. First, consider the case of an American company planning an investment in Britain. One of the factors that will have to be considered is the fate of similar ventures in the past. On the whole these have been remarkably successful. Since the Second

World War, US firms have, with few exceptions, done consistently well in the British market, which has shown itself receptive to ideas and products from across the Atlantic. Experience, therefore, suggests a high probability of success.

On the risk/reward front, on the other hand, the idea of a substantial long-term investment in sterling may not be considered to be an attractive one – the currency, already subject to sudden tremors whenever speculators get an attack of nerves, could decline rapidly once the benefits of North Sea oil production diminish or when there is a change of government. But account must also be taken of the fact that, in comparison with most other possible sites for investment, Britain is a model of political reliability and social stability. Overall a reasonable but not a sensational reward could be expected in return for taking a negligible risk.

Now consider the problem in reverse – from the point of view of a British firm contemplating an investment in the US. Again, stability could be taken for granted here, if anywhere. And there is the added attraction of investing in the world's largest and perhaps most resilient economy and in one of its safer currencies. The reward looks good, the risks seem low.

But against all these factors must be weighed the record of previous British involvement in the US market, a record which is, with a few brilliant exceptions (the success of Hanson Trust and, more recently, of Jaguar come to mind), not particularly exciting. The British style of management, compensation and legal practice, it seems, seldom works satisfactorily in American conditions or the American competitive environment. (Imperial Tobacco's acquisition of Howard Johnson and the dismal forays of some British banks on to the American banking scene serve as reminders of what can go wrong.)

The prospect of exciting US rewards may be persuasive, but unless the company concerned feels confident that it has identified and solved the problems which many other British firms failed to solve, it may well be that the probability of failure is too high.

Finally, what sort of calculation might either an American or a British firm make when contemplating a similar investment in Japan? Again, the prospects are in theory excellent – a sound economy with an unequalled record of growth, a political and social background that seems stable, a currency that should certainly continue to be strong. The rewards, in other words, look appetizing. But a glance at the record, which shows that few foreign firms, British or American, have ever really succeeded in breaking – on their own – into any *vital* sector of the Japanese market, suggests that the risks, in terms of money and waste of executive talent, are staggering.

In the case of Japan it is not a question of there being a possibility, or even a probability, that things might go wrong – if past experience is any guide it is almost certain that they will. And I say this, in spite of the fact that Japan has recently announced that it will be opening its market wider to foreign competitors. The internal cultural and commercial differences are just too vast to be overcome quickly.

To sum up then, too many decisions go wrong because managers fail, beforehand, to submit their decisions to *two* predictive calculations. In an uncertain world no important decisions should ever be taken without a careful and intuitive look at both the estimated *probabilities of success* and the *balance between risk and reward*. You do not always have to make the choice that this often subjective arithmetic dictates, but you would be foolish to make any choice at all without first taking a long, cool look at the special arithmetic of the decision-making stage of the decision-thinking process.

★

I started this book by attacking the over-emphasis which our culture places upon doing as opposed to thinking. By this point I hope that you will have been persuaded that, whenever complex issues are at stake, there must be a *conscious* effort to bring decision-thinking skills to bear on them. But decision-thinking is a preparation for action, not a substitute for it. The wisest decision, the best-laid plan, will amount to no more than a waste of talent and time if it is not implemented with all the care, energy and skill which the individual or the organization can command.

During decision-thinking one must be open-minded – afterward, single-minded. Thus, once the decision is taken and contingency plans prepared, the rules change. Then doubt has to be put aside and the action has to be taken with precision and enthusiasm, if it is not to be ineffective. As Zen teaching might put it: 'When you think, think; when you act, act'.

The greatest danger facing us today comes from organizations which often act without thinking through the consequences of their actions; but the threat posed by organizations which are unable to put their thoughts into action effectively is also great.

Again, the root of the problem, to come full circle, lies in the way in which we in the West arrive at our decisions, for how we make our decisions affects directly how we implement those decisions. Depending on how we manage it, the circle which links decision and action can be either vicious or virtuous.

With far too many Western managements a decision, it seems, is not the point at which debate is concluded and action commences, but merely the bell which signals the start of a new round of internal strife. In such organizations, for every person who accepts the decision and tries to implement it effectively, there will be another person who will try to render the decision ineffective by delaying or even sabotaging its implementation, and yet another who will set out, covertly or otherwise, to get the decision rescinded or changed. Not surprisingly, few decisions taken under such circumstances achieve what is expected of them. All the energy that should go into implementing them is instead expended in Machiavellian manoeuvres, and cynicism flourishes in place of enthusiasm.

Even the most important decisions are often not perceived as expressing a single-minded commitment by an organization, but the views, dictatorial or otherwise, of some faction or interest within that organization. They are seen, in other words, not as the product of the organization's decision-thinking efforts, but as the product of arbitrary decision making by a person or people within that organization.

It would be foolish to suggest that everyone within an organization should, or could, agree with everyone else – opinions about both means and ends are bound to be divided at times. But it must be recognized that it is the responsibility of management to lead the *entire* organization, not a faction, even a ruling faction.

Peter Drucker has shown★ how Japanese companies delay the actual moment of decision and involve as many people and departments as possible in the discussions which precede it. By so doing they ensure that a decision, when taken, is supported by a consensus that is as wide and general as possible. In effect, everyone involved knows what the decision will be before it is taken and most, probably, supports it. Even those who opposed it are satisfied that they have had a fair hearing and are, as far as possible, reconciled to implementing the inevitable.

Yes, the successful implementation of a decision will be far more easily achieved if the decision making has been done with care and respect. But I would go further and argue that the seeds of effective implementation are sown throughout the *entire* decision-thinking process. An organization which wants to act together needs first to think together.

★

Sound decision-thinking practices lead to sound decision-making choices – which must, in turn, be followed by the effective implementation of those choices. If that chain is broken, sooner or later something goes wrong. If the decision-thinking is poor, the ultimate decision will be inadequate, and whether the implementation of that decision is effective or not will matter little. If the thinking effort is sound but the wrong decision is made, then again whatever happens at the implementation stage will be harmful. And, finally, good thinking and wise decision making will both be wasted if the implementation is handed

★ Peter F. Drucker, *Management: Tasks, Practices, Responsibilities*, Harper & Row, 1974.

over to people who lack the basic qualities needed to lead people into effective action.

What I have wished to do in these last four chapters is to analyze the process of judgment and identify its key rules and practices. It has often been said that people are born with or without good powers of judgment. Some, it may be, are blessed with a mental make up and personality which make it natural for them to follow a thinking process similar to the one I have described before making a decision. But I would argue that everyone can give himself a better chance of exercising good judgment by consciously following the route described.

Professionally managed decision-thinking provides us with the best method for coping with complexity, change and future uncertainties. All of us, organizations and individuals alike, need to be clear about where we are going and how we intend to get there. Nothing is so great a danger to itself, and, in many instances, to the rest of us as well, as the aimless organization. No one is less useful and few are less happy than the person without a purpose.

Yet we in the West are often unclear about our collective aims and, individually, are lacking in plan and purpose. These are not handicaps from which some of our competitors and enemies suffer. Unless we soon learn to think, and therefore plan, more thoroughly, there is a very real danger that other people's aims will be achieved and other people's purposes will prevail – with consequences which we will not enjoy. We will only avoid this fate if our decision-thinking, decision making and, in turn, decision implementing are all more professionally managed. The first step toward achieving that goal must be to master the management of our own minds and the minds of our organizations, which is the subject of the rest of this book.

Before we go on in the second part of the book to consider how, in practice, the decision-thinking process should be managed and how individual managers can analyze and improve their performance, there are certain obstacles that have to be removed. In the next chapter I shall highlight some crucial truths about decision-thinking, truths which must be faced up to, even if they are uncomfortable. Then, in chapter 9, I shall examine some of the attitudes and assumptions which are widely shared by Western managers and which, it seems to me, are serious impediments to the professional management of the decision-thinking process.

Summary

Before you attempt to reach an important decision, make one last check that:

the right question has been asked in the most complete and the richest way;

all credible alternatives have been considered;

the possible consequences of each alternative have been imagined and thought through; and

all foreseeable contingencies have been, as far as possible, provided for.

Then, before deciding upon any course of action always carefully assess two quite separate and, often, subjective factors:

the estimated probability that it will be successful; and

the balance between the risk involved and the reward predicted.

Until these two important calculations have been consciously made and clearly spelled out, never make any decision.

★

Properly managed, the decision-thinking process not only helps to create the best decision, it also helps secure the support needed for effective implementation. The reverse is also true.

Before a decision is reached, open-mindedness is vital; once it has been taken, the time for debate is over. When you think, think. When you decide to act, act.

8

The Unique Characteristics of Decision-Thinking

Life can only be understood backward, but it must be lived forward.

S. Kierkegaard

It is the future that dictates the present . . . People act in the present according to their judgment about what the future will hold.

Gordon O. Pehrson

No child can resist the temptation to fiddle – to play with matches, to tease the cat, to play indoors with a hard ball. Sooner or later the inevitable happens, fingers get burned, the cat scratches, a window is broken, and an angry adult arrives on the scene. The dialogue that follows usually goes something like this:

CHILD (*eager to explain that it was all due to a simple misfortune that might have happened to anyone*): I'm sorry, I didn't think that . . .

ADULT (*interrupting*): I know you didn't think. That's your problem, you *never* seem to think.

What really arouses the anger and incomprehension of the
grown-up is, of course, the child's inability to foresee that a
certain action would have consequences which were almost
inevitable.

Most of us, happily, do grow up to learn that playing with
fire is dangerous, that, teased enough, the best-mannered cat
will turn on its tormentor, and that the right place for a hard
ball is the baseball field. But few of us really come to terms with
the idea, which is at the heart of decision-thinking, that we must
always make an effort to predict the future consequences of an
action, however difficult to calculate they may be, *before* taking
the decision to act.

Naturally, when the issues at stake are complex, it is not
sufficient to look at just one option, predict the consequences
and move ahead. Like the chess player, the decision-thinker
must try to see every possible move and must calculate the
consequences of each as far ahead as he can see.

The manager who thinks only in the short-term and de-
velops no strategy for the medium- and long-term future is like
a novice chess player who sees only the obvious, immediate
moves and, as a result, falls easily into the traps that are set by
his opponent. But the manager is matched not just against his
competitors, but also against the whims of circumstance and
luck. If he is to outwit his opponents and avoid the pitfalls
which booby-trap the future, he will need all the skills and
instincts of a grand master. But, unlike the grand master, he
cannot, even in principle, forecast the consequences of any move
with total certainty.

This may seem obvious enough in theory, but it is something which many managers find difficult to acknowledge in
practice. For organizations, which have to justify their decisions
to their shareholders, electors or the general public, are deeply
unhappy about acting or, even worse, being seen to act on the
basis of possibilities and probabilities.

Anyone who has ever been involved in working with large organizations on matters of policy will know how great can be the pressure to provide predictions which are definite: to say that if A is done, then B *will* happen, rather than if A is done, it is likely/probable/possible or there is an x per cent chance that B will happen. If the person providing advice can be persuaded to commit himself in a conclusive fashion, then those taking the advice seem, somehow, to be spared the knowledge that they are taking a gamble.

This is, of course, a dangerous illusion. As I have pointed out in the previous chapter, all management decisions are, in one way or another, gambles – that is, calculated bets on the proposition that there is one version of the future which is more likely to come about than all the other possible versions. This is just another way of saying that *any* decision, whether it involves recruitment, firing, promotion, demotion, strategy, finance or allocation of resources, will be based on an estimation of probabilities and of risk and reward. This is the first reason why decision-thinking must be treated as a separate subject – a unique use of our thinking skills.

There is no system of decision-thinking which guarantees infallibility. There will always be future risks and those risks will always have to be balanced against the possible future rewards they offer. Sound decision-thinking does not allow us to avoid risk, nor does it ensure reward: what it does do is help us to assess both factors more clearly and to select and hedge our bets – that is, our decisions – more intelligently.

★

The human factor is another unique aspect of decision-thinking which, though it compounds the uncertainties, must always be taken into account. Indeed, one of the key elements which needs to be anticipated in making any major decision is the way in which other people are going to react to it. Human reactions are notoriously influenced by prejudice, perceived self-interest and even sheer stupidity. None of these factors is easily measured; all must, nevertheless, be anticipated and allowed for.

Decision-thinking, in this respect, is not unlike poker – it often matters not only what you think, but also what others think you think and what you think they think you think. Interestingly poker, that most subjective of games, has often been of considerable interest to people who are, by any standards, good thinkers.

The great mathematician John von Neumann was, among his many other accomplishments, one of the originators of games theory. In particular, he showed that all games fall into one of two classes: there are what he called 'games of *perfect information*', games like chess which are meant to involve no element of concealment, bluff or luck – games where the players can, in principle, discover the best move by the application of pure logic to the available data. Then there are 'games of *imperfect information*', like poker, in which it is impossible to know, in advance, that one course of action is better than another.

One of the most dangerous illusions about business (or, indeed, any activity involving human beings and human institutions) is that it can be treated as a game of perfect information. Quite the reverse. Business, politics, life itself are games which we must normally play with very imperfect information. Many a business decision involves odds that would make a professional poker player shudder, for the number and extent of the unknown and unknowable factors are themselves often incalculable. But, as I have wished to point out, few organizations find it comfortable or congenial to admit that they are gambling, and many still prefer to delude themselves that they are playing a sober, responsible game of chess and are not engaged, as is often the case, in a fling at the poker table.

To take but one obvious and topical example: in the 1970s and early 1980s US banks lent tens of billions of dollars to countries like Brazil, Mexico and Argentina, which now threaten – and will continue to threaten for some time to come – to bring down or seriously disrupt the US banking system by reneging on their debts. If, before the end of this century, most major American banks are nationalized or bailed out *à la*

Continental Illinois, it will in all likelihood be because of these debts.

The bankers acted as they did because they persuaded each other that they were playing a game in which it was simply against the rules for whole nations to contemplate or threaten insolvency. Lending to governments (as opposed to lending to corporations or individuals) was supposed to be completely safe. 'Governments don't go belly up,' we were told.

Thus the banks, which were prevented by law from committing disproportionate amounts of their capital to any single corporate customer – be it as solid as General Motors, IBM or Sears Roebuck – were able and willing to lend (that is to gamble with their own capital plus their depositors' money) *ad lib* to governments which patently lacked the means to service, let alone repay, their debts.

Even today, when most bankers would admit that their policy was a disastrous mistake, few would acknowledge that it was anyone's fault. After all, they followed conventional wisdom. It *should* not have been wrong. It did not *seem* like a gamble. Their reaction has been, in fact, a little like that of a novice poker player who, because he was told that a full house is usually a good hand, assumed that it is always a winning hand. Alas, sometimes it turns out that the other guy, no matter how desperate his situation might at first appear, can end up with four of a kind or better.

One of the first steps that we can take to improve our decision-thinking performance in business – and, indeed, elsewhere in practical affairs, from government to our own personal life – is to face up to the fact that when we make important decisions (or our leaders make them for us) we are normally engaged in a game of imperfect information, a game in which there are always complex conditions and assumptions, most of which are subject to change without warning.

★

If the unique features of decision-thinking create difficulties for us, it is, I believe, because they run counter to our instincts about what constitutes logical thinking, and the basic ideas and emotional attitudes we developed about thinking in childhood.

As I have said at the beginning of this book in chapter 1 – but I believe it bears repeating here – until we come to grips with the fact that when we want to make a decision, which will lead to (or avoid) action in the practical world, we need to call upon a very special and unique use of our thinking skills, the vital role of thinking in our practical life will remain unclear – and, hence, neglected. And all our mental efforts – whether scientific, religious, mathematical, artistic or action-oriented – will continue to be lumped together and analyzed under the all too vague and now, therefore, meaningless heading of 'thinking'.

Instead, when it comes to the complex subject and practice of decision-thinking – as with *all* uses of thinking – we need consciously to understand what we are doing and why we are doing it. In other words, as managers and private citizens, we need to understand how our decision-thinking should be managed just as a scientist needs to understand how his scientific thinking should be managed.

The point is that the decision-thinker, unlike the scientist or the logician, cannot hope, even in principle, to determine what will be true in the future. The scientists who planned the recent missions to Halley's comet for example, could predict both the comet's course and the earth's orbit with total certainty. They could therefore calculate the exact trajectory that a space-craft launched from a given position on earth at a given time in the future would have to follow in order to intercept the comet many months later.

Contrast this with the situation of the manufacturer who plans to launch, let us say, a new personal computer on to the market in six months' time. On the face of it his position is not unlike that of the scientists. He wants to know at what 'speed' he should launch the product (i.e. what inventory he should build up before the launch, what rate of production to plan for over the months that follow, how much he should spend on advertising and promotion, etc.) in order to arrive at a given target at a given time (say, a twenty per cent per annum return on his investment within two years).

He too may start with one 'scientific fact' provided by his engineers who say that if he builds a computer to their design it will be 50 per cent faster than existing models. But there the similarities end, as there are few other 'facts' of which he can feel really confident.

He may, it is true, know something about the present in that he can ascertain with reasonable accuracy how many such machines are currently being sold in his target market each month and what share of the market is currently held by his competitors. But when he tries to look into the future he will find himself beset by a host of uncertainties.

He may calculate that the advances in technology built into his product should gain him say 15 per cent of the market: but that is only an assumption. Will the market be the same size six months hence? Will his potential customers agree that his is a better machine? How much will they be swayed by the consideration that, if they do buy his computer, they will also have to buy new software?

Moreover, he has to accept that even his knowledge of the present is far from complete. For he has no means of knowing that one of his competitors is not even now developing a machine that will be as good, or better than, his. Nor can he be sure that the customers, who he has assumed are looking for a faster machine, would not in fact be even more eager to buy computers with, say, greater compatibility or more 'user friendliness'.

Now the manufacturer can of course set his accountants to work and ask them to forecast the outcomes of a range of different options. And suppose they recommend that the optimum course of action involves pricing the computer at $500, building up an inventory of 50,000 units before launching and planning to produce 100,000 units a month for the first three months. This, they say, will ensure that the R&D costs are recovered within the three months' period and also ensure that the project stays within budget and starts to show a good return on investment. Fine. That recommendation is a product of mathematical thinking and – since they are good accountants – all the figures are right and the calculations are totally self-consistent.

But it is quite impossible to guarantee that the outcome will actually be as forecast. Suppose, for example, that there is a downturn in the market and the sales after two months only amount to 100,000 units. Now the manufacturer is looking at an inventory of 150,000 computers, a commitment to buy components for another 100,000 and, as a result, a budget that is in tatters.

Or suppose that the launch is unexpectedly successful; then a completely different set of problems arise. Can the company find the cash to increase the rate of production? Should resources be diverted from other product lines? What can be done to placate the retailers who are complaining that they have thousands of unsatisfied customers?

The manufacturer cannot ignore these possibilities. Indeed, even if he accepts his accountant's recommendations, he cannot simply sit back and wait for them to come true. Instead he must make plans to deal with the possibility that they will turn out to have been ill-founded, either on the up-side or the down-side. But here the essential point is that mathematical thinking, or any other branch of logic, can only tell a manager what will happen *if* a particular set of assumptions prove to be correct.

Now, the answer to the really crucial question 'Should we do it?' can only be determined by decision-thinking. And the manager will be fooling no one except himself if he pretends that there is any way of coming up with an answer which has the guaranteed predictive power of scientific thinking or the logical rigor of mathematical thinking.

But just because decision-thinking is an inexact, risky, imprecise and often intuitive discipline, unlike any other human thinking effort, it does not mean that we cannot learn to manage each of its four stages so that we can do it more effectively and wisely. Indeed, in my opinion, we have no choice but to plan quickly to do just that.

Summary

There are seven special features which, when taken together, separate professional decision-thinking from all other important forms of thinking. They are:

1. Decision-thinking is a game of imperfect information, involving the future, change and human action and reaction.

2. Because none of us lives outside the stream of time, we are obliged to try to *predict* the future short-, medium- and long-term consequences of every decision before we make it, even though those consequences cannot be predicted with certainty.

3. Since we cannot 'know' the future, we also have to hedge against our decision going wrong by trying, in advance, to create *contingency* plans.

4. Most of the important decisions we make are *not* dealing with problems that will have right or wrong answers, but rather only better or worse solutions – hence our need for debate, devil's advocates and rigorous, dispassionate and intuitive thinking.

5. The results of most of our decisions will, as in poker, depend upon how other people *react* to them, be they family members, friends, employees, the media, our boss, our competitors, our shareholders, our bankers or public officials; and those reactions have to be predicted *before* we make our decisions.

6. *Probability* estimates always need to be made, again in advance, of the chances of our decision succeeding.

7. Lastly, *risk/reward* calculations also have to be predicted beforehand to find out if it will be worthwhile to try to achieve our objective – even if it is highly probable that we will successfully carry out our decision. We always need to remember before we make any decision that 'something not worth doing, is not worth doing well. '

9

Western Myths About
Decision-Thinking

*A bottom-line philosophy and short-term goals have triggered a
disastrous movement in the US electronics industry that endangers
its survival.*

Wisse Dekker, former president, Philips NV

*Some American banking institutions already have been eclipsed
by their Japanese rivals. No longer are American banks the
world's largest. No longer are American banks' balance sheets the
soundest. No longer are American banks' foreign assets the biggest.
Japan is now tops in all those categories, thanks to an un-
precedented concentration of wealth in Japanese hands in the last
three years.*

Los Angeles Times, March 16, 1986

Decision-thinking, decision making, and inspiring other
people to implement those decisions effectively, in business,
government and even in our own private lives, are all inter-
woven. If we fail in any one of them, we will also fail to achieve
our objectives. In the West a great deal has been said and written
about all of these subjects – except thinking.

In business, for example, the assumption is often made that

if the organizational structure, accounting responsibilities and management practices are sound, the thinking will take care of itself. Sometimes it does, but often it does not. All of us have known or read about important companies, in such fields as financial services, air travel or 'high' technology, where morale was high and where management was well organized and proficient at having their decisions faithfully and efficiently implemented. Nevertheless, these same companies, because they did not think through their decisions in the first place, followed the wrong strategy and caused, as a result, a great deal of grief and loss.

Lifting our eyes to wider horizons for a moment, the need for better thinking – and hence better planning – in each of several different areas is painfully obvious. Even if we ignore for the moment the ultimate challenge of peace or annihilation, any one of a whole range of problems could become severe enough to cause disaster if we do not think and plan how to deal with them intelligently. High unemployment, overpopulation, mass starvation, excessive permissiveness, rampant crime and drug abuse, mediocre educational policies, our special relationship with Mexico and its citizens, the US trade deficit and possible trade wars, ecological imbalance or major financial collapse, whether at the corporate, state or national government level, are just a few of the most obvious.

But to see how ingrained our disregard, even distrust, of thinking in practical affairs has become, we need look no farther than the political arena. In choosing whom we elect to manage our communities and our countries, we no longer seriously consider what we know of the quality of their thinking or, more importantly, their ability to manage other people's thinking. Indeed, a reputation for being clever or, worse still, a reflective thinker may be a considerable handicap. Often, it seems to be electorally advantageous actually to appeal to public dislike and distrust of thinking and thinkers.

In our personal lives the explosive growth of self-help psychology has also encouraged the belief that our thoughts are of little value compared to our feelings. Self-improvement used to mean self-education, the painstaking acquisition of knowledge and the cultivation of careful, creative and critical thinking. Today it is generally taken to mean the latest in an apparently unending succession of 'quick fixes' which can painlessly 'improve' one's personality. Style, not substance, is what matters.

★

But it is in the field of business that the cost of our failure to take thinking profoundly seriously is being brought home to us most obviously and expensively. The American and European economies, and the men and women responsible for managing them, are today in direct competition with industries that are guided by very different sets of values and priorities – most notably those of Japan, a nation whose whole cultural tradition encourages reverence for practical thought and respect for those who do the thinking.

Already the Japanese have provided some impressive object lessons in what can be achieved by precise and sustained attention to thinking. They have also shown, with concepts such as 'quality circles' and 'bottom-up' participation in thinking, that the management of an organization's thinking processes and its productivity cannot be separated. If we ignore those lessons ourselves, we may be sure that there are others, especially in the emerging economies of Asia, upon whom they are not being lost.

The most celebrated and exemplary lesson thus far is probably that administered to the US and European car makers over the past twenty years. In 1960 Western companies still totally dominated the world car market. By all the rules it was pure fantasy for the Japanese, with none of the raw materials to hand and no established tradition or reputation in the automobile business, to consider competing with the American and European firms in the world market, let alone taking them on in their own domestic markets. For a Japanese heavy engineering business like Mitsubishi to try to sell cars in Chicago, Paris or Manchester seemed as unreal as for Levi Strauss to start marketing kimonos in Tokyo. Yet by the end of the 1970s, the Japanese were a major force in the car market and a threat to the very survival of some European and American manufacturers.

In retrospect it is clear that the single most important advantage which the Japanese could put in the balance against a daunting set of disadvantages was their ability to *think* through an audacious yet meticulously calculated plan and to implement it over a period of years – never losing sight of their objective, yet always retaining sufficient flexibility in their thinking to ensure that they could react to changes in circumstance. Their second most important advantage was the inability of their American and European competitors to see the market facts or to think about them clearly, even when those facts and the conclusions which should be drawn from them were staring them in the face.

It may be objected that the Japanese had lucky breaks, notably the great oil price increase of 1973. But the point is that they were sufficiently fast-thinking and flexible to take the chances when they came. Post-1973, for instance, it was clear that in the United States enormous advantages would accrue to manufacturers who sent small cars into the showrooms fast and in quantity. The Japanese, unlike the Europeans (who also had the experience and the tooling to produce the cars), saw the opportunity and took it. The toehold they gained in the US market quickly became a foothold. It then threatened to turn into a stranglehold, just because the American car-makers failed to think through the consequences of what had occurred.

Several years ago I had an experience which seemed strikingly to illustrate the difference between Japanese attitudes and the sort of complacent thinking which often prevails in the West. While flying from Geneva to London I fell into conversation with my neighbor who was, it turned out, a member of a group from the Tokyo Stock Exchange which was making a tour of the world's leading stock exchanges. This was, he explained, something that he and his colleagues did at regular intervals, for they had found that there was always something they could learn from the practices and technology developed elsewhere which could usefully be applied back home in Tokyo.

Intrigued, I asked if managers from the leading Western

stock exchanges ever came to Japan to see what, if anything, they could learn from their Japanese counterparts. He thought for a moment and then replied, 'Very seldom.' When I replied, 'That doesn't seem very smart,' he smiled as he answered, 'Well, that's their problem.' How right he was.

But it is, of course, not true to say that only the Japanese have shown themselves capable of good business thinking, or that they alone have reaped the rewards of it.* To stick with the motor industry, the extraordinary turnaround at Chrysler engineered by Lee Iacocca and, on a smaller scale, at Jaguar by Sir John Egan offer encouraging evidence that we in the West can do it if we try.

If, however, we are to do it on a large enough scale quickly enough and thoroughly enough to matter, we will have to gain a clear understanding of the rules of the decision-thinking process and learn how to be more professional in applying them to our particular problems. In doing this we will have to rid ourselves of some deeply embedded myths about the nature of managers and their role and functions within an organization. Our society does not have to adore its managers, but unless it learns to respect their thinking skills – and unless they, in turn, make those skills worthy of respect – it is now unlikely to develop wisely.

*

There seem to be at least three separate myths which have contributed to the creation of our unhealthy attitude toward thinking. First, there is the myth that a manager's thinking involves no more than the application of ordinary common

---

* Nor would it be wise to forecast that the Japanese will not make mistakes in *judgment* in the future, as they have in the past. But their respect for thinking and some of their thinking practices are what we should *learn* from them – plus the very practical and profound concept, which is implicit in all their effective management actions: the careful and attentive management of an organization's thinking practices is critical to the successful implementation of any important decision.

sense to some specialized data. It is assumed that the right sort of person (the one, that is, with enough of the intangible qualities like judgment, determination and charisma) will quickly master the thinking skills involved in being a manager.

To illustrate the point, consider the mass of literature which tells the aspiring manager how to be assertive, how to influence people, how to be successful, popular, loved or powerful, and compare it with the paucity of material discussing the manager's most important responsibility, thinking – the source of all of his strategies, policies, decisions and actions. The attitude seems to be that while managers may welcome advice on how to make an after-dinner speech, get the best table in a fashionable restaurant, keep their figures slim, imitate the management ideas employed by other companies, or climb their way up the corporate tree, they have no need of any instruction at all in thinking – everyone who achieves executive rank is assumed to be able to do *that*.

The second myth is that those managers and companies who do take their thinking responsibilities seriously are, somehow, behaving in a way which is unfair or unmanly. One of the most interesting aspects of the Japanese success in capturing markets which were previously dominated by American and European firms is the way in which many aggrieved Westerners have reacted. They are, of course, worried and chastened by the defeat; but what they seem to find really outrageous is that the Japanese so obviously sat down and planned it all. Rather like the French legal system, which is indulgent to the husband or lover who commits a *crime passionnel*, but merciless toward the perpetrator of a premeditated murder, Western business seems to find something reprehensible about success that comes as a result of careful thought, carefully implemented.

The point is well made by Iacocca in his autobiography. Pondering the refusal of so many Americans to accept the need for their government to have an industrial policy, he asks: 'Don't they want America to be strong and healthy?' He goes on: 'Sure they do. But they want it to happen without any planning. They want America to be great *by accident*.'

The really damaging aspect of this second myth is precisely

the one Iacocca pinpoints: we are, it seems deeply prejudiced against planning, especially against large-scale planning or planning that looks beyond the immediate future or the short-term advantage. Economic or industrial planning has, quite falsely and simplistically, become associated in our minds with socialist systems and thus with inefficient and unresponsive bureaucracies.

The lesson we must draw from the failure of such planning is not that planning itself is bad, but that bad planning is bad. Those who feel that planning of any kind is alien to the capitalist system should consider where IBM, Honda and a hundred other successful businesses would be today if they had not committed themselves to sound planning.

It has been my experience that any organization which does not take planning seriously does not take thinking seriously. They go together and cannot be separated. Or, as that apparently simple but profound saying puts it: 'If you don't know where you are going, any road will take you there.' The only way we are going to cope with change and complexity is through effective planning. And all our plans are products of our thoughts and decisions.

Thirdly, there is what might be called the myth – or more accurately the disease – of the *macho* manager. This undermines many of the management principles which are today essential to effective decision-thinking. For example, to show that they are doing a good job, many managers feel they must put on a display of ostentatious, non-stop, decisive 'busy-ness'. Action is what matters; not thought.

At best this belief in what could be called 'management by perspiration' leads to irritating stupidities, such as constantly interrupting meetings to take 'vital' calls. At worst it leads to dangerous folly, such as the idea that it is feasible, even admirable, to jet halfway round the world and immediately take a jetlagged mind straight into an important meeting. Another symptom of the same disease is the compulsion to demonstrate 'decisiveness', to be the fastest gun in the executive suite, even at the cost of hitting the wrong target.

Those who believe that a decision, any decision, today is

always better than waiting until tomorrow to produce a decision should again take a look at the Japanese example. Unlike their Western counterparts, Japanese managers do not pride themselves on their decisiveness. In fact, they actually loathe making decisions and tend to put them off as long as possible for one very good reason. In a country where you cannot easily change employers, declare bankruptcy and, like the phoenix, rise again, or have lawyers at your beck and call to shield you from your thinking mistakes, the price of making a wrong decision, in terms of career prospects and loss of face, can indeed be horrendous.

But the best Japanese companies do not waste the time during which a decision is being delayed and pondered – a process which uninitiated Westerners who are trying to deal with them for the first time find frustrating and, wrongly, consider evidence of incompetence. Instead they use that time to do more thinking and, even more importantly, to obtain the benefit of their colleagues' thinking. As a result, by the time a decision is taken it will, as was discussed in chapter 7, not only have been thought through more thoroughly – it will also be a decision in which many individuals and departments have participated and which is, therefore, more likely to command the support of the organization as a whole when the time comes to implement it.

The final element in the macho myth is the image of the manager as an isolated figure, the individual with whom 'the buck stops'. Ultimately, of course, one person does have to make decisions and take responsibility for them. But that does not mean that only one person should be involved in the thinking which precedes those decisions. On the contrary, it is vital for a manager to recognize that all decision-thinking is a *collaborative* process. It is a process which requires constant attention and careful management. It is also a process to which different people, with different talents, backgrounds and casts of mind, have different skills to contribute – people who provide the raw material, the ideas, from which any decision will be constructed.

Summary

If we are to become professional decision-thinkers involved in a unique branch of thinking, we must learn new thinking and management skills. But first we must discard some of our society's existing myths and prejudices. In particular we must not:

undervalue practical thinking -- that is, decision-thinking – and those who do it;

neglect careful planning (planning is how we think our way into the future; managers who do not take planning seriously will not take decision-thinking seriously);

believe naively that blind market forces are good in themselves, or that, if we make a decision-thinking mistake, its damaging future consequences can quickly and painlessly be corrected. (Note: OPEC armtwisting, Vietnam, our leading banks' Third World debt, Challenger, our growing dependency on Japanese savings to help finance our own national debt, and the insidious and widespread evils of drug use.)

We must also recognize that ostentatious 'busy-ness' is no substitute for thinking.

Nor is macho decisiveness a virtue by itself. Any fool can make a decision. It is making the best decision that is difficult.

The buck may stop on the manager's desk, but, if it is not accompanied by the collective wisdom of his organization, he has failed to do his job. Remember, every manager will get the thinking he deserves.

PART II

Managing Our Decision-Thinking Process

The question remains as to whether or not we can influence human destiny constructively. It seems evident that if anything can be done, it will require that the human mind act upon itself, in the sense that the minds of human beings act upon each other.

Jonas Salk

We as a species have become a major source of change through our activities and technologies, and we have brought upon ourselves a new responsibility.

Lester R. Brown

10

Models – What We Think About

At the time we are conceived, the requirement that we satisfy our basic needs is built into our genetic instructions, but when we are born, we have not the slightest idea of what these needs are or how to fulfill them. To satisfy them, even before birth, we begin to create what is best described as a picture album in our heads and begin to fill it with detailed pictures of what we want. Our whole lives will be spent enlarging these albums. . . . Our personal picture albums are never hazy or general; they always contain very specific pictures of what will satisfy our needs right now.

Dr. William Glasser

. . . the important thing was not to be caught up in one's own lies or to be fooled by anyone else's.

Anthony West

Part I of this book was concerned with achieving three objectives: first, to show how urgent is our need for a clear understanding of the principles and practice of decision-thinking; secondly, to give a stage-by-stage analysis of the process of decision-thinking; and thirdly, to identify the features which are unique to that process so that decision-thinking can be perceived and studied, as it should be, as a separate subject.

Having described the theory of decision-thinking, I now turn, in Part II, to the question of how we can prepare and equip ourselves to put that theory into practice. I start, in this chapter, by considering the models of reality which incorporate both our perceptions of the past and our expectations about the future. This is followed by an evaluation of the three principal thinking instruments – experience, imagination and reason – which we employ to construct and interpret our models. Chapter 12 will then offer specific proposals aimed at helping you, the reader, to assess your own strengths and weaknesses as a decision-thinker. I then move on, in the following chapters, to identify the practical steps which a manager can take both to sharpen his perception of other people's decision-thinking abilities and to develop the skills and attitudes he needs to use, as a *professional*, to manage the decision-thinking process within his own organization.

We can only learn to improve our individual and collective decision-thinking performance if we are prepared to analyze the actual mechanics of our thinking. We must strip away the veil of confusion and mystification which surrounds it and look upon it as a practical human activity like any other. The fact that the physiological processes which underlie our thinking abilities are still imperfectly understood should not deter us from making an effort to 'know' those aspects of our own minds which are open to inspection and introspection. We do not, after all, have any real idea what makes a natural athlete natural. But that does not mean that inborn athletic talent cannot be developed and shaped by training and coaching.

★

In the most literal sense the tools we use in decision-thinking – or, indeed, in any other kind of thinking – are our brains, physiological mechanisms the workings of which we have barely begun to comprehend. A paper produced by the Salk Institute in California gives some idea of the awe which is felt by even the best-qualified scientists when they contemplate the mysterious processes by which chemical and electrical events in a few cubic inches of gray matter give rise to the phenomenon we call 'thinking'. To put things in perspective, let us first pause for a moment to ponder these mysteries.

The human brain is the most complex structure known to man in the universe. Beside it, the most up-to-date and elaborate computer is a crude, puny and stupid adding machine. In the three pounds of gray matter folded up in our skulls are ten billion nerve cells embedded in a matrix of a hundred billion supporting cells. Every one of these nerve cells, as far as our present knowledge allows us to judge, is independently capable of making separate connections with hundreds, perhaps thousands of other nerve cells. There is no way to adequately comprehend the complexity of such a system. But its essence must lie, so brain researchers believe, in the nature of those inter-cell connections, in the wiring pattern of the brain.

Consider a nerve cell somewhere deep down in the brain. Bathed in fluid that brings it nourishment and oxygen and removes its wastes, the cell lives a long life, perhaps as long as its owner's. Unlike most cells in the body, which assume a compact rounded shape, the nerve cell sends out long shoots in all directions. These fibers make contact with other cells and, where they touch, establish working connections called synapses. It is across these synapses that communication between the connected cells takes place. A minute pulse of electric current racing down a nerve fiber reaches the synapse, and there causes the discharge of a chemical known as a transmitter. The transmitter is released from tiny packages into the junction between the nerve fiber and the cell it is resting upon. The membrane of the receiving cell possesses receptors capable of recognizing the transmitter substance, and binding it to themselves. This act of binding triggers a response in the receiving cell. Typically this response might be excitatory, setting off another electrical discharge; or inhibitory, suppressing the spontaneous electrical firing of the cell. The response depends on the nature of the transmitter substance and – probably – of the cell that received it.

One cell sits like a spider at the center of its web of fibers, dabs of transmitter being deposited onto its membrane where the fibers from other cells form synapses upon its surface, in turn responding by releasing the transmitter from the ends of its own nerve fibers onto the cells it contacts. Multiply this picture by ten billion times, and one begins to form an image of the working brain. It is this constant chemical and electrical cross-talk between the cells of the brain that allows it to run the rest of our body, reason, dream, emote, compose music, [decide] and devise experiments by which to understand itself. ★

'. . . The most complex structure known to man in the universe.' Clearly, we must reconcile ourselves to the fact that, however dramatic the progress of brain research may be, we may not know for years or even centuries to come what happens in our brain when we add 2 and 2 and make 4, recognize a familiar face or make a simple decision, let alone how Shakespeare came to write *Hamlet*, Darwin to discover the theory of evolution or Einstein the theory of relativity.

Our ignorance of the brain's workings may, however, be less of a handicap than might at first appear, for we are still able to understand and manage what a mechanism does, even if we do not understand how it does it. Many people, for example, are rightly confident of their ability to understand and control what a motorcar does as it travels along the highway, even though their grasp of what is going on underneath the hood can be at best sketchy.

Thus instead of looking primarily at the brain itself, we have to look at what it does, as manifested by our own thoughts and the thoughts of other people. And we have to judge the quality of individual thoughts and decisions not by where they come from, but rather by their utility and their effects upon the real world. Impressive as it is, the brain is but an instrument.

★ *The Brain: A Quest to Understand*, The Salk Institute for Biological Studies; San Diego, California, 1978.

What it *is* we may never fully understand; but understanding what we can *do* with it matters a great deal.

Whether we simply call each separate product of a brain a 'thought' or, more comprehensively, lump all the thinking done by an individual together and call it that person's 'mind', it is clear that there is a level at which we can discuss what a brain *does* both usefully and intelligently. We not only understand, for example, the mathematical rules we apply when we calculate that 5 plus 4 equals 9, we can even build machines which implement extremely complex versions of those rules far faster and more reliably than we are able to. We may not know what, physiologically speaking, is going on in our brains when we choose salmon rather than steak, plan a journey or read a book, but we can develop – if we try – a reasonably precise understanding of the steps by which our minds can reach a decision or create an alternative.

In fact, much of our confusion and ignorance about thinking stems from an imprecise use of one of the most important words in our language – 'mind.' To avoid such confusion I should make it clear that I shall use the word simply as a form of shorthand for the thinking efforts required to implement the decision-thinking process – that is, to describe what our brain does and produces when we think about making a decision, just as the scientist could use the word 'mind' to describe what his brain does and produces when thinking about solving a scientific problem.

★

But I do not wish to trespass further into the philosophical minefield which surrounds the subject of the brain and the mind than is strictly necessary for our purposes. Certainly, I do not wish to confuse matters by considering the many different branches of thought – aesthetics, metaphysics or pure mathematics, to name but three examples – which are remote from, and largely irrelevant to, decision-thinking.

What distinguishes decision-thinking from other uses of

thought? Above all it is characterized, as I have explained in Part I, by being directed toward the solution of practical problems in the real world of human interactions and relations. It is therefore always focused on the possibility of human action and human reaction. Unlike algebra, say, or music, it has no point or purpose if done simply for its own sake and, unlike philosophy or physics, it has little to say about abstract ideas or any world other than the everyday one which surrounds us.

It follows that if we are to perform effectively as decision-thinkers, our first priority must be to ensure that we are indeed thinking about the world as it really is and not about some partial or distorted version of it.

This is, however, more easily said than done. Except in the most trivial circumstances, we rarely think *directly* about the real world as it impinges on our senses. We may, it is true, react instinctively when we touch something that is too hot or see something that frightens us – but we have all, nevertheless, reached for or flinched from things which we thought to be there, but were not. For most of the time, and certainly when we are concerned with the complex processes of decision-thinking, what we are thinking about is not the real world but our own *model* of that world.

We experience, think and decide – that is, create our questions and alternatives, and make our predictions and decisions – about the world through a model of it which mirrors both our own personal experience and such knowledge of other people's experiences as we have been able to gather from conversation, books, films, newspapers, reports and all the other sources of information available to us. As we accumulate experience and add to our store of information, so our model of reality changes and expands to take this new material into account.

But our model, our accumulated perception of the world, is not a haphazard pile of facts stacked one on top of another. We all have a fundamental need to make sense of events and this leads us to try to fit them together in order to create a structure that is intelligible to us.

The need to make sense of events and to construct a model of reality which yields accurate and useful predictions about the future, is a fundamental human requirement. The obvious danger is that, faced with the monumental complexities of today's world, we may try to cope with them either by devising models which are simplistic and artificially rigid, or by shutting our eyes to reality and constructing a model of the world which shows it as we would like it to be rather than as it actually is. Naturally, if we start relying upon inaccurate or inappropriate models of the past, we will inevitably place a false interpretation upon present events – thus further distorting our model of reality – and consequently make predictions about the future which are unrealistic.

★

Those of us who have to cope with the practical problems of managing an organization and planning for its future are all striving to understand events as they unfold and to apply that understanding to our thinking about the future. If we are to do this effectively we must appreciate that our need to structure our knowledge and experience shapes all our thinking. If we have no model of the world, no working hypothesis that allows us to explain what has happened in the past, and to simulate and then predict what is likely to happen in the future, we will be helpless.

Now, if you feel that this talk of models of reality may be all very well for philosophers, but that it is a bit airy-fairy for practical decision-thinkers, I would draw your attention to a recent article in the *Harvard Business Review*. The author, Pierre Wack, was formerly head of the Business Environment Division of Royal Dutch Shell's Group Planning Department, where he helped to develop that company's approach to 'scenario planning'.

In his paper Mr Wack emphasizes that the real battle he and his colleagues had in trying to persuade senior management to adapt to the rapidly changing business conditions of the 1970s and 1980s centered upon the need to change their perceptions of the business environment as a whole. As he puts it:

Scenarios deal with two worlds: the world of facts and the world of perceptions. They explore for facts but they aim at perceptions inside the heads of decision makers. Their purpose is to gather and transform information of strategic importance into fresh perceptions. This transformation process is not trivial – more often than not it does not happen. When it works it is a creative experience that generates a heartfelt 'Aha' from your managers and leads to strategic insights beyond the mind's previous reach.

I have found that getting to the management 'Aha' is the real challenge of scenario analysis. It does not simply leap at you when you've presented all the possible alternatives, no matter how eloquent your expression or how beautifully drawn your charts. It happens when your message reaches the microcosms of decision makers, obliges them to question their assumptions about how their business world works, and leads them to change and reorganize *their inner models of reality*.*

The article goes on to explain how Shell benefited from the insights which Mr Wack and his colleagues were able to achieve and communicate to those responsible for the giant corporation's decision making. But even at much less powerful levels of business the need for managers to update and revise their models of the world is no less urgent.

Shell may have been concerned with problems of Middle East politics and world demand for oil in a period when the business cycle was seesawing; but in a rapidly changing world much smaller businesses can be seriously affected if their managers' perceptions are overtaken by events. The store owner who failed to foresee and come to terms with the impact of electronics on consumer products, or the farmer who borrowed heavily against the value of his land in the late 1970s, have discovered, to their cost, that they too could fall victim to changes which rendered their model of the business environment outdated.

The way in which we use our models of reality must also

* Pierre Wack, 'Scenarios: Uncharted Waters Ahead', *Harvard Business Review*, September/October 1985, pp. 73–89; 'Scenarios: Shooting the Rapids', *Harvard Business Review*, November/December 1985, pp. 139–150. (My italics.)

take account of the fact that other people's models may be very different from our own. One may find today, in the same country, even the same town, people for whom a journey across the Atlantic is a routine affair and others for whom a 20-mile trip to the seaside is the most complex event of the year. The two groups may intermingle, talk to one another, do business with each other without ever realizing that each is operating with a model of reality which the other would find unrecognizable.

Most of you who read this book will share with me a model of reality in which personal property is something to be respected and honesty is a quality without which society could not function. But we will, unless we are exceptionally naive, have learned that there are those amongst our neighbors who view property, other people's property anyway, as something to be stolen whenever the opportunity presents itself and for whom honesty is a mug's game.

Thus the way in which we view the world and, in particular, the extent to which our models of it accurately capture the shapes and subtleties of reality will largely determine how well we are able to cope with the real world in which decisions have to be made and implemented.

To illustrate the point further, take the case of a European company with which a friend of mine happens to be familiar. They had a deceptively simple problem which became deeply worrying and extremely expensive to them. Over the years they had established in Europe a successful range of branded consumer drinks. They had therefore felt confident when they turned to the American market that they knew exactly what US consumers wanted in their field and that they were well-equipped to provide and market it. But after they had spent considerable sums on launching one of their products in America, it soon became evident that the venture, if continued, could turn into a multi-million-dollar catastrophe.

The root of the problem, when it emerged, was almost too simple. All the senior management of the company and all their faithful customers in Europe had grown up in a world in which a certain ingredient, let us call it 'wow', was a familiar feature of many drinks – all kids drank some products containing wow and 99.9 per cent of them liked it. A drink with wow in it had, therefore, a pretty good chance of succeeding and that, among other reasons, was why the company's attack on the American market had been spearheaded by a brand in which wow was the predominant flavor.

Unfortunately in the American market wow was an exotic and little-known taste. In the supermarkets and corner stores where the company expected to sell its goods, any drink with wow in it was treated with reserve and suspicion. Wow, which almost ensured success in Europe, could be a recipe for failure in America. In fact, if one really wanted to have a hope of selling the product in America, it would have been necessary to present it as an exotic novelty, rather as one might go about trying to sell British beer, say, or the Mexican delicacy the cactus worm *gusano de maguey* which represent equally alien and unfamiliar tastes.

Those in charge of the company were in danger of behaving in a paranoid fashion. They decided that initial consumer resistance could be overcome and they could, by simply throwing money at the problem, advertise their way out of trouble. As things got worse they persisted in imagining all sorts of elaborate explanations for their problem, instead of realizing that it was in essence attributable to the fact that they, and the customers they hoped to sell to, had models of reality which differed in one significant respect. No one in the company could imagine living in a world in which the flavor of wow was not a familiar and welcome feature of everyday life. But almost no one in the American market they were attacking had ever lived in such a world. Eventually the drink had to be removed from the market, but only after a great deal of money had been lost.

Another example illustrates the way in which perfectly valid models of the past may, if misapplied, lead to false expectations about the future. A company we were advising some years ago was deeply involved in the British dairy industry which, almost alone in the world, had maintained the tradition of the daily doorstep delivery. At the time in question, the early

1970s, over 90 per cent of British milk was delivered to the consumer's doorstep by the milkman and his electric float. Our clients, obviously, had to consider whether this state of affairs was going to continue or whether in Britain, as in so many other countries, there would be a switch to a system in which milk was sold over the counter along with other groceries.

After a good deal of research and some careful thought my associates and I came to the conclusion that, in this respect at least, Britain was likely to remain 'different' and change much more slowly. The reasons behind our thinking were complex, ranging from the fact that British refrigerators, as compared with those in countries with hotter climates, are small, through the British preference for really fresh milk which is not homogenized and has cream on top, to the conservative nature of the British consumer. But however cogent our reasoning, our conclusion was not universally accepted.

In their anxiety to ensure the accuracy of what was, for them, a quite crucial exercise in prediction which would affect their medium- and long-term plans at every level, the company sought the opinion of a leading American marketing authority.

His approach was very different to ours. He knew little of the particular circumstances of the British dairy market, but he knew a great deal about the forces which had made doorstep delivery of milk in the US a comparative rarity. And he was confident that those forces would make themselves felt in Britain within the near future with utterly predictable results.

His advice was therefore diametrically opposed to ours. Our model of Britain suggested that the dairy industry would stay pretty much as it was; his model, based upon American experience, suggested otherwise. He could not, in fact, envisage circumstances in which the forces for change, which he understood so well, would be defeated by conservative forces which were absent from his model of the dairy industry and consumer behavior.

Well, that was more than thirteen years ago now, and the last figures I saw showed that more than 80 per cent of the milk consumed in Britain was still being delivered to British doorsteps. And, incidentally, a lot of traditional and new grocery items, such as fruit juices, mineral waters and pet foods, are also now being delivered along with the milk.

This particular case history provides a useful example of the way in which an organization's future success or failure can depend upon its ability to choose correctly between two totally different models of the future, each of them based upon a perfectly logical, but totally contrasting interpretation of the past and present. Happily, our clients opted for our model which has so far proved to be the more accurate.

This is not, however, to say that our model will continue to hold good indefinitely. Currently, for example, Britain is under strong pressure from its Common Market partners to allow the importation of price-competitive fresh milk from the Continent, something that could well involve the company in rethinking their whole strategy and building a new model with new assumptions for the future.

Finally, let us examine the example of a model which will be familiar to everyone since it has played a major part in shaping the economic history of our times. The model of reality with which we are concerned in this case is that shared by virtually all those who were involved in formulating American foreign and defence policy in the quarter-century from 1948 to 1973. Whatever models you might have looked at during that period, whether those of liberal Democrats or right-wing Republicans, of State Department officials or Pentagon brass, you would have found two constant features: (i) the main threat faced by the US was seen to be Soviet military might and (ii) it was assumed that oil would be plentiful and cheap.

Few gave thought to the fact that, with the Western economies hooked on oil, an awesome weapon had been placed in the hands of a few Middle Eastern nations which were increasingly cutting themselves free from the apron strings of the colonial powers and the Seven Sisters of the oil industry. Thus, when the Arabs used the weapon which fate had handed them, the US lacked the means to react, and even more importantly, the plans and the will to react. Until recently, at least, the Western world was still struggling to come to terms with this failure – a failure to build a model with assumptions that would predict accurately that the Americans and their allies had *also* to protect themselves from a major threat that was quite unrelated to the Soviets.

★

Practical people may still ask, 'Why do we have to bother with models? Why can't we just experience and react to the real world directly?'

In the first place, there is very little of the outside world which we can experience directly and immediately: heat, cold, pain, noise, light, dark, smell, taste, blows, caresses are about all; and even these are, as it were, contaminated by being interpreted in the light of our preconceived models. The same smell may be appetizing when it comes from the cheese board and revolting if it comes from the dessert tray.

If this is true of something simple, like a smell right under our noses, how much more must it be true of more complex matters in our private and working lives. We cannot just look at a piece of fissile uranium and see that if it were a bit bigger it could destroy a large city. We have to 'look' at it using an enormously complex symbolic verbal model to 'see' that it is uranium, that it is fissile, that this means that it is made of particular kinds of atoms in particular proportions, which will predictably produce an explosive chain reaction, releasing a predictable quantity of energy, as soon as the mass is super-critical. And *that* model, which is based on common sense plus the whole of science and engineering knowledge, took many thousands of people many hundreds of years to develop.

Similarly an executive cannot just look at his business, spread multinationally over the globe, and see what is going right, what is going wrong, who to praise or punish, and how, if necessary, to change its course. He has to 'look' at the business using a complex *model* of the environment it is operating in and of the way businesses in general and his business in particular are supposed to 'work'. All he can see will be things like tables, charts, reports, budgets and plans. He cannot even see all the real events that underlie such documents – the nearest he can get to them is to make a symbolic model which he *can* see and experimentally manipulate in their stead.

There is an ever present danger that those who have to rely upon symbolic models of reality may work with models which are wholly misconceived. Just because the president of a major corporation has a nice neat chart on his wall depicting the managerial structure, showing who reports to whom, where the profit centers are and at which level day-to-day decisions should be taken, it does not mean that the business is actually working that way. It is perfectly possible that the chart is little more than an abstract fantasy, a model of the organization that has little basis in reality.

John Brown, the titular head of a major division, may, for example, be leaving all the hard decisions to Dick Smith, his deputy; and Dick may have become so disillusioned with his boss that he has taken to making informal reports direct to Bill Jones, his senior executive friend at corporate headquarters, who, recognizing the realities of the situation, sends his most important orders verbally direct to Dick, leaving John Brown to worry about his golf handicap.

It may, furthermore, be in everyone's interests to perpetuate this situation. John Brown gets to play golf three days a week and is not a bad front man and public speaker; Dick Smith is able to get on with running the division in practice, if not in theory; and Bill Jones figures that this arrangement makes for a quiet, effective life, and if his own boss is happy to believe that his wallchart represents reality, why disillusion him? If it works, it works. But how do you *control* it?

If the people at the top of an organization allow themselves to become divorced from reality in this way, then sooner or later trouble will occur. They will normally discover too late that they have been managing not an organization, but a model of an organization which no longer resembles the real thing.

When they try to put matters right, they find that the business does not work in practice as it should do in theory. It is rather as if they are driving a car and find, when they are cruising along the highway surrounded by heavy trucks and other perils, that their instruments are all malfunctioning – the temperature gauge is reading normal while the radiator boils, the petrol dial is indicating half-full while the engine stutters for lack of gas, nor do any of the controls work properly – stamping on the brake causes the car to accelerate and when the indicator switch is turned the windscreen wipers come on.

Our models of the future – that is, our predictions and plans, together with their associated contingency plans – will only have a chance to be practicable and realistic if they are based upon accurate models of the past and the present. But although that is vital, it is not by itself sufficient. When we think about the future, we must consider not only how the world is, but also how it *might* change and, as far as our own affairs are concerned, how also we *want* to change it.

★

In decision-thinking we should never fall into the trap of assuming that one model, and one model only, embraces all aspects of a problem. Suppose, for example, that a company is debating whether or not to build a new factory on a greenfields site in a foreign country. Many of the points at issue can, clearly, be considered within the bounds of a model which encompasses just the firm's own finances and future plans – the accountants can work out, given the right projections, when the investment will be recovered and whether the return will be sufficient to justify making it. But to decide the matter solely within the context of that model might be quite dangerous. For it could well be to beg any one of a dozen questions, each arising within the context of a different model, which might be vital to the project's fate.

Could it be, for instance, that the site has features which are of interest to conservationists and that the arrival of the first bulldozer will signal the start of a long and damaging confrontation? Or is the locality so lacking in schools and other amenities that it will be almost impossible to attract the professional staff the plant will require? Or might it be that the current government, so anxious to woo foreign investors, is about to be supplanted by one which will be hostile to them? Each time a new model – be it ecological, social or political – is examined, potential problems become evident which would have never been spotted if the decision had been considered only within the company's own restricted world view.

In order to cope with such considerations a manager needs to be aware of a whole range of issues and of the way in which they are likely to affect the future business environment. As Shell's former Chairman, C.C. Pocock, said when discussing the company's use of the scenario planning techniques mentioned earlier: '. . . we believe in planning, not in numerical forecasts but in hard thought that aims to identify a consistent pattern of economic and social development.'

One of the great advantages of treating decision-thinking as a *collaborative* effort is that everyone will have a slightly different model or, rather, set of models, and will look at ideas, therefore, from a different point of view. Like a navigator plotting a course on a chart, the manager can use other people's models to obtain cross-bearings which will ensure that he gets a regular fix on reality as his thinking progresses.

At each of the four stages of the decision-thinking process different models will be used in different ways. Stage 1 – the question stage – for example, involves the consideration of models which represent an existing set of circumstances. We could be asking ourselves what, given these conditions, should we do to solve a specific problem? Or how, if our business is currently in this situation, will it be faring in three years' time? Clearly it is vital that the model we are considering should correspond as closely as possible with reality. If we employ an inaccurate or oversimplified model, then we will end up asking ourselves a question that misses the real issues.

Success at Stage 2 – the alternatives stage – depends upon our ability to construct the widest possible range of intelligent proposals in response to our Stage 1 model. This, in turn, depends upon the flexibility and inventiveness of the models we bring to the task. The person whose model of the world is rigid and constrained by firm rules about the way things 'ought to be done' or the way people 'should react' will be of little help.

To take some examples – a person's thinking about the problem of overpopulation could be limited by his model of moral behavior, a model which excludes birth control; a pacifist's ideas about the problems of international relations will exclude the option of war; a cattleman contemplating the need to extend his ranching business might dismiss the possibility of buying a flock of sheep as simply unthinkable. The people who excel at Stage 2 are those whose models have no preset limits, who do not take anything for granted or assume that something cannot be done simply because it has never been done before.

The models initially generated in the course of Stage 2 will usually be relatively crude and simplistic – broad, impressionistic outlines which may or may not prove to be workable. Stage 3 – the predicting stage – involves taking these rather basic models and testing them (often to destruction) by seeing what happens when they are incorporated in a wider, more general model or scenario of the future, which includes predictions about the influences and reactions of other people and organizations, and about the effect of extraneous and uncontrollable factors. The model-building skills required at this stage are those of the patient thinker who, as each bit is added, tests it for strength and accuracy and ruthlessly rejects it if it proves inadequate.

Finally, at Stage 4– the decision stage – the decision maker looks at all the models coming out of Stage 2 which have been expanded and survived Stage 3, assesses their relative strengths and weaknesses, attractions and disadvantages, risks and rewards, and chooses the one which he judges to be preferable. Where there is a possibility of snags emerging, and these can be foreseen, he tries to provide for them by adopting hedging policies and contingency plans. But he will, or should, be aware that, in reaching a decision, he has been making a choice not between alternative versions of future reality – there is, after all, only one version which will actually come to exist, objectively speaking – but between alternative models, based on specific assumptions about future reality, none of which can possibly be guaranteed in advance to be accurate.

★

Throughout the four-stage decision-thinking process, then, the minds of the participants are focused upon a whole variety of different models – made of words, numbers and visual displays. Each model and its assumptions will reflect some aspect of the world as it is or as it might become. Existing models are being examined, tested for accuracy, comprehensiveness and future reliability. New models, together with their assumptions, are being created, refined and projected into the future. These alternative models are then being tested by simulation and those which prove unsatisfactory are being discarded or modified. Finally models are being compared with one another to assess the chances that they can be realized, as well as the risks that are involved and the rewards that are envisaged. This thinking process will continue until, at the final stage, one of the models is selected – that is, decided upon – and the organization's energy and resources are then focused on transforming it into reality.

If we accept that models are the basic currency of our thought, then the following issues must be considered: what are the principal mental instruments that we use to construct, manipulate and interpret our models? How can we make sure that those instruments are kept in good shape? And how can we learn, individually and collectively, to make the best use of them?

Summary

Since decision-thinking is concerned with finding practicable solutions to real problems in the real world, our perception of reality must be as accurate as possible.

But we do not perceive most of reality directly, rather

what we perceive are our own models of reality, which we have created or borrowed from other people.

Our models are shaped by the way in which we interpret our experience, and they allow us to anticipate what will or could happen in the future. But if we place a false interpretation on the past or present, or if we are insensitive and unimaginative about the future, our vision of the future will be faulty.

In considering any complex problem, we must recognize that one model seldom encompasses all the relevant factors.

Because different people have different experiences and, therefore, different models, collaborative decision-thinking can help us to get a better fix or cross-bearing on past, present and future reality. These cross-bearings can also help us to develop each of the four stages of the decision-thinking process.

We use models to build the plans which we need to guide us into the future. Our plans are, therefore, only as good as our models.

11

The Instruments of Our Mind –
What We Think With

I see myself becoming a teacher of these branches of natural science, choosing the theoretical part of these sciences. Here are the causes which have led me to this plan. . . . It is above all my personal disposition toward abstract thought and mathematics, lack of imagination and of practical talent.

Albert Einstein, at the age of sixteen

To become professional decision-thinkers we now need to do some model-building of our own. First, let us imagine the four-stage decision-thinking process as a symphony of the mind. Each of the stages can then be likened to a separate movement, having its own theme and tempo, while also contributing to the development of a common theme – the answer to the question. The manager is, as it were, the conductor of the composition. The orchestra which is being conducted may exist entirely within the manager's own mind or it may include the minds of many players within his organization.

Just as an orchestra is divided into sections – strings, percussion, woodwind, etc. – so the decision-thinking orchestra contains a variety of conscious mental instruments. They are composed of three main sections: experience, imagination and reason.

Experience is our accumulated knowledge of how the world around us has worked in the past – our existing model of reality, if you will. Imagination is what allows us to envisage how it might work in the future – to construct alternative models. Reason is the formal set of thinking rules which we use to codify our experience, discipline our imagination, and test the effectiveness and accuracy of our models of the past, present and future.

It is rare for any of these three sections of the mental orchestra to play alone, but, even when playing together the balance between them often changes. The manager must ensure that each section plays in harmony with the others, even though first one and then another section predominates. To do this he must understand the strengths and weaknesses of each section and must know how to deploy them both separately and in concert.

★

Our personal, first-hand experience is perhaps our single most important thinking resource. It represents hard-won and invaluable knowledge which can be supplemented, but never altogether replaced, by second-hand experience. There are many managerial skills which, like the knack of swimming or riding a bicycle, can never be learned except by trial and error. You can learn what you are supposed to do easily enough from reading a book or listening to a lecture, but you will never *know* how to do it until you have actually done it.

It is, of course, a fatal mistake to assume that wisdom automatically comes with experience. As the saying warns us, there is no fool like an old fool. Experience is of no use, unless we think about it and learn from it. But true wisdom can never develop without experience. The young, if lacking in experience, may be brilliant, brave, inventive and energetic, but they will not be wise decision-thinkers. Wisdom comes from the university of hard knocks and from nowhere else.

Yet I am often amazed at how ruthlessly and wastefully

we in the West squander experience, that most valuable and irreplaceable of resources. I have good reason to appreciate the benefits that it can bring to decision-thinking and the extent to which those benefits are spurned in Europe and the United States (though not, let it be noted, in Japan). Our own advisory business has relied heavily upon associates who have retired, or been forced to retire, just at the point when their experience, accumulated over long and distinguished careers, was reaching its peak. They are people who have run international businesses, made acquisitions, fought off predators and advised important companies; some were involved in the management of government agencies.

Of course, their experience does not guarantee that they will see the problems and opportunities of our clients more clearly and more accurately than other, younger members of the firm. Often their experience provides just one contribution among many to our thinking.

It is, nevertheless, a contribution which is both crucial and irreplaceable. We could go out tomorrow and hire a fully qualified accountant or an economic forecaster with a string of degrees after his name, but the strategic expertise we and our clients stand most in need of is not measured in terms of such qualifications. And I am acutely aware that, without the experience of these associates, my own thinking would lack a leavening of wisdom, which could not be replaced from any other source.

Unlike the Japanese, who revere age and the experience that comes with it, Western businessmen often act as if senility sets in overnight once an executive reaches the age of sixty. The figure who, yesterday, was to be feared and obeyed is, today, just another old duffer who can safely be ignored or, at best, humored along.

I am not, I hasten to add, proposing that every CEO should be permitted to remain in power until he himself decides that he is ready to quit; what I am suggesting is that even after they have handed over the responsibility for the running of a company, such people represent a valuable thinking resource of which we can and should make far better use.

I have found that experience makes a particularly import-ant contribution at the third stage of the decision-thinking process. Those who are rich in experience, while being perhaps a little poorer than they once were in energy and drive, are not only well qualified for the sort of thinking involved, they are also temperamentally well suited to it. With experience there often comes the patience needed to think something through, to tease out all its subtleties, implications and potential consequences.

As a person's thinking matures with age and increased experience, so it becomes more reflective. There is less tendency toward impatience and a greater tolerance of complexity and uncertainty. Clarity of mind is less likely to be clouded by ambition, self-interest or personal feelings, and problems be-come interesting for their own sake – which is vital for the pure thinking we need. All of these traits are invaluable in the context of Stage 3, where we are obliged to try to look accurately into the future.

To illustrate this point, just consider the difference between the boilingly ambitious and comparatively simple-minded forty-year-old and the patient, shrewd sixty-year-old Lee Iacocca as revealed in his autobiography.

But what can a young, ambitious manager do if he is lacking in experience? He will hardly be satisfied with the suggestion that he should not engage in decision-thinking until he grows older. The remedy is simple: he must seek out and make use of other people's experience. If arrogance or personal insecurity prevents him from doing this, sooner or later he and his organization will get into trouble. By the same token, older managers often also need to seek out those with experience which complements their own.

This is not to say that experience alone, unaided by imagin-ation and reason, will be enough to allow us to arrive at a good decision. But when experienced people are at hand, a manager who neglects the contribution they can make to his decision-thinking efforts needlessly starves himself of wisdom, a highly precious commodity. We need wisdom in our thinking just as we need vitamins in our diet, not because they are sufficient to ensure health, but because their lack will certainly lead to ill health.

Experience plays a double role: first, it provides the raw material for our models – past, present and future; secondly, we use experience as a tool to help us interpret new experiences and to incorporate them into our existing models.

But just as experience which is correctly interpreted provides us with an accurate model of reality, experience which is poorly interpreted generates a false model of reality. If we start to misinterpret events in the past, we will then begin to anticipate events that will not happen in the future. Past experience alone, moreover, cannot provide us with a complete picture of the future. New experiences will always be lying in wait, and we must therefore always be prepared to re-evaluate and reconstruct our models. We must also accept that surprises will occur and be prepared to initiate events for which we have no previous models.

Thus experience should be our guide and not our dictator. History is littered with examples of people and organizations that came to grief because they took yesterday's experiences as an infallible guide for the future, and such casualties will only multiply as technology and sudden change accelerates us into the future. There were, to take just a few examples at random, the builders of the Maginot Line who thought that a Second World War would be a re-run of the First, the Western industrialists who believed that the Japanese could only make shoddy imitations of other people's products, and, of course, as late as 1972, those policy-makers who imagined that oil would always be cheap and would never be used as an instrument of blackmail.

Experience, then, is a two-edged sword. No manager can do without it; but neither should he rely upon it unquestioningly. What it recommends must be subjected to the cold light of reason and often transformed by the originality and vision of imagination.

★

Coming back for a moment to the analogy with which I began this chapter, I think of experience as the string section of the orchestra: it sets out the theme, carries the melody and provides a background for the other instruments. The role of the imagination, on the other hand, is more akin to that of the brass or percussion sections: its interventions may be infrequent, but they are often dramatic, and may be used to raise the music to a crescendo or to mark a sudden turning point in its development. When a manager asks his thinking team to use their imagination, both tempo and excitement will quicken.

Imagination enables us to modify (or sometimes utterly transform) our models of the world. When imagination takes flight, we can re-examine orthodoxies, reshuffle their elements, and combine them with new ones to build a model which differs radically from that upon which we previously relied.

If we depend upon experience alone, we resign ourselves to the world as it is; we forfeit the chance to think about how we might make it better. If we allow orthodoxies to rule our thinking in any field, be it manufacturing or biology, cosmology or economics, then we miss the lesson that, sooner or later, a Ford or a Darwin, a Galileo or a Keynes will establish a new orthodoxy that supersedes and dissolves the old one.

But we use imagination not only to create new models of reality; we also use it to interpret experience. To clarify this point, consider the case of those people, and we all know some of them, who produce an edited version of the past, a version in which they give themselves the starring role. The politician who is wise after the event, the manager who claims the credit for a subordinate's successful idea, the executive who 'always knew' that a plan would not work (but never argued against it) are not necessarily conscious of deliberately falsifying the record. Such people may simply be allowing their imaginations to censor the aspects of the past that they dislike. Unconsciously they embroider the truth to persuade others, and perhaps even themselves, that their role was more significant or worthy than it actually was.

This practice is not confined to individuals. George Orwell foresaw (and the official histories of Soviet Communism have

confirmed) that nations would promulgate almost entirely
fictional versions of their history.

But our imagination does not invariably, or even normally,
distort the record of our experience. On the contrary, it can
illuminate, enrich and give meaning to experience. Experience
by itself is little more than 'one damn thing after another'. With
the help of imagination – and reason – we can relate experiences
to each other, interpret them and decide what they mean.

If, for example, an advertising campaign misfires or we
lose a sale that seemed assured, something may nevertheless be
gained from the experience if we take time both to reflect and
to imagine why things went wrong. Why did our predictions
turn out to be wrong? Why did people react in a way that had
not been anticipated? What contingency planning should we
have proposed?

These questions will not be answered unless we use both
imagination and reason. Experience records what happened,
but imagination and reason reveal why it happened and, by
improving our model of the world, enhance the odds that on
the next occasion we will succeed.

But imagination also has a vital role in helping us to
construct our new models of the future – that is, our plans. I
have already emphasized its importance in the second and third
stages of the decision-thinking process. In Stage 2 we use the
creative powers of imagination to generate alternative answers;
in Stage 3 we use imagination to foresee the consequences of
these alternatives and to provide a basis for assessing their
relative merits.

Managers often have a bias against the use of the imagination or, to put it another way, a suspicion that people who are
'imaginative' are impractical creatures with wild appearances
and visionary dreams. Such people even try to distinguish
'imaginative' fiction (science fiction and fantasy) from 'realistic'
fiction – as if *Huckleberry Finn* or *Oliver Twist* were unimaginative works.

A person with a vivid and creative imagination is not
necessarily impractical; many imaginative people I know have
their feet firmly planted on the ground. They think about

the real world, not imaginary worlds, but they bring to their thinking an originality and verve which makes their ideas new and exciting. There are far too many people who congratulate themselves on being 'realists', and who are reconciled to dealing with things as they are, when they should be regretting the fact that they lack the skill to imagine how things could or should be changed.

Because imaginative thinking is so often viewed with suspicion and considered to be somehow unsound, managers sometimes push imaginative people aside into the backwaters of an organization and treat them as a species of licensed eccentrics or incompetents – full of interesting ideas, no doubt, but not to be taken seriously. Many managers make this thinking mistake.

The truth is that imagination needs to be treated with respect and brought into the mainstream of *any* decision-thinking task. Without imagination managers will become trapped into short-term, reactive thinking. They become pre-occupied with the need only to respond to events; they fail to realize that, if they used their own imagination and the collective imagination of the mind of their organization, they might seize the initiative and, for a change, make things happen or prevent some unpleasant events from occurring.

As I have already stressed, the creation of mental waste at Stage 2, in the form of more alternatives than will be needed, is inseparable from the use of our imagination. While it is often possible to see in retrospect which ideas were bad, and therefore where time and energy were wasted in debate that was ultimately unproductive, it is impossible to decide whether any serious proposal is bad or good unless it is first examined in some detail. Managers who try to avoid waste will end up, at best, with pretty unimaginative thinking – they may have avoided the waste involved in discussing bad ideas, but they will also deny themselves and their colleagues the chance of hitting on a really valuable idea.

When we move on to Stage 3, moreover, there is a real danger that we will concentrate only upon forecasting those prospects which we find pleasing or congenial. In most cases that means we will follow the primrose paths in our imagination which show everything going right and ignore the murky, muddy trails where things can go wrong.

For most of us, imagining a future in which things go wrong, and then creating a variety of plans and contingency plans to prevent this, is more laborious and less enjoyable than imagining a happy future in which things go right. Yet it is also, of course, necessary to carry out that more difficult task.

I emphasize this point because otherwise it is easy to conclude that 'imagining' the future is, somehow, an easy, relaxed and enjoyable sort of thinking in which we pleasantly daydream our way into the future. In the context of decision-thinking this is not so. The manager must steer his imagination and that of his colleagues, correct it when it begins to stray into improbability or self-indulgence, insist that it confront unpleasant possibilities, and require it often to explore territory which seems tedious or unrewarding.

To make good plans a manager must also predict how other people and other organizations will react to his initiatives. Imagination enables him to do this by helping him to think his way into other people's minds. To understand another person's model of reality, we first must make an effort to see the world as he does. We must imagine his assumptions, positions, needs, desires and other motives. In some cases this will be beyond our powers – for example, we probably can never know what it would be like to be, say, a Hindu holy man or a Japanese kamikaze pilot, because their models of reality differ so radically from ours. But in most cases our imagination enables us to empathize with the people who will influence the success or failure of our plans.

We can all imagine, for example, what it is like to be fired or to be denied a wage increase; we can imagine how the stock market will react to a bad set of quarterly figures or how the boss will greet the news that we have failed to meet budget. We can also envisage the confidence that our bankers will feel when a loan is repaid before it falls due, the enthusiasm that a well-timed word of encouragement may kindle in a subordinate, or, with the help of some research, the eagerness with which consumers will react to a new product or the sales force to a new bonus scheme.

On the other hand, we need only look at the bewildering variety of motives – desires, fears, hopes and needs – which guide our own actions to see that people often behave in ways that are complex and frequently illogical. To approximate how other people – voters, consumers, employees – and how other organizations – competitors, unions and government services – will behave in reaction to our decisions, therefore, requires a genuinely creative imagination.

Some people have a far greater aptitude than others for solving these kinds of puzzles. The novelist, the professional negotiator and the psychiatrist must develop the necessary skills as part of their professional equipment, but they will succeed only if they start out with considerable native talent.

The manager blessed with the imaginative knack of putting himself in other people's shoes is indeed fortunate. But those who lack it need not necessarily suffer thereby, provided, that is, they are willing to seek out and heed the advice of colleagues who do have this gift. Today, without such input it is almost impossible for any decision-thinking effort to be considered professional.

★

For all their importance, experience and imagination are difficult to define, and what they tell us is not always relevant or useful. But reason, surely, is above suspicion. What is reasonable must be right – or is it?

Anyone who followed the TV series, *Startrek*, will remember that the logical Vulcan, Mr Spock, was always reasonable – and usually wrong. Does this furnish a clue to our real attitude toward reason? For all that we pay lipservice to the powers of reason, our culture, as reflected in the imagination of Hollywood, rates it pretty poorly as an instrument of decision making. It was, you will remember, the imaginative Captain Kirk who usually came up with the right answers.

In my opinion we are right to be suspicious of reason, but only because we often ascribe to it a power it does not have. In the first flush of our love affair with the computer, that eminently reasonable machine, it was credited with powers that were almost magical. If a product was tested by a computer, a fact confirmed by a computer, a result predicted by a computer, then it was somehow *guaranteed* to be right. As we became wiser, of course, we saw through the fallacy and recognized that if a computer started with garbage, it would, quite reasonably, process it into more garbage. What all of us need to recognize is that the same principle governs our own reasoning powers.

We can use reason to manipulate experience and, in doing so, we hope to have new truths revealed to us. But, if the model of reality which we are using to reason with is an inaccurate one, then the result will be a structure as misleading or more misleading than the undigested experience. We can reason about a non-existent world as easily and logically as about a real one. Perhaps even more dangerously, we can displace reason from its proper sphere altogether and use it in ways that are not appropriate.

To take an extreme case, consider the world of mathematics. Using principles which are relentlessly reasonable, mathematicians explore worlds that have no connection with everyday life. If they deal with quantum mechanics, they can reason about the motion of electrons in a space having infinitely many dimensions. Their results predict events not predictable in a mathematics employing only three dimensions. But the reasoning used in quantum mechanics does not help us to understand the ordinary world; indeed, if we used the mathematics of quantum mechanics in the calculation of compound interest or the behavior of commodity markets, the results would be gibberish.

In the business world reason can be overrated and its confident, arrogant voice allowed to drown out the subtler tones of experience and imagination. Those who insist that all analysis be quantified, or those who will not even consider an idea unless it can be expressed to three places of decimals, see the world naively as a machine in which other people are like puppets without feeling, thought, imagination or ambition.

In that model of the world no one's judgment is influenced by a bad oyster eaten the night before or by the prospect of going on holiday tomorrow; no one backs a hunch, bears a grudge, or acts out of friendship or compassion. In reality, of course, people do these things all the time, and reason is of little help in predicting their behavior.

Reason alone, or reason which starts from false assumptions, is treacherous, shifting ground upon which to stand. Whether we are reasoning about the nature of the atom, the behavior of the price of pork belly futures or the outcome of the next presidential election, the conclusion we reach will depend upon the assumptions with which we started. And in decision-thinking the most important assumption, from which each of us starts, is our own existing model of reality. We will, therefore, use reason more wisely if we include in our model the assumption that, distressing as it may be, people can often act irrationally.

Once we abandon the notion that reason governs all human affairs, we recognize its value as an instrument for monitoring and interpreting experience. Reason checks our internal models against the external world and alerts us if the two begin to diverge from one another. Reason asks, 'Are you sure that is really what you saw?' 'Is that really what is going to happen, or is it what you want to believe?' 'Were you really so clever, or was it just a bit of luck that came your way?' and so on.

Reason helps us prepare our question in Stage 1 and identifies the information we need to create our alternative answers. In Stage 2 and Stage 3, reason analyzes our previous experience to help us create alternatives; it also censors our imaginings and sounds the alarm when they stray too far from what is probable. Reason – aided by intuition, that *sub-conscious* instrument of our thinking, of which I shall have more to say in chapter 16 – calculates the odds in favor of success and those against it. And reason, again aided by our intuition, quantifies the rewards and weighs up the risks in Stage 4 of our decision-thinking process.

★

Experience, reason and imagination, then, are the *inter-dependent*, conscious mental instruments poised for action and interaction as the manager raises his baton and signals the first beat of the decision-thinking symphony. As the conductor, he must feel confident that the instruments are tuned, that the musicians have rehearsed and that they will follow his beat and accept his interpretation. The manager, in short, must have brought the instruments of his own mind and of those of his subordinates together into a single orchestra responsive to his demands, yet not so disciplined or mechanical in its performances that all originality and excitement is lost.

It is not to be expected that any manager will have a mind that contains the perfect blend of talents wanted for decision-thinking – a rich, well-ordered experience, balanced by a prolific yet disciplined imagination, and both of these governed by a clear and exact reason. Certainly, no manager should perceive his role in the organization as a one-man-band – a master of all the instruments of the mind, capable of solving every sort of problem by his own, unaided efforts. Rather like any good conductor, he should aim to build up an orchestra in which each section includes people of talent, and he should devote himself to rehearsing and encouraging the orchestra until each player is contributing his own mental gifts in full measure.

A professional manager, in other words, cannot excel in every aspect of thinking; if he is to succeed, he must excel at recognizing thinking talent, attracting it to his thinking orchestra, and ensuring that all the members of the orchestra work fruitfully together. He will, of course, have ideas of his own to contribute, and, ultimately, the responsibility for the final decision must be his. But he should never confuse his role as conductor with his role as performer.

★

If you want to improve your own abilities as a decision-thinker, you may benefit from using the two models described in this chapter as well as the one that will be discussed in chapters 14 and 15. These models are, first, the model of the manager as conductor of an orchestra of thinkers using the conscious mental instruments of experience, imagination and reason to realize their performance; secondly, the model of the decision-thinking process as a four-movement symphony of the mind which the manager must conduct his orchestra to play; and thirdly, a new model of a manager also as a coach of a team of thinkers.* If you consciously and conscientiously apply these models, I believe that you will find them apposite and helpful.

But, before you can assemble and manage the talents that will compose your thinking team, you first must take the measure of your own mind. In decision-thinking, as with the rest of life, 'Know thyself' is the first commandment, whether you aspire to manage more effectively either your *own* mind or the *collective* thinking efforts of both yourself and your colleagues within the mind of your organization.

Summary

To become professional decision-thinkers we need to build some models of our own. Thus we need to perceive that a decision-thinking orchestra is made up of three main sections: experience, imagination and reason. The symphony that orchestra must play consists of the

---

* The reader will note that in the following chapters I change the model for managing the decision-thinking process. Hereafter I will compare the management of that process to the management of a team engaged in a sport such as baseball or football. In this chapter the orchestra metaphor fits better with the mental *functions* being discussed. But, I think the mental *interactions* between a manager and his colleagues, which will shortly be considered, can best be analyzed when using the model of a coach and his team of players.

four movements – that is, the four stages – of the decision-thinking process. It is the manager's responsibility to conduct this orchestra through the four stages within both his own mind and the mind of his organization in order to arrive at the best decisions.

Never underrate the value of experience, because it is the only source of true wisdom. Whenever you lack experience, seek out and make use of other people's – but only from those people who have bothered to learn from their own experiences.

Because imagination can help you to understand and interpret your experience, it is essential in allowing you to create alternative answers to any complex problem. It is also essential to effective thinking about the future, to predicting the consequences and the reactions of others to each alternative you are considering, and to preparing hedging and contingency plans. So make sure you always bring the instrument of imagination into the mainstream of your organization's thinking.

Beware of the tyranny of reason; other people seldom act – or react – totally reasonably. Rather, use reason to make sense of your experience and to discipline and test the products of your imagination and intuition.

No one person, not even an Einstein, can expect to have the perfect blend of experience, imagination and reason, but a good decision-thinking team can achieve something close to it. It is a professional manager's responsibility to first build, and then manage, such a team.

12

Know Thy Thinking Self

One must 'know thyself'. This (with 'nothing too much') was the favorite dictum of the Greeks and yet their greatest thinker fell short of outlining a technique whereby we go about to fulfill it. Something of going about to catch oneself in one's inevitable evasions of self-candor. Something of experimenting in the possibilities of one's traits. Something of frankly taking pride in one's merits.

Thornton Wilder

We in America feel a compulsion to be constantly measuring and quantifying the level of performance we achieve in almost every department of life. Baseball players are graded according to their batting averages, workers according to their salaries, citizens by their credit ratings, politicians by their standing in the opinion polls, children by their school grades, companies by their P/E ratios. Almost anything, it seems, even a woman's attractiveness, can be reduced to a set of vital statistics.

But in almost every case in which such measurements are applied to human worth or talent, the result is crude, simplistic and misleading. At best they allow us to make facile judgements, at worst they encourage the use of standards that are utterly phoney.

One of the most futile and dangerous examples of this whole attitude is the idea that a person's intelligence or thinking ability can be measured and expressed as a single number in the form of an IQ. Most of us will know people whose lives have been highly successful, but who, according to the intelligence testers, are probably of no more than average intelligence. Some of us have also had the misfortune to work with people who, despite having IQs in the genius or near genius range, have displayed a practical incompetence and a lack of judgment that have bewildered less intelligent folk.

Whatever value or interest IQ tests and similar formulas for quantifying people's mental capacities may have for the psychologist (and psychology is increasingly discarding such methods as crude and unreliable), they are useless as a yardstick with which to measure an individual's potential for coping with the practical problems that confront the decision-thinker.

In fact, if taken seriously they are not just useless, but positively harmful. No one is more confident of his own abilities, and with less cause, than the man who places his faith and value in his own high IQ – who demands, in effect, that his mind should be respected and admired not for what it *does*, but for what it is. This is an attitude, moreover, that not only causes the individual concerned to overrate his own abilities; it almost inevitably, and justifiably, earns him the suspicion and dislike of his colleagues.

No matter whether you are attempting to assess your own thinking abilities or trying to weigh up other people's, you will not get very far if you assume that they can be placed somewhere on a single scale running from 'brilliant' to 'dumb'. Decision-thinking demands a range of talents, and it is very unlikely indeed that any single mind will contain them all in equal measure – no more likely, in fact, than that an Olympic weight-lifter will also be a world-beating sprinter. The decathlon competitor who is good at a wide range of events is seldom outstanding at any one of them.

I have started this chapter by emphasizing my distrust of systems which purport to measure people's thinking abilities by any single yardstick because I do not want anything that follows to be misunderstood. In proposing that you, the reader, should make an assessment of your own abilities as a thinker, I am not suggesting that you should try to determine how 'good' or 'bad' your mind is, let alone that you should grade your intelligence as being so many points above or below some abstract standard. What I am proposing is that you should try, first, to arrive at a realistic and objective appreciation of your own particular strengths and weaknesses, and then to understand the way in which these influence your total decision-thinking performance.

In the previous chapter I drew a parallel between the instruments of an orchestra and the conscious instruments of our mind – experience, imagination and reason. To suggest that John Dreamer, with his vivid imagination but comparatively weak reasoning powers, is automatically a better or worse decision-thinker than Bill Reason, with his incisive analytical mind which has about as much imagination as a calculating machine, is absurd – as absurd as arguing that the woodwind section of the orchestra is more important than the strings.

No musician, of course, expects to master every instrument in the orchestra, and even if we are sometimes forced to rely solely upon the instruments of our own mind, we should be aware that we cannot normally play them all with equal skill. Therefore, whenever possible we need to seek help from those whose abilities complement our own. Every instrument has its virtuosos, but one-man bands do not play symphonies.

The manager responsible for conducting any decision-thinking performance – be that his own or that of his organization – must therefore start with a sound and shrewd assessment of his own thinking abilities. Only if he knows his own *thinking* strengths and weaknesses can he start to build upon the former and, as far as is possible, remedy or compensate for the latter. Only when he understands where his own talents lie can he look around for the indispensable talents that will balance and complement them. And only after he has assessed his own skills as a manager, motivator and assessor of other people's thinking efforts can he set about improving those skills.

Thus, 'to know thyself' or, more precisely in our context, 'thy thinking self' is certainly the first step toward the effective management of your own mind, the improvement of your own skills as a decision-thinker and, ultimately, your development as a professional manager of other people's thinking efforts.

★

What I have to say in this and the following chapter is the product not of psychological theorizing but of my own experience, both in private life and in the practical world of business. What I wish to do is to persuade you that:

1.   Each of us has different personal characteristics which affect our approach to thinking.

2.   Most of these characteristics have a vital role to play in one or more stages of the decision-thinking process.

3.   The more clearly you understand – through self-questioning, self-examination and conversations with family members and friends – your approach both to your own thinking efforts and to those of other individuals, the better you will be able to manage your own thinking and to cooperate with the thinking efforts of other people.

4.   It is, therefore, within your powers to improve your decision-thinking (in just the same way as you are free to improve your mental arithmetic or your golf swing) by study and practice.

How, then, should we go about measuring the quality of our own thinking? If it cannot be expressed as a figure, like an athlete's personal best for the mile, or as a statistic, like a baseball player's batting average for the current season, then what sort of yardstick should we be applying and what sort of answer should we be seeking?

What is needed, I believe, is a profile which reveals the overall shape of an individual's decision-thinking abilities; both the peaks, the areas where confidence is justified, and the troughs, which give cause for concern.

I have designed the questionnaire on pp. 173–175 (which has been reproduced at the end of this book as an appendix in case you wish to detach it) to help you construct a self-portrait of your own thinking profile to highlight those aspects of its performance which are relevant to your decision-thinking.* In order to complete it you need to assess your own characteristics as a decision-thinker under twenty-one separate headings and, in each case, rate yourself on a scale.

The scale, as you will see, does not always run from bad to good, from desirable to undesirable, but from one extreme to the contrasting one. Thus in some cases one extreme might be considered 'better' than the other, but in many instances this is not so. There is, therefore, nothing to be gained by adding up your 'score' – in fact, it removes the point of the whole exercise, which is not destined to obtain some overall rating for your thinking but rather to discover its principal characteristics.

Even if you do not feel that you would place yourself at either extreme on any of the counts, you will recognize, if you are honest with yourself, that you are inclined to lean to one side or the other. And how you lean makes all the difference to your daily approach both to your personal and your collective decision-thinking responsibilities.

It is not very easy for any of us to see clearly into our own mind or to report what we find there with complete objectivity. So it may well be worthwhile double-checking your own findings by asking relatives, friends and trustworthy colleagues to run through the table with you and give you their frank opinions on where they rate you on each count. Their views may not

---

* The questionnaire can also be used by a manager to evaluate the decision-thinking characteristics of his colleagues, as well as to estimate the decision-thinking qualities of people before they are hired or promoted. The manager may well find their replies highly illuminating – there can be a big difference between the way the manager sees other thinkers and the way they see themselves.

always be more accurate than your own, but any major discrep-
ancies should at least alert you to the possibility that you may
need to reconsider some of your opinions about yourself.

★

Once the questionnaire is completed, stand back and look
at the profile you have constructed. Consider the strengths and
weaknesses it reveals and the ways in which they may affect your
competence in each of the four stages of the decision-thinking
process. Consider, too, the characteristics that are needed to
complement your strengths and make up for your weaknesses,
which is a factor that will be of particular importance whenever
you want to assemble around you a well-balanced thinking
team.

For example your strengths, as you rate them, may be in
objective, analytical and decisive thinking, qualities that are
extremely valuable at Stages 1 and 4 of the decision-thinking
process. But these qualities may well be counter-balanced, as
they often are, by a lack of the imagination and patience that
are needed at Stages 2 and 3. On the other hand, if you feel that
you are a good listener and considerate of other people's feelings,
you are likely to be a good member or manager of a thinking
team, but you might have to beware of being too readily
influenced by the opinions of others or you may find it difficult
to be decisive.

Cautious thinking, and moderately pessimistic thinking
suggest that you are effective in the role of a devil's advocate,
but extreme leanings under these headings should alert you to
the risk of being unnecessarily negative.

Thus, each one of the headings highlights a significant
element in your decision-thinking which needs to be taken into
account. There is not, I repeat, any ideal shape for your profile;
everyone will be different and yet be none the worse for it. Only
the extreme ratings in some instances need signal a danger. Yet,
even if someone marks himself as 0 right down the middle on
every count, he has something to worry about − if only the

Your Decision-Thinking Profile

A. *Personal Decision-Thinking Characteristics*

5 - 4 - 3 - 2 - 1 - 0 - 1 - 2 - 3 - 4 - 5

1.	Enjoy decision-thinking		Find decision-thinking disagreeable
2.	Adventurous thinker		Cautious thinker
3.	Can concentrate		Mind wanders easily
4.	Easily discouraged in thinking tasks		Persevering in thinking tasks
5.	Intuitively biased		Analytically biased
6.	Good at working with numbers		Poor at working with numbers
7.	Optimistic		Pessimistic
8.	Like taking thinking initiatives		Prefer reacting to the thinking of others

5 - 4 - 3 - 2 - 1 - 0 - 1 - 2 - 3 - 4 - 5

B. Personal Factors Directly Relevant to the Four-Stage Process

		5 - 4 - 3 - 2 - 1 - 0 - 1 - 2 - 3 - 4 - 5	
9.	Tend to accept the question as posed (Stage 1)	I - I - I - I - I - I - I - I - I - I - I	Tend to query the assumptions underlying the question
10.	Like marshalling information (Stage 1)	I - I - I - I - I - I - I - I - I - I - I	Dislike marshalling information
11.	Dislike creating alternatives (Stage 2)	I - I - I - I - I - I - I - I - I - I - I	Like creating alternatives
12.	Dislike thinking about future consequences (Stages 1 and 3)	I - I - I - I - I - I - I - I - I - I - I	Conscientious worrier about future consequences
13.	Like making decisions (Stages 1 and 4)	I - I - I - I - I - I - I - I - I - I - I	Dislike making decisions
		5 - 4 - 3 - 2 - 1 - 0 - 1 - 2 - 3 - 4 - 5	

C. *Personal Factors Relevant to Managing and Cooperating with Other Decision-Thinkers*

5 - 4 - 3 - 2 - 1 - 0 - 1 - 2 - 3 - 4 - 5

#			
14.	Self-Centered (Ego Mind) approach to thinking	— — — — — — — — — — —	Team approach to thinking
15.	Manipulative (Machiavellian Mind) approach to thinking tasks	— — — — — — — — — — —	Open and objective approach to thinking tasks
16.	Receptive to other people's ideas	— — — — — — — — — — —	Not-invented-here mentality (Rigid Mind)
17.	Poor listener	— — — — — — — — — — —	Good listener
18.	Willing to seek advice of others	— — — — — — — — — — —	Reluctant to seek advice of others
19.	Unable to accept criticism and admit thinking mistakes	— — — — — — — — — — —	Willing to accept criticism and admit thinking mistakes
20.	Poor at stimulating other people to think	— — — — — — — — — — —	Good at stimulating other people to think
21.	Not careful of other people's feelings when considering their ideas	— — — — — — — — — — —	Respectful of other people's feelings when considering their ideas

5 - 4 - 3 - 2 - 1 - 0 - 1 - 2 - 3 - 4 - 5

★   ★   ★

degree of honesty with which he has marked his score. The idea is to get a realistic and clear picture of your decision-thinking characteristics in this essential context. If you do not, you will, as the Greeks warned, be kidding no one but yourself.

★

The results of this self-analysis should lead you to consider two questions. First, what can you do to correct the defects revealed in your profile; and second, how can you balance your strengths and your weaknesses when enlisting other thinkers to form an important decision-thinking team?

As in every other field of endeavor, the first step toward improving your decision-thinking is to identify those aspects of your present performance which should be worked on. The professional tennis player or golfer whose game goes off the boil will look to a coach to diagnose the trouble and prescribe a remedy. The decision-thinker may not always be able to get disinterested criticism and advice from colleagues within his own organization. This is especially the case if he happens to be the boss. Few of us would feel comfortable, if our boss asked us to tell him our real opinion of his thinking skills and practices. That makes it all the more important that any professional manager's analysis of his own thinking profile should be especially rigorous and honest.

There are some common decision-thinking weaknesses which can be treated, or even cured, provided that they are tackled with determination and self-discipline. No one, for example, has to be stuck for ever with a 'not invented here' mind. After all, it was more or less built into the Japanese national psyche until the late nineteenth century that all foreigners and foreign ways were intrinsically inferior. Then, quite suddenly, Japan ceased despising the West and started to try to compete with America and Europe on their own terms – the rest, as we know, is an awful lot of history. If an entire nation can get rid of the 'not invented here' attitude, then there is no reason to believe that organizations and individual managers cannot do so as well.

A thinking weakness is not cured, it should be added, by going to the opposite extreme. The manager who carries numeracy to the point at which he will not consider any argument that is not expressed as an equation is as dangerous as the one who cannot read a balance sheet. The manager who always agrees with the last person who spoke to him is just as foolish as the boss who never listens to anyone else's opinion at all.

But even where a weakness cannot be totally eliminated or cured, we can still counter-balance it or compensate for it by making sure that we are aware of its existence and constantly on guard against its effects. The habitual pessimist can learn to discount his pessimism; the person who places too much reliance upon intuition can make a habit of checking and then double-checking every time he is tempted to follow a hunch. Above all, of course, knowledge of our own thinking weaknesses should guide us in our choice of colleagues, aides and advisers, and influence the way in which we collaborate with them.

Often enough the mere recognition that a problem exists will go far toward minimizing its impact. It would, of course, be absurd to suppose that the individual who is lumbered with an unimaginative nature can, simply by acknowledging the fact, liberate hidden reserves of creativity, or that someone who is chronically indecisive can become bold and resolute overnight. But acknowledging that you are lacking in imagination should encourage you to stand aside while other people let theirs rip. And if you know that you are indecisive, then you should also know that you need help from people who do not share that particular problem.

If you know that you are prone to over-optimism, you will be aware of your need to have some conscientious worriers around you. If you find that you suffer from a lazy or a wandering mind, then (apart, of course, from doing your best to discipline it) you can seek out the help of people who are by nature cautious and meticulous in their thinking habits.

Patience and understanding will be needed if such collaborations of opposites are to be fruitful – others will be as irritated by you as you are by them, and if either party indulges its feelings, then matters can go badly awry. But however congenial it might be to have a decision-thinking team in which everyone's mind worked alike, it would be about as much use as a basketball team made up entirely of centers or guards.

The British, who have perhaps the most varied selection of beautiful racecourses in the world – flat, undulating, clockwise, counterclockwise, uphill finishes, downhill finishes, etc. – have a saying which is quite relevant to the management of decision-thinking: 'Horses for courses.' By this they mean that some horses will run better on certain types of courses than on others. They also apply this phrase in everyday life to practical human situations, when they want to say in effect: 'Let this person do what he can do best' or 'Joe is not suited to the task, but Jennifer is.'

So it is with thinking. Each of the four stages of the decision-thinking process is a different sort of course, which requires particular qualities in those who run it. In assembling a team of thinkers – and *all* major decision-thinking efforts require a *team* of thinkers – the aim must be to achieve a mix of talents which not only balance each other, but also cover the specific needs of *each* of the four stages. And, please remember here and in what follows, I am referring to a *thinking* team to formulate strategies, plans and policies, not a management team to implement and administer them.

★

Our personal approach to thinking is a fundamental part of our whole way of living and (as the existentialists say) of 'being in the world'. That seems obvious, but not enough attention has been paid to this basic point. Not only does each of us need to understand his thinking self in order to become a more effective manager of his own mind and the mind of his organization, he also needs to understand how his thinking personality fits into his total character. In other words, how we think and how we approach decision-thinking is an integral part of our total being.

Our own personal approach to decision-thinking is also at the center of our relationship to other people. If we are too rigid in our thinking, if we are poor listeners, or if we adopt a calculating, Machiavellian approach to every issue we deal with, this will obviously affect, fundamentally, our own rapport with other people.

Nobody likes to have his ideas rejected. If done brutally ('Don't be stupid', 'What's new about that', etc.), it seems to jar our whole system both mentally and physically. And yet in any complex thinking effort certain ideas will have to be thrown out – wasted. How we deal with other people when they reject *our* thinking and how we deal with them when we reject *their* thinking lie at the heart of how well we manage our mind on the job and in our own personal relationships.

Most conflicts in organizations, and even in family life, revolve around just these issues. The more skilled understanding you have of your own decision-thinking profile, as well as those of others with whom you need to carry out a collective thinking task, the better you will be able to deal with any four-stage decision-thinking effort.

I believe you will find that a personal analysis based on the table on pp. 173–175 will give you a clearer picture of your own thinking characteristics and your strengths and weaknesses. If you have the courage to be honest about it, you will come quickly to know your thinking self better, and in turn you will then have the opportunity to become a better decision-thinker. You will also learn about a part of yourself that is normally not revealed on the psychoanalyst's couch.

Once established, this foundation of self-knowledge will serve a further purpose. It will equip you with at least some of the insights that are needed to weigh up the quality and characteristics of other people's minds and will help you determine the sort of thinking talents you will need to complement your own decision-thinking skills in order to build around you the best thinking team you can.

Summary

To know thy thinking self is the first commandment for all managers. On the road to becoming a true professional, every decision-thinker (and we are all decision-thinkers) must begin by making an objective assessment of the characteristics of his own thinking.

Do not fall into the simplistic trap of trying to rate your decision-thinking abilities on a single scale; it is an overall profile, not a score like an IQ, which you are trying to establish.

Have you been honest with yourself? Double-check your findings on pp. 173–175 by consulting relatives, friends and colleagues

Once you come to know your own strengths and weaknesses as a decision-thinker, you can take steps to:

capitalize on the strengths;

remedy, compensate for and be on your guard against the weaknesses; and

find other thinking talents which complement, but do not weaken, your own.

13

Three Mental Poisons

*The human race walks around enveloped in an aura of narcissism
that would be laughable to any other animal bright enough to
appreciate it.*

Lance Morrow

To expect that you can get to know someone else's mind
in detail or determine how well it will mesh with your own in
the course of a couple of interviews is no more realistic than to
imagine that you can choose your ideal soulmate by chatting to
the guests at a cocktail party.

The sort of diffidence which many people display during
a job interview may, for example, be quite superficial and caused
merely by a lack of the social skills needed to deal with strangers,
in which case it will probably cease to be a problem once you
cease to be a stranger. But it may also be deep-rooted and make
it very difficult for the individual concerned to get his point of
view across to colleagues who have become accustomed to a
more aggressive or abrasive style. Similarly, assertiveness may
be a reflection of a person's genuine confidence in his own
ability or just bluster which camouflages a fundamental lack of
confidence. The man who radiates charm and expresses himself
with wit may indeed be charming, but is his wit the product of

a quick, alert mind? Or is it a glossy facade that disguises shallowness and lack of commitment?

One of the real problems we face when we try to weigh up for the first time the quality of someone else's mind is that we must also look into the future in order to see how it will develop. We want to know whether it will be equal to the challenges which it will face in our own organization. But the circumstances in which we must make the assessment are inevitably artificial. We are perhaps seeing that mind on its best behavior, so to speak. It is a little like trying to pick the winner of a two-mile horse race by watching the runners walk round the paddock. It is very easy to be overly impressed by superficialities and to miss the hidden thinking virtues and vices which will, in the long run, count for far more.

★

There are three thinking vices which I would rate as being so dangerous to the entire decision-thinking process of *any* team effort that the slightest sign of their presence – in yourself, in the people who work with or for you or in the people you are interviewing – should cause a red light to flash on without delay.

I call them, for ease of reference, the *Rigid Mind*, the *Ego Mind* and the *Machiavellian Mind*. These thinking vices are not always obvious or easily detected; indeed, some of those who are cursed with one or more of them may become very adept at concealing the fact. But any one of the three can today act upon an organization like a slow poison, paralyzing or corrupting its thinking and often doing damage which may be out of all proportion to the rank or position of the individual concerned.

The first of these afflictions, the Rigid Mind, is the thinking approach adopted by a person whose values and models of the world are set or stereotyped. He finds it impossible to accept that the thoughts of others might be of value, especially if they conflict with his own preconceived ideas and models of what is correct or important.

Here I am not talking about the kind of single-mindedness

and determination that is required to implement a decision effectively once it is taken. Rather, I am describing a mental approach that continuously blocks the openness of the decision-thinking effort which is required *before* a meaningful decision can be taken.

We have all met the Rigid Mind in one or other of its guises. Often it wears a uniform, sits behind a desk and tells us that this or that is quite impossible because the rules or tradition forbid it – or simply, 'It just cannot be done.' On other occasions it dons a cassock, climbs into the pulpit and authoritatively tells us what 'dogma' is to be believed. Far too often, alas, it is to be found in the boardroom of some large and well-established corporation.

One problem with the Rigid Mind is that it insists on believing simple 'truths' and seeking easy answers, while rejecting novelty, doubt or complexity. A classic example of Rigid Minds in action and a reminder of the terrible price they may exact is the war on the Western Front between 1914 and 1918. The commanders on both sides clung desperately to the conviction that the war could only be won by attacking 'over the top' at Verdun, on the Somme or at Ypres, because to think otherwise would be to undermine the established orthodoxies around which their careers had been built. They were unable to grasp the fact that the machine gun had rendered their concept of warfare obsolete. This inability to come to terms with *change* is one of the commonest characteristics – and failings – of the Rigid Mind.

The Rigid Mind also greets new ideas with suspicion and obstinacy. Many people were opposed to the New Deal, for example, because it threatened to overturn established economic verities. They preferred to believe that one set of economic laws was true, even if it meant that millions of their fellow citizens must suffer poverty, rather than facing up to the possibility that President Roosevelt's new ideas might work. And those new ideas, which they had resisted, in turn crystallized into a new dogma which then governed the Rigid Minds among a new generation of economists and politicians.

The Rigid Mind is clearly about as much use in decision-thinking as a straitjacket would be in gymnastics – worse, in fact, because it not only lacks imagination itself but, if put in authority, stifles it in others. The problem is not so much that the Rigid Mind is suspicious or critical of new ideas, but rather that it is afraid of them. It resists the new not because it might be wrong, but simply because it is new. It believes in the orthodox not because it is true, but because it is familiar and therefore safe.

Rigid Minds flourish and attain great power in bureaucratic systems, such as the Soviet one, where it is more important to be safe than successful, and where the correct answer is not something you arrive at by thinking, but something that is handed down from on high. The Soviet economy can, in fact, be seen as a sort of perverse monument to the Rigid Mind.

A competitive, capitalist economy provides far less fertile ground for the Rigid Mind, for a failure to come to terms with change, to adapt to new market conditions, to develop new products will ultimately prove fatal. From an objective standpoint, a system in which Rigid Minds bring about their own downfall must be considered more healthy than one in which they have the power to perpetuate themselves. But this is little comfort to those who find themselves working for an organization in which the Rigid Mind holds sway.

We should not confuse a person cursed with a Rigid Mind with a devil's advocate. Although the two may seem outwardly similar, the differences are vital. A Rigid Mind is instinctively and unreasoningly hostile to the new, the unusual or the unorthodox. A devil's advocate is sceptical and justifies that scepticism by reasoned and well-imagined argument. A Rigid Mind clings desperately to one set of ideas and rejects all thoughts which challenge or threaten those ideas. A devil's advocate acts as a control upon, and stimulant to, our own thinking by doubting and questioning our assumptions and proposals. In fact, a good thinker is his own devil's advocate and most ruthless critic.

Nor should it be thought that Rigid Minds are always unchanging. Often indeed they seem to experience conversions that are almost mystical in their intensity. The trouble is that, having seen the light on the road to Damascus, so to speak, they then cling to the new faith with, if anything, even more rigidity than the old. Everything is always black or white.

★

The second major enemy of professional decision-thinking is the Ego Mind. It reacts, often unconsciously, to the elements of a problem *only* in terms of self-interest and self-importance. Since weighing other people's reactions and assessing the way in which a decision will affect other people are essential elements in all decision-thinking, the Ego Mind is dangerously prone to misjudgment. It also creates serious obstacles to cooperating with others in any common thinking effort. Furthermore, it prevents one from dealing objectively with each stage of the decision-thinking process. 'Pride cometh before a fall' applies to the world of thinking just as well as to the world of action.

Unless we are saints, we all suffer from selfishness to some degree. And I do not want to suggest that there is anything wrong or harmful in a healthy degree of self-interest. But the person lumbered with a genuine Ego Mind differs fundamentally from the average individual who has a fair amount of ambition, a desire to make good and a reasonably high opinion of his own abilities. For the Ego Mind is not merely concerned to look after number one, it is obsessed with itself to the exclusion of all other considerations. Ultimately it prefers to take the leading role in a tragedy rather than play a bit part in a play with a happy ending.

Since the Ego Mind is totally uninterested in other minds, can spare little attention for what other people think and pays little heed to what they say, it is an unsociable beast with nothing to contribute to a collective thinking effort except pomposity or self-aggrandizement. Indeed, given the chance an Ego Mind will totally destroy the spirit of cooperation and goodwill which is the basis of any team effort. For its owner will see everything in terms of his own interests and reputation, and he will pass the buck or steal the credit ruthlessly.

When things go well, he will effortlessly rewrite history in order to make sure that the record shows him in a starring role. If they go badly, his first priority will be to make sure that he cannot possibly be blamed. He will not hesitate to betray his colleagues or even the organization for which he works if such a step seems likely to serve his own ends. He will, of course, have no difficulty at all in justifying all these actions to himself on the only grounds he recognizes – they are in his own interest.

For all these reasons an Ego Mind is about as welcome in a thinking team as a player who refuses to pass is in a basketball squad. It is not just that it contributes nothing of value itself, but also that it continually undermines the efforts of others. People will only think well together if they believe that they share the same goals and that other members of the team are pulling their weight. If they get the feeling that they are being used to forward someone else's personal ambitions, or that they will not get legitimate credit for their brainchildren, then they will soon mentally switch off or fight back with sabotage.

The most dangerous aspect of the Ego Mind is that its sheer, obsessive determination and its blinkered view of the world often give it an impressive, if crude, bulldozer power. Because it wants its own way, and feels entitled to it more strongly than other minds, it often tends to get it. Many first generation entrepreneurs, who founded and guided their own business, were helped by having something of an Ego Mind. There is no doubt that it is a powerful motor for driving a one-man band.

The problems come, however, when it is time to expand the business or to pass it on to a new generation of managers. Then the Ego Mind's strength of purpose manifests itself as intolerance of other people's thoughts and unwillingness to delegate or share power. Too often the Ego Mind of the entrepreneur, the very force which drove him to create a business, destroys that same business.

★

One thing at least can be said for the Ego Mind: it is usually relatively easy to spot. By its very nature it is not given to dissimulation or to hiding its light under a bushel. But the final member of our unholy trinity, the Machiavellian Mind, is a very different matter.

The Machiavellian* Mind is shrewder than the Ego Mind and therefore less common, but it is equally dangerous. In large bureaucracies and political life this style of thinking actually flourishes. It is one that is adept at perceiving how the feelings and ambitions of other people can be manipulated with finesse or even outright deception. It is vital that anyone whose self-examination leads him to see that he has a strong leaning toward this approach should learn how to control it in his own decision-thinking.

A modicum of Machiavellianism is, of course, a considerable thinking asset in organizational life. The ability to work out the consequences and potential moves on the chessboard of corporate politics can help to ensure personal survival. But it often ends up – and this is the critical point – by being so compelling an approach at *all* times that it seriously obstructs the directness and objectivity needed to arrive at the best decisions. If every thought is finessed and hidden in ambiguity and deception, then little will be achieved. Bucks will be passed, a second-guesser will be present at every meeting and decisions will be shirked. And, of course, such a mental approach, unless backed up by either exceptional intimidation or exceptional reward, can hardly inspire other people to cross the street, let alone make a whole-hearted commitment to a common thinking task.

Thus the genuine Machiavellian Mind is obsessed by internal politics and politicking. It sees everything in terms of power and powerplays. It is adept at manipulating behind the scenes, at playing upon others' hopes and fears and at covering its own tracks. The Machiavellian Mind seldom comes out into

---

* Here I have chosen to use the word 'Machiavellian' in its popular sense to describe the thinking approach of the devious and calculating individual. I am not referring to the practical wisdom contained in the writings of Machiavelli, the man.

the open and says what it really thinks, and the evidence that one is at work is often circumstantial and indirect. But when you find an organization in which people are constantly worrying about their status and perpetually currying favor among their superiors and harboring suspicions of their subordinates, then you will know that you have crossed the tracks left by a Machiavellian Mind.

Every organization, naturally, needs minds that are subtle, ingenious and even cunning. What makes the Machiavellian Mind so dangerous is not that it possesses these characteristics, but that it employs them exclusively in the pursuit of its ends within an organization. One of the most important tasks for the person at the head of any organization is, therefore, to ensure that his organization does not offer fertile ground to would-be Machiavellis. This means that there must be no kitchen cabinets; no secrets shared with some members of the team and withheld from others simply as a mechanism for showing or withholding favor; and no favoritism that undermines the cooperative effort of any thinking team.

This is not to say that everyone must always be involved in every discussion and privy to every confidence. What it does mean is that a system in which the boss behaves arbitrarily – has favorites or schemes with one employee behind another's back – will soon become infested with Machiavellian Minds. Conspiracies, clandestine meetings and secret deals are meat and drink to scheming people at every level and, in an organization in which devious behavior becomes the norm, everyone will soon lose the capacity to think disinterestedly and, therefore, clearly about anything.

There are, of course, other harmful styles of thinking – 'negative' minds, 'not-invented-here' minds, 'I want to be popular, at all costs' minds and so on. But the three thinking approaches discussed above are today so pervasive and so damaging that they must be recognized and dealt with – that is neutralized and managed. They normally lie at the heart of the worst decisions that have been made by the organizations which control or influence most of our lives.

What professional decision-thinking requires is what I call

pure thinking – thinking that is objective, creative and disinterested. How to get such thinking is the *perpetual* challenge that all managers face. A professional manager must therefore learn how to eliminate – if necessary, ruthlessly – all mental poisons from any important decision-thinking effort.

★

I have discussed these negative and dangerous approaches to decision-thinking at some length because I have seen, at first hand, the harm they can do. But I do not want to leave you with the impression that a manager's only, or indeed his prime, concern is to control or avoid hiring defective thinkers. Keeping the organizational garden free of such insidious weeds is a necessary precaution, but the first priority must always be to discover talent and to coax and encourage it into bloom.

If decision-thinking demanded no more than a brilliant intellect, as measured by an IQ test say, then talent would presumably shine out like a beacon in the night and spotting it would be a simple enough affair. But the talent-spotter who allows himself to be drawn like a moth to the brightest and most obvious lights will almost certainly fail in his quest. For as I have already stressed, in decision-thinking we are concerned *not* with one, general-purpose kind of thinking talent, but with a whole variety of different and often contrasting kinds, the presence of which may not always be recognized even by those who are fortunate enough to possess them.

Where a particular thinking talent does exist, moreover, it will almost certainly be balanced by other, less desirable, thinking traits. It may well be that these negative aspects of a person's thinking profile will be more immediately obvious than the positive ones. It is also quite common for decision-thinking talent to be deliberately concealed for a whole variety of reasons: because to display it would antagonize colleagues; because the person concerned is afraid of the risks that would be involved in thinking out loud or in writing about a complex issue littered with pitfalls; or perhaps, because there are no very clear rewards which could be gained by exercizing the talent.

In order to identify thinking talent where it does exist and to make the best use of it, a manager must learn to concentrate upon those aspects of other people's characters which are relevant to the business of decision-thinking, and to disregard or put aside others which are irrelevant or of negative or only peripheral importance. This normally involves a considerable effort of will and leadership and the abandonment of attitudes and prejudices which are deeply engrained, for the qualities of mind required in decision-thinking are not always ones which most of us would find desirable in friends or acquaintances. By the same token, there are certain characteristics which we might find understandable or even endearing in a friend but which cannot be tolerated in a professional colleague.

A conscientious worrier, for example, may be the last person in the world with whom you would want to spend a holiday. And the idea of sharing your private life with someone who likes playing the devil's advocate might be your idea of purgatory. But this should not blind you to the fact that, when it comes to decision-thinking, people with both these characteristics have a vital part to play. Or, in times of relaxation you may positively enjoy the company of friends who are frivolous and happy-go-lucky, but this should not encourage you to believe that similar people have anything to contribute to your professional life.

The professional manager, in other words, must try to set aside many of the considerations which normally influence our opinions of other people and concentrate on *only* those mental factors which are vital for his purposes – the ways in which their minds work, the quality of their thinking as it relates to one or more stages of the decision-thinking process, and their ability to cooperate and interact with other members of a decision-thinking team. The essential trick is to perceive both yourself and your colleagues as thinkers.

In order to demonstrate how the principles of managing decision-thinkers can be applied in practice, I shall introduce in the next chapter a representative selection of people, such as might be found in any organization, and show how each might be viewed by a manager faced with the task of welding them together into a *decision-thinking* team. Then in chapter 15 I shall move on to discuss the main skills involved in managing such team efforts.

Summary

In decision-thinking there are three kinds of destructive 'minds' which must be avoided at all costs:

the Rigid Mind, because it stifles originality, ignores change and encourages complacency;

the Ego Mind, because it destroys objectivity and makes thinking collaboration impossible;

and the Machiavellian Mind, because it turns all thinkers into bureaucratic connivers and all thinking into 'political' thinking.

Most thinking mistakes arise when one or more of these 'minds' take over the decision-thinking process.

Learn to manage, or if necessary avoid, people whose thinking is dominated by any of these destructive mental poisons and be on your guard against any of them infecting your own thinking.

Decision-thinking, to be successful, must be as objective, imaginative and as pure as possible. It is a primary responsibility of a professional manager to elicit such thinking.

14

Perceiving Your Colleagues as Thinkers

The conductor is only as good as his orchestra. That's not hyperbole. That's fact.

André Previn

Let us suppose that you, the reader, are the new chief executive of a business with growing pains and a lot of problems to solve. You are now to meet together for the first time with the executive team which is going to have to help you think of the solutions. They represent a cross section of the sort of thinking styles that any manager has to be able to cope with and manage. Now you will need to get to know them as thinkers and weld them into a thinking team.

I have chosen a meeting as the venue to introduce you to your new colleagues because it is in meetings, formal and informal, that most organizational thinking takes place. Meetings also highlight the inter-relationships between people and, consequently, it is there that their thinking strengths and weaknesses show up most clearly.

A thinking meeting – as opposed to a meeting called to communicate policy or information – should be the forum where an organization's policy is openly debated and decided. It is the manager's responsibility to make sure that it functions as such. This not only means that he must be an effective chairman, keeping the discussion moving forward, ensuring that it does not degenerate into a series of wrangles, and intervening if and when it strays off the point. It also involves treating each of the participants as an individual who has a particular set of thinking characteristics – a particular decision-thinking profile as discussed in chapter 12 – and who must be helped to create and communicate his ideas as effectively as possible.

In a meeting there will always be those who are ready to shoot from the hip as soon as a problem is identified. They must be encouraged to think twice before they speak. There will be others who are reluctant to commit themselves to an opinion or hesitant about criticizing their colleagues' ideas. The manager must decide whether this is because they genuinely need time to think or because they are simply waiting to see which way the wind is going to blow in order to make sure that they come out on the winning side. Some people are naturally articulate and forceful, but they should not be allowed to exercise their talent for persuasion at the expense of those who find that words come less easily to their lips.

The role of the manager leading a formal or informal thinking meeting, in other words, is like that of a football coach. He must have the measure of each of his 'players' and know how and when to play them.

You, the new chief executive, will need the support of all your executives as thinkers and you must make sure that you get the best thoughts out of them. But you will not be able to do that unless you understand what makes them tick as thinkers and use all the wiles and skills at your disposal to guide, motivate and encourage them. They, as individuals, may all be competent as individual players, but they will only become a thinking team if you do your job properly.

It is now widely accepted that a manager must consider his executives and employees as human beings as well as operators or doers, and manage their working lives accordingly. But in our context we are concerned particularly with your management of their thinking lives. This demands both a different set of skills and a different set of perceptions. How people behave when they *work* for you is one thing; how they behave when they *think* for you can be quite another.

Managing, in the fullest sense of the word, does not just mean controlling people and seeing that they do their jobs. It also means getting them to come across with the best contributions they can offer to the *collective* thinking efforts of your team in solving important problems and creating short-, medium- or long-term plans for the future development of the business.

Many problems arise because the majority of the people in any thinking team will have originally been hired not as thinkers, but as executives. They are department heads or specialists in one field or another first, and members of central management only second. They will have been recruited for their managerial qualities and/or their particular expertise, *not* for their ability to contribute to the collective mental work of a thinking team.

This means that you will often find yourself trying to fill a whole series of round holes with human pegs who remain obstinately square. The very confidence and self-assertiveness that makes one man a good sales manager, or the impatience and drive which makes another a good production manager, may become grave handicaps when they take their seats in your management committee and address the decision-thinking problems that are faced by your organization as a whole.

If you believe that I am being unduly negative about some of the characters I am about to introduce, bear in mind that I am setting aside the executive aspects of their talents and concentrating on their qualities as thinkers and as members of your thinking team. These qualities are of vital concern because these people cannot be excluded from the decision-thinking process; their position and status within the organization requires that they be involved in it; moreover, you need their special knowledge and experience. Equally important is the fact that the decisions you make will not be properly implemented unless your key executives have been fully involved in the deliberations that led up to them.

Inevitably it is the heads of the major departments or divisions who will form the core of your thinking team. But there will also be other members who are coopted because they have particular knowledge or expertise or because they are concerned with particular issues. Thus, the make-up of the team will not always be the same – indeed you will need several different teams, each with a slightly different composition and each concerned with a different range of issues. You will also need some players who are kept in reserve and brought on to the thinking field only when you need their particular talent or feel that they may be able to bring new ideas to bear on an issue that threatens to become bogged down.

*

So bearing these points in mind, let me take you into the meeting and introduce you to your new colleagues. I am going to overdraw these pen portraits in order to make my points clearly. I should, therefore, add that all these people will have good thinking qualities or else they would not be there; but in most cases it is their thinking weaknesses that you will have to worry about.

Jack is intelligent and articulate – but a fence-sitter. He likes reacting to other people's thinking, but not creating ideas for those same people to evaluate or criticize. He will always come up with arguments on both sides of the question or merely try to duck the issues. But ask him to plump for one or the other of two solutions and he will wriggle and writhe in an agony of indecision. You are not going to change Jack's thinking personality overnight, but you have got to get him off that fence – by shoving him off if need be.

Persistent fence-sitting is normally a symptom of insecurity or deviousness. Jack's thinking problem is that he does not want to take the responsibility of expressing any opinion which might subsequently prove to be wrong.

But do not let Jack's thinking faults blind you to his potential thinking virtues. A man who devotes so much trouble to picking holes in his own arguments may, if set loose on other people's arguments, turn out to be a natural devil's advocate. But you need to be careful. If Jack is allowed to be a full-time critic of other people's thinking and is never forced to stick his own neck out, he will become resented and may be seen as no more than your tame hatchetman.

Even though Jack has to be pushed off that fence, you can bolster his confidence by showing him that there are thinking contributions which he is uniquely qualified to make, and that they will be valued and appreciated. He must also be made to understand that you appreciate that all the members of your team as they search for the best decisions, will make 'thinking mistakes' and that without those 'mistakes', including Jack's, you are never going to get close to the best decision. Remind him that all good decisions require that more thoughts be created than will be used.

Dick is a bulldozer and suffers from the Rigid Mind syndrome. He is totally confident that he has all the answers and he will, given half a chance, drive them through the meeting by sheer force of character. Dick, clearly, is a dangerous fellow to have around when you are trying to deal with thinking problems which are not clear-cut and straightforward. If not halted, his bull-headed approach could quickly wreck your management china shop. He must be told, therefore, that if he wants to play at being an irresistible force, then you, his boss, will turn out to be an immovable object.

Initially, at least, Dick will need to be confronted on a one-to-one basis in a friendly manner. He should be told that you do not always share his confidence in his own infallibility and that, even if you did, you would still disapprove of his brutal thinking tactics, which simply have the effect of cutting off or stifling the other contributors to the decision-thinking process whom you want and need to hear from. He should be warned that he will be pulled up smartly at the first sign that he is ignoring your counsel.

Again, there is a positive side to be considered. Dick's boundless confidence and energy should be harnessed and used, not destroyed. So if you do have occasion to pull him up publicly in the course of a meeting, take him aside afterward and explain why you had to do it – that you were not just pulling rank on him, but that you genuinely felt his behavior was making your thinking task more difficult.

There are some people like Dick, of course, who do not take kindly to being disciplined and who may, if push comes to shove, have to be sent roaring off to demolish some other organization's thinking efforts. But surprisingly often in my experience, a bulldozer can – if well managed – also turn out to be a good team player. Bulldozers, after all, are powerful and tenacious, not easily diverted from their objectives and, if disciplined, good to have on your side.

Ted comes dangerously close to having an Ego Mind and is a real Lone Ranger. He finds it hard *ever* to look beyond his own self-interest in order to consider other people's viewpoints or the wider problems of the organization. If, for example, he is appointed to run a department, he will be quite unable to take off his department chief's hat and exchange it for a member-of-the-executive-committee hat. He will also be unable to imagine any circumstances in which his department should give rather than take. He will certainly never admit he or it has made a mistake.

Somehow, if you are to get the full value of his brilliant potential as a team member, Ted is going to have to be persuaded to drop his blinkers. One way of speeding up the process is to make certain that the *thinking* assignments he is given force him to look at the bigger picture. Another is to take some examples of his narrow, blinkered thinking and go through them in detail with him, making it clear that you have seen through his attempts to dress up personal or departmental interests in the garb of general ones, and explaining why this sort of approach will, if he continues with it, diminish rather than enhance your regard for both him and his department.

Ted's case is also one that can be used to illustrate a more general point: the importance of getting people to put their thinking in writing. There are at least three excellent reasons for insisting that this be done. First, the actual process of writing aids clear and careful thinking. By slowing the mind down, so to speak, to the speed of the pen or the typewriter, you may force it to examine an argument in greater detail and, in doing so, help it to detect flaws, which can easily be glossed over in speech. Secondly, a complex problem is often seen more clearly when set out in writing, because nobody can keep all the issues clearly in mind when it comes to openly debating the subject. Thirdly, and this is the prime reason for adopting the tactic in Ted's case, it is very much more difficult to disguise partial or biased thinking when it is put down on paper and, of course, also far less easy for the person responsible to deny the charges when he is confronted with evidence in black and white.

So you should make it a rule that every time you find Ted advancing an argument or a point of view which you suspect is narrow or self-interested, he should be asked to produce a paper in support of it – but one which must show *both* the pros and cons. This discipline need not be imposed oppressively or offensively; it can easily be handled with tact and courtesy: 'Yes, Ted, that's a new angle on the issue which I would really like to mull over. Could I ask you to summarize it, together with its possible pitfalls, in a couple of pages by, let's say, Friday?' If there is real thinking talent beneath Ted's egotistical surface, this technique should quickly force him to confront his own limitations.

Peter is a playback artist and a latent Machiavellian. He belongs to the 'to get along, you go along' school. At meetings and in discussions he keeps his head well down and has little to contribute until he has a firm sense of which way the wind is blowing. Then and only then does he weigh in on what he has decided is likely to be the winning side. If Peter's arguments often sound familiar to you, do not be surprised: they are almost certainly your own arguments being played back to you.

It is, of course, very easy to lead Peter up the garden path, to let him think that you are going to jump one way and, just when he has committed himself, to jump the other. But such sport will soon lose its savor and may do little to achieve your objective, which must be to break Peter of his sycophancy and get him to start doing what he is, in part, paid to do – think.

Again, the only way to do this is to be tough. Flush Peter's real opinions out right at the beginning of a meeting, before he has had a chance to see how other people are lining up, and do not let him get away with vagueness or generalities. From time to time assign him the role of devil's advocate and, if you are not satisfied that he has been through an alternative with a fine and critical tooth comb, make him start over again.

Unless you can change Peter fairly rapidly, he will make no real contribution to your organization's thinking. For unlike Jack, Dick and even Ted, Peter may have no thinking virtues to compensate for his vices. The only thing he seems really good at is telling you what you should already know, your own mind.

This may be a case where, as a last resort, you should adopt a tactic that has to be handled with skill and good judgment – the loss of temper. This is, I emphasize, a step that should be taken only after careful consideration. Nothing is less effective or, in the long run, less conducive to good thinking than a bad-tempered manager whose temperament hangs over everyone like an ever present cloud.

But a blow-up on the part of a manager who is normally courteous and friendly is all the more impressive for its rarity value. And it may just be what is needed to save Peter from himself, though I personally doubt it. Peter, I fear, is a natural sycophant, in which case your next step is clear. If Peter cannot or will not develop a mind of his own, out he must go. Or if that cannot be done, then just remember to keep him on the sidelines when major thinking tasks are being assigned.

Dave is somebody who puts all his faith in numbers. He believes the only factors worthy of consideration are those which can be measured, quantified and balanced against each other. For Dave the marketplace is not the sum of individual decisions motivated by greed and fear, courage and caution, but a well-oiled machine which will *always* behave in a fashion that is statistically predictable.

It would be helpful, clearly, if Dave could be made to see that human fallibility and personality may have to be considered and assessed with just the same care and attention as, say, the current economic indicators or raw material price trends. But in all probability he really cannot help thinking the way he does; if you are wise, you will try to use his mind in areas where his strengths are valuable and his weaknesses unimportant. What you must never do is to allow Dave to persuade you that his narrow, quantitative view of the world is anything more than a partial one, which must always be balanced against other, more subjective and yet equally realistic, ones.

Nevertheless Dave has the potential to become an extremely useful member of the team, and will probably make a particularly valuable contribution at Stage 3, where the quantitative implications of any possible course of action always need to be forecast with meticulous care. Every team needs at least one person who is good with numbers. Dave will only become a threat to the organization's future if his restricted 'bottom line' view of the world comes to dictate your strategy, rather than being just one factor among the many which should guide it.

Tom is another person with a thinking problem, but one that can be dealt with reasonably easily. He has, as soon becomes evident, an original and inventive mind which is good for Stage 2 and Stage 3 thinking; but he is very hesitant about putting forward his ideas. It may be that in the past Dick has dismissed them prematurely or that Jack has sensed his insecurity and has nit-picked his way through Tom's proposals before he has had an opportunity to explain them fully.

It may be useful on occasion to cast Tom in the role of a devil's advocate and get him to criticize ideas put forward by, say, Jack or Dick. It will do him good to be on the attacking side for a change and it will do the other two no harm to see what it is like to be on the receiving end. Moreover, because Tom has an inventive and creative mind, he may well be able to find ways around the problems which he identifies or he may be able to take someone else's idea and develop it in a new and unexpected direction.

What Tom clearly needs more than anything else is encouragement. So when he next comes up with a bright idea, go out of your way to emphasize that you think it is worthy of serious consideration and be prepared to offer a word of thanks. But do not go overboard. If you treat Tom as a favorite and greet his every suggestion with an indulgent smile, you will only make it more difficult for him to work with the other members of the team.

Jim earns a place on your thinking team not because he has a line position within the organization, but because of his specialist knowledge. He is the organization's legal adviser. Why, you may ask, not just call him in when you need him? The answer is that if you only involve Jim in your thinking when it has become obvious that a legal problem exists, it may well be too late. Seen properly, his role is not to cope with legal difficulties when they arise, but to make sure that they arise as infrequently as possible.

It is Jim's job to identify the possible legal hazards of every answer proposed at Stage 2 and to make sure that they are thoroughly investigated at Stage 3. If he is good at that job, then he will save you and your colleagues a great deal of wasted thinking and also, it may be, some nasty surprises.

Jim has only one important thinking flaw – which is common to many lawyers and other specialists. He is great at posing problems and telling you, with the arrogance that often accompanies specialist, but limited, knowledge, what you cannot do. You will have to bring him around to the view that you do not want him only to identify problems for you; you also want him to solve them. He is quite capable of doing this, but you will certainly have to prod him.

Finally, there is *Roland*, a cynic. Roland has only a couple more years to go before he is due to retire, and he is already making it clear that he is world-weary and without illusions. While Roland's career has been successful enough to earn him a seat on the management committee, he has not achieved the eminence which he feels should have been his due. He is sure that this is because lesser and more foolish people (like you, for example) have conspired against him or, somehow, gained an unfair advantage over him. Roland is certainly not going to help you get even further ahead by giving you the benefit of his hard-won wisdom. In fact, what he would really like to do is to persuade you to be as cynical and pessimistic as he is.

Roland is a real problem. In theory he may well be right in thinking that his experience has equipped him with knowledge and insights which other people still lack. But in practice he is worse than useless because of the way his fatalistic attitude can poison the 'thinking atmosphere'.

He must be persuaded to drop his cynicism and to think

positively, clearly and dispassionately. Perhaps he can be flattered out of it. If he believes that you really want and appreciate what he has to offer, then he may just decide to play ball. At other times he might have to be jolted out of it. If, for example, he is suddenly given a completely novel assignment and told that, even at his advanced age, he must either sink or swim, he might just remember that he is a very good swimmer indeed and strike out with a vigor that is totally unexpected.

In any case, it is certainly worth trying either to cajole or prise Roland out of his bunker of cynicism. But in the last resort, if pride or envy prevent him from coming out, you are just going to have to play it rough and either force him into early retirement or find some backwater where he can serve out his time, while doing the minimum of damage to your organization's thinking efforts.

*

This cast does not by any means exhaust the possibilities. You may find yourself having to deal with a whole variety of other characters: the 'not invented here' fellow who automatically rejects any idea that did not originate within his head or department; the pessimist who always remembers that every proposal has been tried before and failed and never stops to think that circumstances may have changed; or the small-print specialist who can never see the wood for the trees and tries to nip every new idea in the bud; and many, many more.

There will also, I hope for your sake, be some members of the team who need no help from you. They get their facts ready well in advance, marshal their arguments, offer – when requested – sound, objective opinions and are capable of stimulating the thinking of other people. When their ideas are adopted, they are generous in sharing the credit; when the final verdict goes against them, they accept a *thinking* defeat with good grace and set about implementing the decision which has been taken with energy and determination. They will be, we must hope, the bosses of tomorrow.

But few organizations consist entirely of such paragons, nor would it be a good thing if they did, for, as I have stressed throughout this book, people who have noticeable weaknesses as thinkers can also have exceptional strengths. The truly professional manager is the one who *can* remedy or neutralize people's faults, while at the same time nurturing and making good use of their virtues. In decision-thinking it requires many different thinking strengths – different varieties and combinations of imagination, experience and reason – and different thinking types – like introverted dreamers, conscientious worriers and devil's advocates – to bring the entire four-stage decision-thinking process to a competent and professional conclusion.

In short, when it comes to complex decision-thinking, everybody has the strengths of his weaknesses and the weaknesses of his strengths. There is a saying that an engineer is a man who can make a reliable system out of unreliable components; that could very well serve as a job description for the person who has to manage the decision-thinking processes of an organization.

Any new manager will ultimately have to decide, once each team member has been given a fair chance to show his or her thinking paces, who is worth a permanent place in the line-up; who should be kept and coached; and who will have to go or, at least, be kept on the sidelines, so that more useful thinking skills can be brought into the thinking team.

Summary

The very qualities that make someone an effective executive may make him a less effective member of a thinking team. It is the professional manager's task to surmount such difficulties.

Every management team will contain a mix of think-

ing weaknesses and strengths. It is also the manager's responsibility to bring out the best – and suppress the worst – in each member of the team.

This can only be done if the manager recognizes that all the members of the team, apart from being executives responsible for specific departments or functions, are also thinkers, each with his own particular decision-thinking profile.

In order to get the best out of every member of a thinking team, the manager must first assess their characteristics as thinkers and then decide, quite consciously and deliberately, how he is going to manage them as individual thinkers and as members of his thinking team.

It is during the uncertainties of Stages 2 and 3 of the decision-thinking process that the thinking weaknesses in a thinking team are most likely to become evident. The professional manager must overcome these weaknesses, if necessary by introducing to his team new members who have the requisite thinking skills.

15

Managing a Thinking Team: The Key to Coping with Complexity and Change

> *If you think of a giant human memory bank in operation, each of those General Managers Meetings [at ITT] had an average of 120 highly competent men, each with more than twenty years of business experience from all parts of the world and in different product lines. That's 2400 years of business managerial experience on hand for each of our meetings. And we had two of them, every month.*
>
> *As we listened to the points of view of one another, each of us became more sophisticated in our own knowledge of the marketplace, world economics, world trade, international law, engineering, and, of course, the techniques of business management. Moreover, we were all on one team. We became, in effect, a working 'think tank', a problem-solving mechanism in business management.*
>
> Harold Geneen

What are the secrets of successful management? Is it possible to identify a set of common factors that make some businesses or other organizations more innovative and effective than others? These are questions that are perennially fascinating, and books and articles which try to provide answers to them have flowed from the printing presses in a steady stream for the past century or more.

Today's executives read *The One-Minute Manager*, their fathers or grandfathers read Dale Carnegie's *How to Win Friends and Influence People*, their great-grandfathers probably read Samuel Smiles' *Self-Help*. Managers and would-be managers, it sometimes seems, are as ready to put their faith in the latest fashionable formula for success as slimmers are to believe that the next diet will, finally, be the one that works.

My own career has given me the opportunity to work with a wide variety of organizations, some highly successful, others less so. If there is one thing I have learned, it is that if there is a secret of success, then it is a very open one. For the one feature that all the most successful organizations I have been concerned with have shared is, quite simply, the ability to think better than their rivals. In every case the high quality of the organization's thinking has been directly reflected in the way in which the management tackled its responsibilities, set its priorities, managed its people, arrived at its decisions and had those decisions implemented. The successful organizations were smarter organizations. But why were they smarter?

The key to an organization's sustained success, I believe, has been that its managers have mastered the art of orchestrating collective thinking. It is not just that they and their colleagues have been able to think their way more imaginatively, productively and accurately into the future, but that they have done so as a team. In organizational life success is seldom due to the skill or flair of one person's thinking. What is needed is consistent, high quality and motivated thinking on the part of every member of the team whose job it is to think about the organization and its future.

In the last resort there can be no doubt that the ultimate responsibility for ensuring that the decision-thinking effort is complete and effective lies with the boss. For every boss, as I have already pointed out, gets the thinking he deserves, be it from his production manager, his sales director or his finance department. How, then, can a professional manager set about making sure that he deserves and gets the best thinking?

★

Although it has become hackneyed to the point of losing virtually all its original force, Harry Truman's point, that the office where the buck finally stops is different from every other office, remains 100 per cent true. Whatever the size of an organization, whether it be the federal government or a family business in rural America, the person who heads it will always be separated from those who work for it, at however exalted a level, by the knowledge that he has to bear the final responsibility for success or failure.

The interests of the boss, in other words, are much more likely to coincide with the interests of the organization than are the interests of the other people within the organization. Whereas those people may choose to give or withhold their best thinking according to their mood, their interest in the issue concerned, the time or energy they feel they have to spare, or their perceptions of what is likely to be in their own best interests as individuals, the boss needs everyone's best thinking on every issue.

This is not to say that there will not be occasions when even a boss does not have the best long-term interests of an organization at heart. He may, for example, be aiming at a better job as boss of a larger organization; in which case personal image-making needs and short-term performance may well take priority over the thinking needs of his current organization. Equally dangerous, paradoxically, are those chief executives with, perhaps, only a couple of years remaining before retirement. They often feel an irresistible temptation to try to ensure that their career will, as the French put it, *terminer en beauté*. Unfortunately, when engineering a wave in order that they may go out on the crest of it, they frequently adopt the reckless attitude toward the future that is summed up in another apt French phrase: *après moi, le déluge*.

But what about the manager who is happy in his present position, anxious to nurture the growth of his organization and, therefore, eager to manage the organization's thinking as skillfully as possible? Where should he start?

Every organization will have a hierarchy of executives, a team of 'doers'. And as I have already pointed out, the manager's first priority is to transform this group of people also into a *team of thinkers*.★

These executives have, therefore, two responsibilities. They must see that the organization's policies and plans are successfully carried out; but, first, they must make their contributions to creating the best possible decisions regarding those policies and plans. Much has been said and written about the 'doing' responsibilities of an executive; not enough about how that executive must meet his *collective* thinking responsibilities. In fact, most executives are selected for their professional ability to get a job done – to be a member of the doing team. But if they want to contribute to the thinking that is required to formulate the policies and decisions they are going to implement, they will also have to become effective members of the thinking team. And here is where many, otherwise successful, executives come unstuck.

The success of a thinking team, like that of any other kind of team, depends crucially on two things: how it is managed and who belongs to it. It is the manager's job to provide leadership; but he must also pick not just the best players but rather the best team. As any coach knows, the two are far from being the same. A soccer team, for example, in which all eleven members want to be goal-scoring strikers or, in American football, a team in which everyone wants to score touchdowns and no one is interested in being a blocker will never succeed. In the same way an executive committee in which everyone is

★ Although I will discuss in this chapter primarily one team of thinkers, it is obvious that a manager will have to manage various teams of thinkers – depending on the subject to be considered, the specialists whose views are required and any thinking gaps (as was discussed in the previous chapter) in his main executive thinking team that need to be filled. This being said, the core of any single thinking team will remain those executives with 'doing' responsibilities who report directly to the manager.

set on playing the role of a Harold Geneen or a Lee Iacocca will not just be ineffective, it will also be unbearable.

All of us have known or read about brilliant people who were outstanding at their own job, but ultimately failed because they could not effectively work *and* think together with other people. The skill involved in picking the right man or woman for the right job is so crucial a part of the management of an organization's thinking that 'people-thinking' must be considered a vital part of any decision-thinking effort.

But even with the best possible team, thinking, good thinking, cannot be manufactured and delivered to order like a sandwich in a coffee shop. If talented people are to give of their best, they have to be given some motive beyond merely doing what they are told; they have to be truly managed. Traditionally managers have two powerful incentives at their disposal, money and the sack; the carrot and the stick. There will be many occasions in any manager's life when the use of one or the other of these is called for. But the best thinking, in my experience, is done out of neither greed nor fear but simply because the person concerned has become absorbed in the problem. The great managers are those who are able to get their colleagues and subordinates to share their own commitment to arriving at the best possible decision.

Exactly how a manager is able to bring the best thinking out of this thinking team is not easy to define – leadership, force of character, the ability to create and sustain interest and excitement in others, these are all matters which involve the chemistry of personal relationships. There are none the less five practical rules that, if applied consciously and consistently, will help a manager to get the best out of any thinking team.

★

The *first* rule is to spell out the *objectives* of the thinking game precisely. A manager must explain without equivocation that he needs and expects to get open, creative and above all, objective thinking on every issue. If he fails to do so, he will not receive it, certainly does not deserve it, and should not be surprised if his subordinates turn their minds to bickering with each other and conspiring against him.

For a manager must face the fact that no matter how skillfully he picks his team, *any* organization – if not properly led – will foster dangerous and debilitating bureaucratic and internal political diseases. These diseases, if left untreated, will discourage, even destroy, good thinking. Good thinking is, by definition, objective and disinterested, but the people who have to do that thinking are almost inevitably going to be part of some hierarchy, and where there is an hierarchy, there will also be competition to move up.

Once office politicking is allowed to get a grip on an organization's thinking, it will quickly pervert or paralyze the entire collective thinking process. Work may get done, but professional decision-thinking will not. The ones who are making power plays will be looking for openings; the ones who are not will be protecting their backs. Neither will be looking at the real world outside the building, which the business has to understand if it is to survive. Scorpions in a bottle are fun for sadists to watch, but they are not good for a business.

Even when people are persuaded to address the needs and problems of the organization, their thinking, if not professionally managed, can easily become colored by political considerations. A will support a project because it takes some turf from B. B will naturally fight back. But A and B will unite to block the hiring of any new talent worth hiring, who might get ahead of them in the succession struggle. X draws up a plan to make himself look good and Y bad. When X's plan misfires, Y sees this as a victory for him rather than as a defeat for the business. No business can survive for long, if the manager lets such intrigues to take hold.

Thus in order to ensure that everyone thinks first of the collective good of the organization, it is necessary to make it clear, from the start, that a firm line will be drawn between the sort of overt and legitimate competitiveness, which lends zest and excitement to an organization's thinking, and the covert manoeuvring and manipulation which damages or destroys it.

Anyone who strays across that line must be pulled up sharply and warned that the manager cannot and will not tolerate such decision-thinking behavior.

★

The *second* rule is that everyone on the team must have a *clear grasp of the four-stage decision-thinking process* and understand its principles and requirements. Just as a good general will go to considerable trouble to make sure that his troops understand the overall plan of battle as well as their own particular role in it, so the professional manager needs to educate his team in the strategy and tactics of decision-thinking. Simple common sense tells us that people work better, with more enthusiasm and greater sense of purpose, if they not only know *what* they are doing but also understand *why* they are doing it.

Moreover, if everyone understands the decision-thinking process, the function of the different stages, and the roles that they and their colleagues are expected to play within those stages, there will be far less scope for misunderstanding and misdirected thinking. The imaginative thinker who comes up with a promising suggestion will appreciate that the team-mate who acts as devil's advocate and identifies the weak points in the proposal is not trying to put him down in front of the boss, but is simply doing his job.

Similarly, the conscientious worrier who spots a potential risk will feel no hesitation in drawing attention to it, in the confidence that his colleagues will recognize that, although his contribution may be a negative one, it is none the less valuable for that. Again, each member of the team will feel able to speak his mind for or against any proposal without the fear that he will subsequently be blamed if his views, honestly held and frankly expressed, turn out to have been wrong.

The manager must not only ensure that every member of the team understands the requirements of the decision-thinking process as a whole right at the outset, he must also keep his colleagues up to date as it progresses. Each thinker should be aware of the stage that has been reached, and of the way in which the process is developing. At the end of Stage 1, for example, it is up to the manager to draw the strings together and say, in effect, 'OK, we have now agreed upon the question that we are going to answer, and this is how it reads.' If subsequently it turns out that the question requires revision or modification, then all those involved must be made aware of the fact.

When Stage 2 is completed, it is up to the manager to have drawn up a list of the alternatives that have been selected for detailed investigation. In the same way, he must make sure, as Stage 3 progresses, that everyone knows of the potential risks that have been identified and are to be made the subject of contingency planning.

★

But this sharing of knowledge and continual updating will only be effective if the *third* rule is observed. This calls for *precision* in the communication of thinking assignments.

We have all, I imagine, sat through long meetings which culminated with the chairman saying something like, 'I guess that we are not going to get any further with this problem today, but I would like everyone to think about it over the coming week and have some new ideas when we reconvene next Wednesday.' Such vague requests or instructions amount to little more than a gesture toward the need for good thinking. The professional manager, heading a team of decision-thinkers which is dedicated to operating the four-stage process, will never be satisfied with such vague exhortations. He will assign well-defined thinking responsibilities to each member and will make sure that everyone understands what they are supposed to be thinking about and why.

Suppose, for example, that the team has been asked to address a completely new issue and is, therefore, faced with defining the question that it will be thinking about over the weeks to come. The initial discussion might conclude with the manager saying something like this:

'Right. We seem to be agreed that we have to consider whether or not to take this new product through to the stage of test marketing. In order to make sure that we do not waste our time trying to answer the wrong question, I would like the following points to be considered in depth. One, are the R&D people right in believing that they have got the bugs out of the production process? Joe, will you look into that and let us have a report next week? Two, we need to think about what damage this new product could do to our existing products. Dave, as marketing manager you are the obvious person to look at that. Again, I would like your thoughts before our next meeting. Paul, I am a bit worried that we are falsely assuming that we have the manufacturing capacity to move on to full production if the test marketing is successful. Could you check up on that? Brian, I thought your point about the implications which the promotional costs of the new product might have for next year's budget was a good one. Why don't you get some figures out on that?' And so on. The point being that, by the time they next meet, the team will be in a position to define the question a lot more closely and, perhaps, enrich it considerably.

The need for thinking assignments to be precise continues throughout the four stages. When the final stage is reached, for example, one group might be allotted the task of assessing the probability of a test marketing effort being successful, while another will perform the risk/reward calculations, and two other members of the team are told to prepare detailed contingency plans for, respectively, moving rapidly ahead to full production if the test exceeds expectations, or aborting the whole project and redistributing the manufacturing capacity to other products if it turns out to be a failure.

If everyone understands the decision-thinking process clearly and is given specific assignments, their thinking will be focused in a way that is simply not possible when the mind of the organization is left free to wander this way and that without system or purpose. But this in itself is still not sufficient. There are two further rules which should be in the forefront of every manager's mind if he wants to get the best out of his thinking team.

★

The *fourth* rule concerns a management quality that, in my opinion, we hear far too little about these days: *courtesy*.

If that sounds far-fetched, and I can imagine some readers' eyebrows rising at the notion that, in our very rough world, good manners are a central factor in management, let me explain. If thinking is to be done properly, then it will inevitably involve the minds of two or more individuals becoming intimately involved with one another. Relations between the manager and his people when they *work* for him may, without causing serious problems, remain formal, but between a manager and his people when they *think* with him there must be a rapport and a trust which go deeper and matter more to all parties.

This is not to say that everyone must be close personal friends. But it does mean that a *thinking* relationship is one in which personal feelings of pride, loyalty and shared ambition become involved. And one of the most powerful weapons which the manager can use in order to ensure that the feelings remain positive is basic courtesy.

Any thinking partnership has to be based on parity of respect. People worth working with do not have to work for you, they can get work anywhere. If you do not treat them as your intellectual equal or if you secretly do not think they are your intellectual equal (which will show), they will not see any point in delivering their best thoughts to you about anything, because they know in advance that whatever they say will be discounted or distorted.

Courtesy should not be confused with weakness. To be courteous does not mean that you cannot also be firm. But, properly employed, courtesy will go a long way toward ensuring that people make a thinking effort not because they are told to, but because they want to. And that difference in motivation is crucial.

A good thinker is interested in the thinking, not in himself. If you do him the honor of giving him a serious, well-researched and well thought-out argument back, you can be as rough about it as you like, and you will both enjoy the fight – *if* it is fought cleanly. A lot of the best thinking gets done when everybody gets their adrenaline up in these constructive debates. You can hire a lot of people to play customer's golf with your thoughts, but it is not always easy to find somebody who thinks your thinking is worth serious criticism.

As I pointed out in chapter 5, people's ideas are their 'brainchildren', of which they feel understandably proud and protective. The manager who goes out of his way to abuse his subordinates' brainchildren will soon find that the supply dries up. Self-interest, then, as well as good manners, requires that if ideas must be rejected, or if they prove, upon examination, to be less wise than they seemed, the manager must still handle the situation with courtesy. It costs very little to say thank you – and mean it – when someone offers you an idea, even if it is inadequate; but failure to do so could cost you their next idea, which might be the one you need. *Every* new idea honestly presented, whether accepted or rejected, must be welcomed as a useful step along the road to a sound decision.

In this area, as in others, Lee Iacocca seems to have an unerring instinct for identifying what matters. 'You don't have to accept every single suggestion,' he points out in discussing how a manager should communicate with his colleagues, 'but if you don't get back to the guy and say, "Hey, that idea was terrific", and pat him on the back, he'll never give you another one.' Even less can the boss expect another idea from the colleague whose brainchild has been snubbed or exposed to ridicule.

Because people normally do not get promoted just because they excel at Stage 2 or Stage 3 thinking, a manager can never afford to forget that the thinking, especially the vital kind of thinking that is required at these essential stages of the decision-thinking process – in which the majority of ideas will ultimately be rejected anyway – can be a pretty *thankless* task. No manager can be expected to feel warmly inclined, for example, toward the devil's advocate who shoots his favorite project full of holes. But if that resentment shows through, then the individual concerned, who has, after all, probably just saved the organization a lot of money or a lot of grief or both, may well decide that enough is enough. If that is all the thanks he is going to get, the next time he may decide to keep his mouth shut and let the boss pay the price of his impatient folly.

Because serious decision-thinking, whether short, medium or long term, involves the construction and consideration of a range of alternative proposals, of which only one (if any) will actually be acted upon, those who contribute to the thinking process will also always lay themselves open to the danger of being eventually shown or proved to be 'wrong'. This was brought home to me forcefully by a couple of recent experiences.

A long-standing client was facing a serious commercial problem on which he had taken professional advice. A certain course of action, which could have had dangerous consequences if things had gone wrong, had been recommended to him as the only solution to his problem. After he had explained the situation to me, I said that, if I were in his position, I would insist on a second opinion before committing myself to so drastic a step.

In the event he decided to ignore my advice, as he had every right to do, and to go ahead on the basis that had been proposed. I was pleased to learn, subsequently, that my misgivings had been unnecessary and that all had gone well. I was less happy, however, when my client wanted me to admit that my advice had been overcautious and therefore wrong.

It is always easy to be wise after the event, but if you do it too often and with too much relish, then you may find it harder to get advice when you need it. Sure, I had been 'wrong' that time. But, as I knew from experience of similar cases, I might well have turned out to be right; in which case, I like to think, I would have had the courtesy to resist the pointless temptation to say 'I told you so.'

The second example concerned another company with which my associates and I have worked for a number of years. On a dozen or more occasions we have accurately predicted the consequences, good or bad, of following a particular course of action. But there was a period of several months during which our client seemed to have forgotten the good advice which we had provided in the past. Instead, whenever we ventured an opinion about the future in the course of a meeting, the client would remind us of one particular recommendation which we made a couple of years before. Let us assume the recommendation concerned gold.

The price of gold at the time was around $370 an ounce and we suggested to our client that he should buy some options or the bullion itself as a hedge, predicting that it would rise sharply in the relatively near future. Our client, as it happened, decided not to follow our advice, and we heard no more on the subject over the following few months while the price of gold rose to around $500. But as soon as it fell back again, our client chose to remember our prediction and to remark, with jocularity and not for the last time, 'That was one you certainly got wrong.'

I could and did point out that if he had taken our advice and then sold at the right time, he would have made a handsome profit on the deal. The point of the story, though, is not to show that we were at least for a period of several months right and the client was wrong to criticize us, but to illustrate just how easy it is for either partner in a *thinking* relationship to poison or weaken it by seeking to score points off the other.

In this instance no lasting damage was done. We have thick skins and quickly cast aside our pique. Others can be less forgiving. But, whatever the circumstances, it is worth remembering that there is seldom anything to be gained in saying such things as 'I told you so' or 'Well, you sure got that one wrong.' It only serves to bolster your own ego at the expense of someone who may be of vital *thinking* help to you in the future.

Rather than harping, justly or unjustly, on what he perceives to have been mistakes, the far-sighted manager will go out of his way to congratulate his people when their ideas and predictions turn out to have been correct. He will also accept that no decision-thinker, however excellent, can guarantee success all the time. If people are doing a genuinely good thinking job, then thanking them when they get it right will encourage them far more than just criticizing them with hindsight when they have been wrong. Brickbats should be saved for those who deserve them. Remember, people are often as sensitive about the thoughts they create, as they are about their own children. Negative criticism will get you nowhere – except to poison the thinking environment of your organization. But constructive criticism will still be required.

★

Though courtesy should be the norm and the aim should always be to encourage and inspire rather than to hector or bully, I do not want to create the impression that the management of thinking is a passive or relaxed affair. On the contrary, one of the problems that any manager will face is the inherent conservatism of organizations. The *fifth* rule is therefore concerned with the need to *guard against rigidity and complacency*.

It is only in the first few years of their existence that mental agility comes naturally to organizations. New, young companies may initially be able to dart hither and thither like a Paris taxi in the rush hour, snatching up an opportunity here, dodging a threat there.

But pretty soon they can get bigger, more complex and more bureaucratically inclined and, like a heavily laden truck, change direction only slowly and ponderously. The people who were once full of bright ideas and eager for change are now always ready with a precedent or a policy that shows why a new idea should be dismissed or why things should not be changed. The antennae which were once aquiver at the slightest hint of an opportunity or the first sign of danger are now blunted. And the organization blunders along in a haze of self-satisfaction, missing chances and falling into traps.

Thus, although I would not normally consider myself a fan of Mao Tse-tung, I do appreciate why he believed that there is a need for 'continuous revolution'. Any organization, such as a communist state and, too often, a big corporation, in which the same set of people hold power for many years and, even when they relinquish it, nominate successors in their own likeness can get into a rut. Mao hoped to find a way round this problem by sending his Red Guards out to discomfort and, if necessary, topple those who had become too powerful and too secure in their positions of authority. In the Western democracies, fortunately, we long ago found a better way of dealing with the problem as it affects politicians – by holding an election.

Some managers can, it is true, also find themselves voted out of power if they fail to deliver – by shareholders, a board of directors or, in the case of public institutions, by politicians or the electorate. But not all organizations are, like government, constantly in the public eye, and not every chief executive's performance is monitored by the press. It is all the more important, therefore, that the thinking of an organization should be monitored and audited internally and that alarm bells should ring at the first sign of complacency.

It is the manager's duty to make sure that his organization has pride, where pride is justifiable, but that its thinking never stagnates and becomes merely complacent. Successful managers seem, in my experience, to have an almost innate talent for keeping themselves and their thinking colleagues on their toes in this respect. Some fundamental, if well-concealed, sense of constructive insecurity is, I suspect, the force which guides most of them.

There is a delicate balance to be struck here, and much depends upon the manager being aware of his own decision-thinking profile and of the effect it has on other people. There are, for example, those whose need for change is so strong that it becomes obsessive, and who are never happy unless they are hiring and firing or changing strategies. Such individuals can, if given free rein, transform any organization into a snakepit in which everyone's energies are totally absorbed in politicking, backstabbing and, not unnaturally, looking for new jobs. One of my favorite anecdotes concerns just such a company, and it goes like this:

On a Friday, the eve of starting a new job, a new executive is invited out for a drink by his predecessor, who has been fired, and who hands him when they part, without comment, three envelopes. On the first envelope is written 'Open on Monday'; on the second 'Open after two months'; and on the third 'Open after nine months'. On Monday the new executive duly opens the first envelope and reads: 'Blame everything on me.' Two months go by and the executive, by now beginning to wonder if he should have accepted the job, opens the second envelope. Again the message is brief: 'Tell them you are reorganizing.' Finally, nine months into the post and at his wits' end, the executive opens the third envelope and unfolds the note inside. It reads: 'Now, prepare three envelopes. . . .'

It goes without saying that an executive who creates a situation in which people are routinely treated in this fashion, as 'flavor of the month' and as mere fools who can do no right thereafter, will both deserve and get mediocre thinking.

But at the other extreme, and in their own way no less dangerous, are the managers who will tolerate and forgive incompetent or inadequate thinking for far too long for the sake of a quiet life or merely to protect their 'good guy' image. They, too, will get mediocre thinking, partly because they never *insist* upon anything better, and partly because they do not understand that, to get the best out of even the most talented people, you will at different times have, like the legendary football coach Knute Rockne of Notre Dame, to encourage, challenge, charm, bully or cajole them.

★

One final note. As was discussed in the previous chapter, the main arena in which any battle for good thinking will be won or lost is the meeting. By meeting I mean not only full-dress affairs with agendas to be got through, minutes to be taken and formal procedures to be followed. I also mean any informal type of meeting when ideas can be created, exchanged and debated – in person, over the phone, in the corridor, on a plane, or over lunch or a drink at the end of the day.

Handling meetings is a subject in its own right, and I do not want here to embark upon a full-scale discussion of it. I do, however, want to stress that the manager who accepts, and gets his thinking team to accept, the model of the four-stage decision-thinking process as the framework for *any* thinking meeting has some enormous advantages.

The fact that the process has an explicit structure which can be understood by all the participants disposes of a problem common to any organization with a lengthy chain of command. However clear a leader may be in his own mind about his thinking objectives, it does not necessarily follow that the people down the line understand what they are supposed to be thinking about, or why. But when a thinking meeting is built around the four-stage model of the decision-thinking process, everyone can be clear about the structure and the practical rules of the process, their own part in it, and where, at any time, they are in that process.

The five rules that I have set out in this chapter are, therefore, intended to be applied very largely in the context of a meeting. But obviously not every meeting is a 'thinking meeting'. There are meetings which take place primarily in order to allow information or instructions to be communicated; there are others which are a forum for negotiation; and there are, alas, yet others that take place for no better reason than 'We have a regular meeting on Friday mornings.' These should not be confused with any meeting of a decision-thinking team which, if the manager is doing his job properly, will have one purpose and one purpose only: to focus the organization's thinking resources on the issues which are crucial to its future and to generate the ideas which are required in order to reach the best possible decisions about that future.

Summary

A professional manager must learn to perceive his colleagues as members of his *thinking* team as well as his *doing* team, just as a coach sees his players as members of his athletic team.

The members of a thinking team may, however, change according to the subject being considered and the different kinds of expertise required. Normally a manager will, therefore, have to manage several thinking teams.

In decision-thinking, where there are strengths, there will also be weaknesses. Do not look for perfection in the individual mind; look rather for a diversity of thinking talent and experience with which to build a thinking team and then develop the attitudes and skills required to manage that team, effectively, as a team.

Some people who are good at getting things done may not be as useful as participating members of a thinking team. Be prepared to recognize this fact and make the additions to your thinking teams, when necessary, to compensate for any gaps.

There are five principal rules that should be followed by anyone managing a thinking team. They are:

1.   Explain precisely the objectives of the thinking game you are going to ask your team to play, and then draw a firm line between the competitiveness which stimulates good decision-thinking and the politicking which destroys it.

2.   Make sure that every participant understands the four-stage decision-thinking process, his or her role in that process and the rules and attitudes that are needed to operate it.

3.   Be precise in assigning thinking responsibilities; make sure that everyone on your thinking team understands what they are supposed to be doing at every stage of the decision-thinking process, and why. (Without such precision any decision-thinking effort will suffer; precision is as important in the decision-thinking process as it is in the manufacturing process.)

4. As a manager courtesy is one of your most important weapons; use it to stimulate and reward good thinking and to keep your thinking team well motivated.

5. Be constantly on your guard against the organizational complacency which threatens good thinking; wise insecurity – based often on a steady flow of 'what if' questions – should be built into all your key thinking assignments.

16

The Eureka Factor and Getting
Out of Your Mind's Way

Fortune favors only the prepared mind.

Louis Pasteur

This chapter and the one which follows may at first sight seem out of place in a book about decision-thinking. They deal with subjects – our sub-conscious thinking instrument of intuition and the vital relationship between our mind and our body – which are rarely considered to be directly relevant to the quality of management decision making. But I make no apologies for introducing them; on the contrary, I hope to persuade you that they have a direct bearing on your performance as a decision-thinker, and that the manager who neglects either of them does so at his peril.

However much we pride ourselves on our ability to think our way through a problem by using our experience, reason and imagination, we must also acknowledge, if we are honest, that we often have a novel idea without being able to explain where it came from or why it arrived at that particular moment.

The nub of the matter seems to be something that is familiar in other fields. Most golfers, for instance, will know that there are times when the harder they try to get their swing right, the wilder it gets. And they will also have discovered that if they can only relax and let their mind and body take over, the chances are that their swing will sort itself out. W. Timothy Gallwey has written with eloquence and insight on this subject in his books on both tennis and golf.★

In much the same way it frequently happens that a door in the mind which has obstinately remained closed when we tried to open it by sheer force of intellect will suddenly swing wide open once we cease pushing against it. Sometimes the effect is so startling and unexpected that we seem to experience an almost audible click. But if we try to backtrack to discover where the key came from or how it was turned, we are at a loss to explain our own cleverness. It is as if the mind is sometimes capable of conjuring a brainwave out of nowhere.

It was no doubt just this sort of sensation that caused Archimedes to leap out of his bath and rush naked through the streets of Syracuse shouting, '*Eureka!*' ('I have found it!'). Today our reactions may be more decorous, but the 'Eureka Factor' is likely to play just as important a role in our thinking as it did in Archimedes' time. And if we are serious about improving our performance as practical thinkers, we cannot afford to ignore it or dismiss it as irrelevant merely because we do not fully understand how and why it works.

On the contrary, we will, if we are wise, do our best both to cultivate it and to recognize that it can play an important role in the thinking efforts of our colleagues.

★

So how do we go about consciously developing the Eureka Factor in our own thinking, as well as in that of our organization?

The first point to make is a cautionary one: the Eureka Factor should never be used as an excuse for lazy or careless thinking. This becomes clearer if we go back for a moment to the analogy of the sports player. The top-class golfer and

★ W. Timothy Gallwey, *The Inner Game of Tennis*, Random House, 1974.

champion tennis player may be aware that the touch of genius which gives them the edge over their opponents on the big occasion is ultimately beyond their control. They may, indeed, recognize that their game goes best when they are relaxed and that the magic touch will desert them if they try too hard to recapture it.

But superior athletes do not neglect the necessity for training and practice; nor do they imagine for a moment that they have no need of coaching. Again and again they will emphasize that those moments of inspired play occur only if they have first done everything within their power to 'earn' them. As Gary Player once put it, 'The harder I practice, the luckier I get.'

If practice, skill and sheer hard work were irrelevant and all that was needed was the ability to relax and let some mysterious 'inner player' take over, then the talented amateur would be as good as the full-time professional. In fact, in sport as in decision-thinking, they are as different as chalk and cheese.

The great French scientist, Louis Pasteur, put the point succinctly and admirably when he remarked that 'Fortune favors only the prepared mind.' In the context of any decision-thinking effort, the prepared mind is the mind which is not only well-experienced and well-informed, but which has also mastered the requirements of *each* stage of the four-stage process, learned to use the instruments of imagination, experience and reason, and understands how best, consciously, to manage its own workings. Only if we come into the thinking stadium properly prepared and thoroughly fit for the decision-thinking game that lies ahead of us can we hope that the Eureka Factor will come to our aid when we need it.

But supposing we have indeed done everything possible to ensure that we are fully equipped to face the challenges of decision-thinking, is there anything further we can do to cultivate the Eureka Factor? Can the fortune of which Pasteur spoke be courted and cultivated? I believe that the answer to this question is an emphatic yes.

We certainly do not as yet know nearly enough about the brain to say that there is an exact parallel to be drawn between the sort of unconscious, intuitive skill that a sportsman relies on and the processes which allow a bright idea to come out of nowhere. But it is credible to suppose that the thinker, like the sportsman, must learn when and how, in a lovely phrase Jonas Salk once used in a conversation with me, 'to get out of our mind's way'.

★

Since different people achieve the necessary relaxation of the mind by different means, the first step toward cultivating the Eureka Factor is to try to make a mental record of when and how it operates in your own case. Even if you instinctively feel that the whole process is arbitrary and inexplicable, you may find that if you make a note of when, where and under what circumstance your next half dozen bright ideas come to you, a clear pattern will begin to emerge.

There are people, for example, who find that many of their best ideas come in the course of conversation or debate. Their minds, presumably, respond to the stimulus of testing their mettle against others. They need a constant flow of talk, a battle of wits and repartee if they are to be stretched. Often such individuals think best in a lively yet relaxed setting such as a dinner party, where the talk is wide ranging and is not overtly directed toward any particular end.

This sort of occasion is also fruitful because one of the principles on which the Eureka Factor operates is the discovery of parallels or analogies between apparently unconnected ideas. It is quite a common experience, for instance, to find that some chance remark about a subject far removed from the practical problem that has been on your mind all day will suddenly enable you to see that problem in a wholly new light. It is almost as if, once the day's worries are set aside, the mind is freed to look at them in a much wider context and to explore comparisons which would seem far-fetched in the formal circumstances of working hours.

A good example of the way in which a brilliant piece of thinking may be sparked off in moments of relaxation or idleness is provided by the case of the bouncing bombs used by the Second World War 'dam-busters' in Germany. The idea of a bomb which would skim over the surface of a lake, thus avoiding the defensive nets in front of a dam, came to the British inventor, Dr Barnes Wallis, while watching children play ducks and drakes with pebbles on a pond. Similarly it has been reported that the basic concept of a float process for manufacturing sheet glass occurred to a member of the Pilkington family (whose company has held the highly profitable patent rights) while helping his wife do the washing up.

Well, we cannot always stand around ponds or beside the sink waiting for inspiration to strike. But we can keep on the alert, take an interest in any task however trivial, and listen to other people talking about what interests them, in the knowledge that, however unlikely it might seem, our mind may suddenly happen upon just the spark it has been waiting for.

★

It is probably because our minds need time to sort through the jumble of material which they have accumulated in search of the half-forgotten item which turns out to have a use after all, or to fit together the bits of a puzzle which, when they were first collected, seemed to be parts of two different puzzles, that the Eureka Factor often operates while we are asleep. Certainly many people have found that it is seldom a mistake to allow themselves a chance to sleep on a problem.

By this I do not, of course, mean lying awake tossing and turning all night trying to see a way through a difficulty. However bad it looks when you go to bed, it will probably look ten times worse by the time you struggle, red-eyed and exhausted, into the bathroom next morning. Nor is it much good actually to try to dismiss the matter from your mind altogether by, so to speak, deliberately dropping it from your mental agenda.

The trick, it seems, is to admit that you will not get any further with it, for the rest of the evening at any rate, by trying to work at it. Instead, do something completely different. Play with the kids, watch TV, go for a walk and let your mind mull the issue over, without either pressing it for any answers or becoming irritated because the subject will not go away. Then go to sleep, and when you wake up with a clear head and the energy to tackle the new day, just pause and see if any new thoughts on the problem have turned up during the night and are waiting to be read off your mental telex machine.

If that sounds absurd or illogical, I can only say that for me and for friends of mine it works. Sometimes, though by no means always, I will find that a rapid review of the question to hand first thing in the morning will reveal ideas that just were not there the night before. So much faith do I put in this system that I make it a rule to conduct a sort of review of my thinking on issues that currently concern me as soon as I wake up. What I do is to note the results of my night's 'thinking' with special care and then look at them again later in the day. It is surprising how often they turn out to be of use.

I also make it a rule, as I am sure many readers do, never to be without that great modern aid to our thinking, the portable dictaphone. I use it to record a memo to myself every time a point crops up that I know I shall want to refer back to, or when an idea occurs to me that I have no time to think about at present, but will want to reflect on at my leisure. This not only saves me the trouble of lugging around a briefcase full of hastily scribbled notes; it also means that my mind is not distracted by the mental effort of struggling to remember ideas which I had when I first woke up, or whenever, but which I will not need to come back to until, say, next week's meeting.

Once I have confided the idea to tape, I can put it out of my mind, knowing that it will be transcribed by my secretary and that when I come to prepare myself for that meeting, I will find a neatly typed memo right at the top of the appropriate file. In a sense, therefore, I am helping to keep my own mind clear (and, I hope, to improve my thinking on the issues that immediately concern me) by using the tape as what a computer engineer would call 'back-up memory'.

★

If you want to get the Eureka Factor to operate in your favor, it is worth repeating one cardinal rule: do not try to force things. The ideas the Eureka Factor produces are often delicate seedlings. If you try to wrest them prematurely out of the fertile mental soil in which they have germinated, they may well wither. We have all had that feeling that there is an idea lurking there somewhere, just out of our reach, rather like that elusive word that is on the tip of the tongue. The more you grope for it, the less likely you are to grasp it. Let it be; maybe it is not quite ripe for the plucking as yet; maybe your mind needs a little more time to work on it.

If we try too hard to force our way through to a solution along the most obvious route, we will not only find that the way is blocked, we will also deny our minds the chance to play with the problem. I use the word 'play' quite deliberately because I think that playfulness is a characteristic of the mind which we all too frequently underrate.

To give an example, one of the more interesting advertising campaigns I have been acquainted with began when an employee in the advertising agency for the travel firm Thomas Cook was riding to work on the London underground and thinking absentmindedly about a forthcoming campaign for his client. He suddenly realized that the last two letters of the company's name were 'OK'. Once you have realized something like that, of course, it is obvious. But it is the sort of idea that might never occur to you if you sat at a desk and beat your brains out for a week. If, on the other hand, you stop trying to be brilliant and just let your mind fool around with an idea, it can sometimes come up with an unexpected idea like building a successful advertising campaign around the name Thomas Cook and the confidence-inspiring phrase 'OK'.

This example, which I have chosen deliberately, may seem trivial when compared with a truly classic case of Eureka, such as Archimedes', but it is important to realize that it is a perfectly valid one. There is no law which says that every bright idea has to be profound. It may take as much ingenuity to discover how to assemble a Chinese puzzle as to unravel a bit of the genetic code. The fact that one achievement will be forgotten within ten minutes, whereas the other will be recorded in biology text-books for the next hundred years, is irrelevant.

I make this point because I often sense that many managers feel that inspiration – which is, after all, just another term for the Eureka Factor – is something that only comes to great minds considering great issues, and that it cannot, therefore, be relevant to their practical work. I certainly do not want to get into a discussion of whether producing a good marketing plan, say, is as truly a creative task as painting a good picture; that is, for our purposes, beside the point. What I want to emphasize is that inspiration is just as likely to come to the rescue of the manager (worried about profits, jobs and continuity) as to the aid of the scientist; and both should take equal pains to cultivate it and show equal gratitude when it arrives.

Whether it is triggered by sheer playfulness or by some-thing more purposeful, the Eureka Factor is unlikely to operate if we allow our thinking on any subject to become too rigid or constrained. In so far as we can keep track of the process by which we arrive at a novel idea, a new perspective on a problem or a way round an apparently insurmountable obstacle, it seems clear that it involves the creation of a stream of thoughts, each of which is very rapidly examined to see if it has anything to offer and, in the majority of cases, equally rapidly dismissed. Only when that first, almost instantaneous, check reveals the possibility of a solution which will fit the problem is a thought pursued further.

Interestingly, the programers who are developing so-called 'expert systems' (computer programs which attempt to capture not just the knowledge possessed by the human expert in some particular field, but also the rules which he follows when apply-ing that knowledge to a particular problem) have hit upon a very similar technique, known as 'generate and test'. Rather than taking all the relevant information (deciding what is relevant is, of course, a problem in its own right) and processing it in order to arrive at a single, 'right' answer, many such programs now generate a whole range of possible answers – following the Darwinian principle of waste discussed in chapter 6 – which, superficially, look as if they might be appropriate. They then proceed to test each one in turn, discarding them as and when they are found to be inadequate.

Clearly success in our own 'generate and test' operations depends upon our mind being *free* to consider every possibility, however apparently outlandish, even if it is dismissed almost immediately. This will not happen if, at a conscious, formal level, we have already decided that one route and one route only should be explored. Again, an open mind should be seen as our thinking ally and a closed mind for what it is – the automatic aborter of any Eurekas that we might be capable of giving birth to.

★

The chance that the mental lightning of the Eureka Factor may strike, against the odds, again and again in the places where it is most needed will be further increased if we understand that it operates in different ways during *each* of the four stages of the decision-thinking process.

At Stage 1 – the question stage – what is clearly required is that sudden insight which turns a question on its head and reveals that the *real* issue is not quite what it appeared to be, or which asks the question in a new way that is more likely to lead to a useful answer. As it happens, Archimedes' problem, the textbook case of the Eureka Factor in operation, provides an excellent example.

The philosopher had been asked by his patron, Hiero, to determine how much base metal was contained in a golden crown. Without melting down the crown, an obvious impossibility from Hiero's point of view, the question seemed insoluble. Until, that is, Archimedes asked himself if there was a relationship between his body's bulk and the extent to which the level of his bathwater rose when he sat down in it. By one of those happy processes of analogy on which the Eureka Factor so often turns, he then deduced that because a given weight of gold (which is heavy) will have a smaller bulk than silver or other inferior metals, and therefore displace less water, adulterated gold of a given weight would displace more than pure gold of the same weight, and the degree of adulteration could be measured by the difference in water displacement.

The relevance of the Eureka Factor at Stage 1 is, therefore, likely to turn upon the possibility of reformulating a question that is impossible, difficult or unprofitable to answer in such a way that it is either more readily answerable or that the answer will address the essential issues more directly.

Stage 2 – when we create our alternative answers to the question posed in Stage 1 – is, of course, the one at which the Eureka Factor most obviously comes into play, in that it specifically demands original and imaginative thinking and is 'creative' in the commonly accepted sense of the word.

But although it may be less obvious, creativity is also required at Stage 3, when we try to forecast the future consequences of each alternative. For thinking what the future might be like, or what we want the future to be like, and what contingencies need to be prepared for is also a task that demands originality and a willingness to consider ideas which may seem improbable. The person who wakes up one morning, for example, asking himself, 'But what happens if . . .' is no less dependent on the mind's ability to explore the by-ways, as well as the highways, than the person who comes up with an original alternative at Stage 2.

This is, in my experience, a point which is too frequently overlooked. Many managers assume that thinking ahead in order to foresee the possible consequences of a course of action is, somehow, a mechanical process. In fact, as I have wished to show, it may well involve a great deal of highly original thinking, as well as the radical rethinking of accepted truths.

An excellent example of what I have in mind was instanced in the articles (already referred to in chapter 10) in which Pierre Wack describes how, under his leadership, Royal Dutch Shell planners drastically revised their techniques for thinking about future conditions in the oil business by introducing scenario planning.

The passage that particularly struck me was one* in which
Wack explained how he and his colleagues came to the realization, early in the 1970s, that the classical market mechanisms
simply did not apply to relations between the Seven Sisters and
the independent oil-producing states. Countries such as Iran and
Saudi Arabia, they recognized, could only absorb so much oil
revenue – their development programs could not be infinitely
expanded at short notice, and if they recycled too many petro-
dollars into the Western economies, they would simply fuel an
inflation that would seriously weaken the value of their assets.
This, coupled with their anxiety to maintain sufficient reserves
in the ground, meant that, rather than a rise in the price of oil
encouraging higher production (as classical economic theory
would predict), it would in fact tend to encourage a decrease in
production, since the producers could then oblige the market to
give them as much cash as they could usefully absorb while
selling less oil.

Now, with the benefit of hindsight, this may seem an
obvious line of reasoning. But, as Wack makes clear, it took
much hard work and ingenuity to persuade the senior management of Shell to accept an argument that ran counter to everything they had become accustomed to believing.

It was, perhaps, largely due to Wack's success in getting his
scenario across that Shell weathered the storms of the seventies in
better shape than most of the other majors. But no one who
reads the paper in question will be in any doubt about the
creativity and Eureka insight required by the sort of thinking
techniques Wack and his department developed for constructing
alternative scenarios of how the future could turn out.

Finally there is Stage 4 – the decision stage of our decision-
thinking process when we are also dependent upon our intuition
and judgment.† After all the alternatives have been reviewed,
the risk/reward factors assessed and the moment has arrived for

* *Harvard Business Review*, September/October 1985, pp. 73–89.
† Readers who are interested in studying more about the role of intuition,
particularly in the fourth stage, may like to refer to *The Intuitive Manager* by
Roy Rowan (Little, Brown and Company, Boston, 1986) which was published
just as the original edition of this book was going to press.

the crucial decision, it can also be of great value, if time permits, to let the mind lie fallow for a while. By sleeping on a decision, or merely giving our thought processes a few hours to mull it over on their own, the Eureka Factor will often come up with what is clearly the best answer. Or again, when a provisional decision has been reached, it can be wise to give the mind, working on its own, one last chance to offer a second opinion.

This is a very different thing from being hesitant or indecisive. In effect the decision maker is no longer facing the question 'What should I do?' Rather, he should be asking, 'This is what I propose to do. Am I sure that it is the best solution?' Normally, if the preceding decision-thinking has been done carefully and conscientiously, there will be little doubt that the answer is yes. But just occasionally given this last chance to intervene, the mind will come up with an intuitive perception which can avert an unfortunate and unnecessary mistake at the eleventh hour. Then comes a moment of truth, when real courage is needed for yesterday's intrepid decision-thinker to say, 'I'm sorry, everybody. I have changed my mind and this is why. . . .'

★

If we try to force the normal rhythm of our thinking to work too quickly or to undertake an excessive load at any one time, we run the inevitable risk that, like a machine, it will break down. We must develop techniques for switching off, for reducing the everyday stress that distracts and distorts clear thinking and for giving our minds the chance to perform effectively. Producing Eurekas is critical to that performance.

There can, of course, never be any guarantee that the Eureka Factor will come to our rescue. Often we shall be forced to apply ourselves to the hard and anxious task of working through the four stages without its help. But as part of our job as professional thinkers and professional managers of thinkers, we need to see to it that the Eureka Factor has at least a *chance* to operate whenever our organization faces a major decision-thinking challenge.

However intensive the four-stage process leading to the final decision, periods of relaxation need to be built into the entire process – as deliberately as they are built into the professional athlete's training program – to allow us to get out of our mind's way and to open our mental doors to the unexpected.

Summary

The Eureka Factor can play a vital part in decision-thinking, but it will only help us if we learn to 'get out of our mind's way'.

Try to work out how, when and where the Eureka Factor operates in your own case, and then deliberately *cultivate* it.

Learn when and how to relax mentally. Try to sleep on a problem whenever possible before making a decision.

As in tennis or golf, learn never to force your thinking. If your mind is not ready with the answer, hassling or rebuking it will do more harm than good.

The same applies to your colleagues, so give them a chance as well to let the Eureka Factor play a role in their thinking.

Brilliant inspirations come after intense preparation and intense thought, not after intense busy-ness or intense stress.

17

Your Mind, Your Body and Your Decision-Thinking

As a physician you have the unique opportunity to see man as he really is – bare and without his many physical and mental façades. He becomes ill (unconsciously) at the time an important decision must be made. He is a gifted leader, but has a serious drinking problem. He is a gifted teacher, but no one knows of his phobias, his insecurities, uncertainties and his problems in coping with himself. He is a political leader with untold powers and secrets. However, he cannot sleep, demands tranquilizers, drinks, is immoral, insensitive and tomorrow could make a decision that could help destroy the world. He is a business leader whose greed is outrageous and who fears losing his position. It appears that man needs more insight not only into the decision-thinking process, but also in evaluating, honestly, the results of his life-style and labor.

Barry W. Frank, M.D, Clinical Professor of Medicine,
University of Colorado, Denver, Colorado

Now we come to the last and most important tool we need to manage to become professional decision-thinkers – our bodies. The purpose of this chapter is not to drive you on to the impossible task of making yourself perfect, but to encourage you to understand your body and its needs and to learn to treat it, if you are not already doing so, in a fashion that will benefit both you and your decision-thinking.

Serious athletes have long understood that success on the track, in the ring or on the court depends at least as much on being mentally prepared for an event as on skill and physical fitness. They know that they cannot expect to get the best out of their bodies unless their minds are clear, alert and free to concentrate upon winning.

Those of us who try to take our thinking responsibilities seriously must, I believe, recognize that the reverse is equally true. The manager who tackles an important decision while suffering from a heavy cold, or after sleeping badly or dining too well, is as prone to make a mistake as the golfer who comes to the first tee preoccupied by personal or financial worries. The difference is that while the golfer probably recognizes the dangers of his situation, the manager too often does not.

Philosophers have argued about the relationship between body and mind for centuries and will, no doubt, continue to do so.* But those of us who have to apply our minds to practical issues are deluding ourselves if we suppose that our state of health and the way in which we treat our bodies does not have a direct and vital influence on our minds. Yet the assumption that our 'state of body' is somehow irrelevant to our 'state of mind' is widespread, and even those who acknowledge that the two may be inter-related often believe that they can neutralize their bodies' problems by sheer strength of character.

★

The idea of an immaterial mind can be the source of much confusion, wasted effort and bad decisions. If we start out, in the world of decision and action, with the assumption that we

---

* When reading this chapter, please remember how I have defined the word 'mind' for our purposes in this book on p. 137 – the word is used to describe what our brain does when we think about making a decision.

need, on the one hand, an immaterial mind and, on the other, a material body to think with, we create for ourselves some wholly unnecessary management problems.

People who have to work in the real world should have little use for the immaterial mind theory. If you are running an airport or a nuclear power installation, in charge of air traffic controllers or plant operators, you are not going to let anybody tell you that your employees have immaterial minds to think with quite separate from their bodies, and that therefore it does not matter how much they have been drinking or drugging when they come on duty.

Many managers, however, often behave as if their bodies do not affect their minds. To illustrate the point, consider the executive who fortifies himself for an important meeting with a three-martini lunch. He may, if pressed, admit that it would be imprudent for him to drive a car. But that, he will argue, is a purely physical problem. He might allow that his reactions have slowed down a bit. On the other hand, he will hotly deny that his mind or his judgment have been impaired. Indeed, he may well claim that he thinks and decides better with a strong drink or two inside him. Most of us know better, I hope, than to believe him.

In fact, the more vehemently he denies that his mind has been affected, the less ready we should be to accept those denials. For experiments have established not only that alcohol blunts our perceptions and diminishes the speed and accuracy with which we react, they have also shown it has the even more insidious effect of bolstering our confidence in our abilities just when such confidence is least justified. Thus the drunken driver who is swerving all over the road is convinced that he is in full control of his vehicle and is handling it with the skill and panache of a Jackie Stewart.

The example is, of course, both extreme and obvious. Few of us would dispute the fact that heavy drinking and good thinking are incompatible. But the underlying misconception, that mind and body should be treated as separate entities, can influence our decision-thinking behavior in circumstances that are far less clear-cut. In what follows I wish to discuss the problems that are created for decision-thinkers when they try to treat their bodies separately from their minds. These problems result from defective eating, drinking, sleeping, relaxing and exercising habits.

★

Many people would swear in all sincerity that they have no drinking problem. But I wonder if they have counted the number of cups of coffee and tea and the cans of cola they consume each day. I am not suggesting that caffeine has effects as serious as alcohol, but the fact that many people claim that they have to have coffee before they can fully wake up suggests that it is a powerful stimulant.

Let us allow that a couple of cups of coffee may be just what is needed to get us going in the morning. But what about the sixth cup of coffee that we take at four o'clock in the afternoon? Is it just keeping us going or is it overstimulating our mind and causing us to become irritable, tense and too eager to be decisive?

The use of tobacco causes a similar concern. Though the long-term damage smoking can do is now established beyond serious dispute, I am quite prepared to believe those people who tell me that they find that it assists their concentration. It is also clear that in a social situation a cigarette may well help people to relax, as indeed a drink can. But when I watch someone chain-smoking throughout a meeting, I wonder whether the cigarettes are relaxing his thinking tensions or exacerbating them.

Positive addictions can also create disabilities in our thinking powers. Consider the young executive, in training for a marathon, who runs six miles each noon. Can he be as alert and as clear-headed as he needs to be in the afternoon?

Drugs present other problems. And I am not talking of the hard drugs, the terrible effects of which are all too painfully apparent, but of soft drugs, like marijuana, which have become socially acceptable in many situations. Whether or not people should be free to use them for pleasure or relaxation is a question for the legislators; but I have seen enough to know that even a mild drug habit can have a bad effect on a user's ability to face up to his decision-thinking responsibilities.

Even more worrying, if only because they are seldom appreciated, are the effects of the perfectly legitimate drugs presented by doctors or purchased over the counter in a drug store. We can probably spot what is wrong with the executive who has treated himself to one drink too many over lunch and is now dozing off as a result. But do we also understand that antihistamines can have similar effects?*

Laws relating to prescription medicines require drug companies to make rigorous tests of new products and, if the tests disclose the possibility of harmful side-effects, require the dispensers of the product to warn consumers of the hazards. I am not aware, however, that these warnings ever cover the possible ill effects on *thinking*. A doctor may advise a patient that a drug could make him feel a bit drowsy, or that he should not drive a car for a few hours after taking a pill, but I have yet to hear of a physician who warns a patient not to make an important decision or to engage in serious negotiations after taking a prescription.

Drug companies and foundations devoted to human health should, to be consistent, make an effort to establish and publicize the effects on our thinking of at least the common drugs. In the meantime, those who must use medicines should make a point of asking their doctors about possible adverse effects on their thinking; they should be alert for any sign that their own decision-thinking is being affected.

---

* There are many other drugs which deserve mentioning. Tranquilizers, anti-depressants and stimulants of all kinds are examples of chemicals which impair the mind. There are others often prescribed by physicians for medical problems that a serious student of decision making should be aware of. Gastro-intestinal medications, anti-hypertension drugs and cardiac medications are but a few. That is not to say they are wholly bad or harmful, but their side-effects should be known and monitored. Again, these side-effects are often such that we will be told not to drive or to operate any other potentially dangerous machine when under their influence, so we must suspect these drugs of also being bad for our thinking in some way.

Obviously, taking medication does not prevent you from being a good decision-thinker, as long as you understand its overall effect. We would be short of a lot of good leaders if this were not so.

★

But we should not imagine that our bodies influence the performance of our thinking only as a result of what we eat, swallow or drink. There are many other mind–body factors which can be equally significant and which we ignore at our peril. Yet ignore them we frequently do.

Not so long ago I watched the British Prime Minister, Margaret Thatcher, being interviewed on television upon her return from a trip around the world, a trip involving her in a series of top-level meetings, culminating in a session with President Reagan at Camp David. She made a point of stressing that her schedule had been a hectic one, and she seemed to be suggesting that her audience should admire the stamina and determination that had made it possible for her, in less than a week, to cover so much ground, meet so many people and discuss so many issues. My own reaction was quite different. How could anyone suppose that this was a sensible way in which to tackle complex problems? Even an 'Iron Lady' like Mrs Thatcher will be adversely affected by frequent, rapid changes in time zones and by living without adequate amounts of sleep, let alone the other stresses to which she is subjected.

Many Japanese executives traveling to the US or Europe on business make it a rule to take, upon arrival, a couple of days off before they set about further widening the trade gap between their host country and their own country.★ If the Japanese, with

★ Given the long distances they must fly from Tokyo and Osaka to reach their most important markets, Japanese executives probably understand the problems associated with jet lag better than most. In fact, the best piece of advice that I was ever given about dealing with the intractable problem of jet lag came from a Japanese executive. I have followed it ever since and have found that I have adjusted more easily to the time differences between, say, all their single-mindedness and efficiency, admit that jet lag is a factor to be taken seriously – a factor, let us remember, which is affecting mankind's decision-thinking for the first time in human history – why do so many Western businessmen and politicians try to prove their managerial virility by ignoring it?

Looking at the question realistically, it would be surprising if we did not react badly to having dinner in London or going to bed in Athens just when, according to our internal clock, we should be getting ready for lunch in Los Angeles. And why should we suppose that our thinking is immune from the disorientation that our body feels? How much damage has been done in recent years, I wonder, by executives and political leaders who gamely marched off a plane and into a long meeting when they should first have been taking things easy, adjusting to changes of time, climate and environment?

Traveling across time zones and working irregular hours are but two of the ways in which working conditions affect our thinking.

It is a standing joke in many an office that when the boss arrives in a bad temper, it is because he had a disturbed night or over-indulged at dinner the previous evening. But how many bosses stop to consider that the overtiredness or the indigestion that causes them to snap at a secretary or give an executive an unnecessary roasting may also have a serious effect upon their ability to handle a meeting or weigh up a decision? And even if they do appreciate that their own irritability or impatience may influence their thinking, how many of them consider asking a colleague to take over the meeting or postponing the decision?

London and Los Angeles or Geneva and Tokyo as a result. His advice was: when you get to your destination, before you go to sleep, try to exhaust yourself *physically*, without reaching the stage of actual discomfort, by doing some form of exercise like tennis, jogging or swimming. As a result you will not only go to sleep, you will stay asleep, even when your *mental* alarm clock is telling you that it is time to get up back home. This advice can, I think, be of help to any one who, having gone to bed at 11 p.m. local time, does not particularly like to wake up at 3 a.m. and then uneasily have to wait for an important meeting until 9 a.m.

Yet if we take the link between state of body and state of mind seriously, such steps are surely no more than common sense.

Turning to yet another mind–body relationship, it is well known that different people are at their best, in their ability to generate ideas and to respond to other people's ideas, at different times of the day. For example, 'morning people', who are alert and refreshed upon awakening, can be a source of puzzlement and irritation to 'evening people', who are further affronted when, just as they are beginning to hit their intellectual stride, the morning people start to yawn and think longingly of going home and relaxing. Most of us recognize that this factor, which doctors tell us is due to variations in metabolism between individuals, plays an important part in our personal lives. But how many of us take this into consideration when organizing our *thinking* work?

One man who did, at least as regards himself, was Winston Churchill, an evening person if ever there was one. The memoirs of those who worked with him during the Second World War describe how he would keep his staff up to all hours, sometimes to engage in brainstorming sessions, at others to watch a favorite movie or simply to listen while the great man held forth. Not all the generals, admirals and political advisers who staggered out from Churchill's war room beneath St James's Park to greet the dawn red-eyed and weary appreciated the arrangement.

But there is no immutable law which says that all serious thinking has to be done during office hours. So if we want to get the best out of our own mind and out of those of our colleagues, we need to pay heed to the metabolic clock that regulates our bodies.

When facing an important decision, if a manager knows that his mind usually is at its sharpest during the morning, he would indeed be ill-advised to allow himself to be scheduled to make the decision during the afternoon. And by the same token he may have to accept that, if he is going to get his deputy to come up with one of those flashes of genius of which he is occasionally capable, then he, the manager, may have to schedule a brainstorming session for late afternoon or early evening, when the deputy is likely to be most creative.

It is dangerously easy for an organization to become the prisoner of a rigid schedule, dictating, for example, that the executive committee must meet at three o'clock on every second Tuesday, even if a majority of the members know that they would produce better thinking at ten o'clock in the morning.

★

The following item appeared in a press article about a 1982 appointee to the US Senate:

Senator Brady, 52, who had never held public office before, somewhat reluctantly agreed to serve in April at the behest of New Jersey Gov. Thomas H. Kean.

In a series of interviews over the last few weeks, he said that he learned several things in Washington:

'Senators are overburdened by things to do and rarely have time to reflect on the important issues on which they must make decisions.

'Senators are preoccupied so often with matters relating to their re-election that they neglect other parts of their job.

'A senator should never count on a good night's sleep.'★

These comments, of course, apply not only to senators but also to our political leaders, business executives and, in many ways, to most of us. And this brings me to yet another physical factor, widely disregarded, which directly influences our thinking: the need for adequate sleep and relaxation. Except in moments of crisis, we should not be patient with managers who pride themselves on working to the point of physical exhaustion and who display the shadows under their eyes as if they were

★ *The Honolulu Advertiser*, December 25, 1982.

awards for hard work and dedication. We would not think very highly of a sprinter, say, who staggered to the starting blocks exhausted from a ten-mile run; why should we admire an executive who arrives at a meeting haggard, short-tempered and fatigued?

Like the sprinter, he is not in a fit state for the task ahead, and the only thing he will have proved is that he is incapable of managing his own life efficiently. To be sure, most of us work better under a bit of pressure. But it is essential to distinguish between the mental pressure which stimulates good thinking and forces the mind to rise to a challenge and the physical pressure which dulls the mind and reduces its activity to a plodding pace.

The manager who takes pride in working a sixteen-hour day and having no time for anything but his work is, in the long run, fooling no one but himself. As the self-imposed drudgery takes its toll of his physical resources, he will soon be doing no more than going through the motions of thinking – reading papers without grasping their content, sitting through meetings without making a contribution and giving speeches that turn people off, not on.

He will, no doubt, claim that he is overworked and suffering from stress, but the chances are that he will also refuse any offer to reduce his workload. He is, in short, a workaholic in the worst sense of the term. He is addicted to work, but he has ceased to get any satisfaction out of it – like the alcoholic who drinks compulsively and has quite forgotten the time when drinking was a source of pleasure.

We have all seen people who are in control of themselves and their surroundings. They always seem to have what they need at their fingertips, and they rarely appear rushed. What is their secret? It is, I believe, a very simple one. They have made a realistic assessment of their physical limitations and their priorities, and have learned to pace themselves: they make sure that they always have some energy in reserve. They have come to know their physical self.

We all get tired at some point or other, either because the continued strain of our normal work wears us down or because a crisis obliges us to work abnormally long hours. A manager, for example, may engage in protracted negotiations for three months and, when the contract is finally signed, may be unable to switch off and forget it. But the wise manager recognizes the symptoms and does not try to ignore them or to conceal them. If a manager stays up half the night waiting for a telephone call from the other side of the world, then he should feel no compunction about taking a nap or going home early and putting himself to bed. If his tiredness is the consequence of a sustained period of hard work, then he should have no hesitation in taking a holiday, even if it is no more than a long weekend.

If you try to force your mind to go on thinking when your body is crying out for a rest, you will quickly realize, if you are honest with yourself, that a law of diminishing returns begins to operate. The harder you try to think, the more difficult the problem will appear; and the more difficult things seem, the more tired you will feel as you struggle to cope with them. The people I have known who have learned to deal successfully with really tough issues are those who refuse to let themselves be trapped into this kind of quagmire. Faced with a stubborn problem, they do not make matters worse by bludgeoning their minds until they are capable of worrying only about the fact that they feel so worried. They know how to get out of their minds' way.

Again, many of us can learn something about managing our minds and bodies from Winston Churchill, who had the composure and self-possession, even at the height of a crisis, to retire for a short nap, after which he would return to the mental struggle relaxed and reinvigorated.

I have, also, always been struck by the fact that one of the recent heroes in American society, Judge John Sirica, the trial judge in the Watergate case, was reported to have had a cot installed in his chambers so that he could daily take a brief nap after lunch. It is not, I know, something that everyone can do. But if you do have the knack of dozing off for ten minutes, you should not feel that you have to apologize for the habit or resist the urge; be glad, rather, that nature has made it possible for you to give your mind a break when it needs it.

There is little doubt that the brain requires sleep just as much as the rest of the body, although we do not as yet fully understand why this should be so. It seems entirely possible that sleep provides an opportunity for us to reorganize our mental filing system, to throw out the rubbish that has accumulated in the course of the day and to establish cross-references that we may have been too occupied to notice during waking hours. Presumably, the Eureka Factor, which can also operate while we are asleep, is a happy by-product of this process. The likelihood that something of this sort is going on while we are asleep is further supported by evidence showing that dreaming plays an important part in our lives.

Experimenters, having established that rapid eye movement (REM) accompanies most dreaming, have been able to determine the effects of depriving human and animal subjects of dreaming sleep. Human subjects, prevented from dreaming for short periods, will compensate by subsequently indulging in longer than usual periods of REM sleep. Animal subjects, deprived of dreaming for longer periods, will begin to indulge in aberrant behavior. These experiments indicate that good sleep accompanied by our dreams is something we all need if we are to think effectively.

After good health, the ability to drop off to sleep easily is probably the most important gift nature can bestow on one who spends much of his working life engaged in decision-thinking.

But when it comes to relaxing, you need actually to *cultivate* the habit of relaxation. However much you are concerned about the problems that have arisen during the day, when you get home try to press the 'off' button which will stop the office program running through your head. Or if you cannot switch the set off altogether, change channels: think about last year's vacation or plan next year's, brood about what to get the kids for Christmas or how you can improve the garden – anything that will set off a new, and a very low-key, train of thought.

A number of stress-reduction techniques – widely taught now – can assist you: simple meditation exercises and breathing and stretching exercises are effective and easy to use. Matters will also be helped if you make sure, as discussed above, that your body as well as your mind is exercised. Reasonable exercise is a wholesome tonic, and it will take your mind off pressing issues and give it an opportunity to relax. Most managers lead sedentary lives – sitting in meetings, cars, airplanes, restaurants and hotels. There is, therefore, all the more reason for them to use exercise to relax, keep fit and cope with stress.

John H. Johnson, president of Johnson Publishing Company, put it well when he explained to an interviewer from *Fortune* magazine why he was using his pedaling machine three times a week for a half hour. 'I don't find exercise boring. I just look forward to thirty minutes in which I solve no problems, think about nothing and let my mind clear. '*

Perhaps you are one of those that find a new quality of relaxed thought when exercising, especially when doing something quiet, like walking, cycling or jogging. For some people this is also Eureka time.

★

Sleepless nights and the inability to relax are symptomatic of an evil which today can afflict almost all decision-thinkers – excessive stress. So too are many of the other problems I have been talking about: over-reliance on alcohol and caffeine, the use of drugs, both medical and 'recreational', heavy smoking, etc. Rarely will anyone in the working world be able to eliminate the environmental sources of exaggerated stress, for its causes are now firmly built into the way we live. Most of us must accept the need to commute to and from a workplace; we must cope, thanks to the telephone, telex and airplane, with events that move at an ever accelerating pace; we cannot realistically expect the crime rate, the divorce rate or the incidence of Murphy's Law to fall dramatically; nor can we expect ourselves or our colleagues to be immune to these causes of tension and anxiety.

If, however, we cannot root out the causes of stress, we

---

* *Fortune*, February 21, 1983, p. 149.

can reduce its impact on our emotions and on our thinking. The key to reducing stress is to think of it not as an enemy out there, getting at you, but rather as part of yourself, a part you can control, even harness for your own ends, if you set about the task methodically. As one book on the subject puts it: 'The effects of stress are not determined by stress itself, but by how we view and handle the stress, by how we appraise and adapt to an event. '*

The war against stress, like other wars, is won primarily by organization. We have all felt at one time or another so heavily laden with duties and obligations that we become disheartened and fearful that we cannot cope with all the contending demands made on us. 'Joe needed that answer yesterday, and the figures still haven't come in from the fourth floor. Bob is expecting me to return his call, and Mary says that if I do not find time to read that contract right now, it will never make the afternoon mail. How on earth am I going to cope with all that and have this report on the boss's desk tomorrow morning? And, oh God, I nearly forgot, I have to be downtown in one hour.'

This common sort of crisis, even if it seems trivial in retrospect, is obviously stressful at the time. You will not make it any less stressful if you try, desperately, to chase the missing figures on one line and ring Bob back on another while glancing through the contract – missing, you feel sure, important points you should be noting.

Better, by far, to summon Mary and get her to chase the figures and make sure they are on your desk in the morning along with the contract, which she will now have to send by courier after you have had a chance to study it; give a quick call to Joe to tell him that he will have his answer before lunch tomorrow for sure; another one to Bob, or maybe Mary can do that, to discover what he wants; put the draft report in your briefcase to be finished off at home; and you still have twenty minutes to get a taxi and make your downtown appointment.

* Richard E. Winter, *Coping with Executive Stress*, McGraw-Hill, 1983, p. 169.

This is a minor but everyday example and I have perhaps cheated by making the solution relatively easy. My point is not that you can necessarily cope with all difficulties by organizing your thoughts properly but, rather, if you do not stop to organize and manage your thoughts and thinking time, you will cope with none of the problems as you should. As a direct result, you will only increase the amount of stress you are under and further weaken your own decision-thinking capabilities.

The risk that you will find yourself too frequently in this sort of situation can only be reduced by careful planning: by making sure that your filing system is efficient and that you have the secretarial back-up that you need; by keeping your correspondence up to date; by using your portable dictaphone intelligently; and by trying never to leave it to the last moment to plan a trip, read a report or catch a plane. These common-sense precautions should be second nature to anyone who takes the war against stress seriously.

But every general knows that, while good staffwork and logistics are vital, when battle is joined everything will depend upon his ability to seize the initiative and keep it, even in the face of the unexpected. So it is with stress. When pressure does intensify (and, no matter how well we organize our working lives, there will be moments of crisis) the one irredeemable error is to give way to the feeling that we cannot cope. To do so is, in effect, to concede victory to stress without even putting up a fight.

If you decide that an issue is so important that you must confront it head on, regardless of the stress this will entail, you must recognize that you are committing not only mental resources but also physical ones. The struggle will take a toll on your body as well as your mind, and your mind will rise to the challenge only if you respect your body's needs. Do not, therefore, delude yourself that you will help matters by staying up all night worrying about the crisis; do not skip meals, and do not overindulge in stimulants such as caffeine. Instead, make a point of trying to get your normal ration of both sleep and nourishment.

Again, I have also found that, at times like this, simple

breathing exercises can help. If I sense that my body is beginning
to rebel at the pressure I am putting on it, if my pulse is going too
fast and I am getting literally twitchy, I force myself to pause for
two or three minutes and to take slow, deep breaths. Invariably I
discover that this reduces tension and clears my mind.

The military services place a high value on drill because
men who might otherwise break and run under the stress of
battle will be steadied if they have learned disciplined procedures
to follow almost automatically when ordered to do so. If the
drill appears absurd to civilians, it is because they do not see
that it is the discipline and self-discipline that is important, not
the drill itself. In much the same way, I think, we all need to
have some exercise which we can follow when we feel our
resolve beginning to crumble under the assault of stress – and
some drill sergeant in the back of our minds who, when pressure
is intense, will step forward and order us to carry out our routine
exercise in order to compose ourselves.

★

Now if we accept that there is a direct relationship between
our body's health and our performance as a thinker, then we
must also accept that the same applies for other people, including
those whose working and thinking lives we are responsible for.
I trust that this is a responsibility which organizations of all
kinds will soon come to take seriously, for their own sake as
well as that of their staff.

My own vision of the office of the future centers on
the concept of the office as a place dedicated to creating an
environment favorable to good thinking. This means that technology, rather than being concerned only with new generations
of computers and telecommunications, which will make it even
easier and faster to store and transmit information, will develop
to the point at which we may be able, as a matter of routine, to
ensure that we realize our full thinking potential.

Not being an engineer or a physician, I can do no more
than speculate on what sort of equipment and techniques will

be available, and when and how they will work. But I can outline a few ideas, some of them based on methods currently in use in other fields, which seem to me to be distinct possibilities.

I believe, for example, that every large office will come to have a sort of 'thinking gymnasium', where a manager can go to keep his mind fit and, perhaps, to limber up his body and mind before any important meeting or vital negotiation. Here those who feel the need for a cat nap will be able to take one without embarrassment or interruption; here one may be able to drop in for five minutes of exercise, say, or get some natural medication that will relieve stress symptoms such as headaches or muscle pains.

There will, I imagine, also be vibrating devices which people can sit or stand on or place their heads in, and which will help them to find quickly the relaxation they need to disperse their stress. Perhaps such devices will also be built into chairs or desks as a matter of course.

Oriental techniques like self-applied *shiatsu* and acupuncture will also be developed to the stage at which they will be available to anyone, just as we can currently have a cup of coffee or light a cigarette when we feel the need either to stimulate or to relax our brain.

Pending the arrival of this Jules Verne world of the office of the future, there is still a lot that any manager can now do to make sure that his people are fit and fully prepared to meet their thinking responsibilities. Above all he can recognize that, as a manager, he has a very direct concern for, and interest in, the good health and well-being of those who think with him or for him.

The manager who drives his team to the point of physical exhaustion is, in the end, simply defeating his own purposes. On the other hand, the manager who goes out of his way to make sure that a colleague gets time off when he has been under pressure, arranges for his people to have short relaxation breaks or insists that an overseas negotiation trip must include time for acclimatization and relaxation, may be spending money in the short run, but in the long run he is making the wisest possible investment in his people's good health and sound thinking.

Summary

Our state of mind (that is, our capacity to think well) is dependent upon our state of body (that is, our capacity to feel well).

Do not deceive yourself or let others deceive you into believing that the way we treat our bodies does not directly affect our thinking.

To make sure that you are fit to face your thinking responsibilities is not self-indulgence; it is elementary common sense. How well you manage your body will help determine how well you manage your own decision-thinking efforts.

Most of us now recognize obvious dangers like drink and drug abuse, but we need to pay sufficient attention to other factors, such as the negative effect of medication, jet lag and workaholic behavior on our decision-thinking.

If you are a morning person or an evening person, recognize that this is a fact of your *thinking* life and try to organize your key thinking time accordingly.

Get the sleep and relaxation you need; going without them in order to think harder will simply cause you to dig a deeper hole and result in the thinking being done poorly.

As a manager, the health of those who think with you must be of vital concern to you. You need to be on the alert for any signs of trouble and ready to take practical and imaginative management steps to avert them. That also is a key part of your thinking responsibilities.

Stress is not caused primarily by events, but by the way in which we react to events. Organization is the key to defeating it. Today, how well you manage stress will play a vital role in determining how well you manage both your own mind and the mind of your organization.

Above all, remember that your mind and your body are *both* part of you – the one can only function effectively if the needs of the other are respected. Your decision-thinking performance will therefore reflect the stresses and strains to which your body is subjected – the food you eat, the amount of sleep you get, the workload you take on, the relaxation you allow yourself, the drinks to which you treat yourself and the medications you take.

Understanding the relationship between your body and your decision-thinking performance is also part of coming to terms with your 'thinking self'.

18

Building Public Demand for Professional Decision-Thinking

We are losing our ability to manage ideas, to contemplate, to think. We are becoming a nation of electronic voyeurs, whose capacity for dialogue is a fading memory . . .

Ted Koppel, ABC Television

We shall have to regard thinking as a skill that we are to teach in schools, rather than as an inevitable consequence of a high IQ acting on a knowledge education.

Edward de Bono

Human history becomes more and more a race between education and catastrophe.

H. G. Wells

Early in 1987 the President, in his State of the Union Message, emphasized the importance of education in combating exterior threats to our prosperity. Secretary of Education William Bennett followed this up with a series of barnstorming sessions in support of the President's theme. Their particular emphasis was on the importance of literacy and numeracy and, of course, the moral dimension of education.

But are literacy and numeracy enough? True, we cannot do without them, but they are no more than two of the indispensable tools which the brain uses to create and guide its thinking. But just using tools haphazardly does not get us very far. It is *how* we use them that matters – and that is where our education system fails us. The real issue is that we are not taught *how* to think. Nor are we taught *how* to manage our decision-thinking efforts and responsibilities when cooperating with other people within organizations.

★

If America is in political and economic trouble (and perhaps heading for greater woes), one fundamental reason is that too many of our managers underestimate or ignore both the importance and the complexity of the particular type of thinking they must employ. If this premise is correct, we should clearly do everything in our power to reverse the trend. But where do we start? And how? And who should take the initiative?

Obviously, much of the responsibility for improving the quality and the management of the thinking that takes place in our government, public institutions and business corporations lies with the managers themselves. But not all of it. For if our society expects its managers to do better, it must also be prepared to play a part in seeing that its expectations are realized.

The object of this part of the book is to outline a plan aimed at creating widespread competence in decision-thinking and widespread demand for managers who are professionals in decision-thinking. To pull America out of its decline as an economic and political power, it will, I believe, be necessary to accomplish both of these goals – quickly.

This chapter first describes briefly why today's environment is one hostile to good thinking. Next, it identifies the positive role that our political leaders and the media can play in

changing that environment. And finally, it proposes an educational program America can and should implement. This last
section is the core of the chapter – for such a program would
achieve the twin goals of both supplying professionally trained
decision-thinkers and creating a widespread demand for managers who are proficient at managing decision-thinking efforts.

If widely implemented, the following program will go a
long way toward changing the present environment from one
that penalizes good thinking practices to one that supports them;
from one in which political leaders dissipate their thinking
energies to one in which they can use their minds more productively for the nation's good; from one in which the media
sensationalizes events to one in which the public will demand
intelligent analysis, balanced comment and, above all, careful
statements regarding the probabilities of success and the risk/
reward considerations involved in *any* major decision.

An Environment Hostile to Professional Decision-Thinking

Managers – whether in business or government – do not
live in isolation from society; they take their cues, to a great
extent, from the rest of us. Today the behavior of too many of
our managers reflects the immature attitudes described in Chapter 9 on Western myths and misconceptions about managers.
Whatever their personal preferences, they often continue to take
a short-term view of their jobs and their responsibilities. Such
managers are 'decisive' in the narrowest sense of the word.
They have become only tacticians, not strategists, and their
organizations are the weaker for it.

Why do we have such managers? Surely our managers
do not lack natural ability, intelligence or aptitude – after all
America has for decades been respected as a nation of good
business managers. The answer lies in the cultural and moral
environment that has rapidly evolved in this country over the last
twenty-five years, an environment that has proven increasingly
hostile to thinking and thoughtful management.

The pressure on managers to produce short-term profits and quick fixes, regardless of long-term consequences, is now endemic in our business, as well as in our political, way of life. So long as next quarter's figures (or next year's election returns) are satisfactory, everyone is happy – the stockholders will see their shares marked up in value, the managers will get their bonuses, and the unions will get a wage increase. Too often, however, someone – and society at large – has to pay a price a few years down the line. In the case of our economic position, for example, we are now beginning to pay the price of just such short-sightedness, a price that can be measured in terms of our budget deficit, trade imbalance and weakening industrial base.

But Wall Street myopia and one-year goals are not the cause of the problem. They are merely a symptom of an attitude that afflicts our society as a whole. Wherever we look in America today we find that people who advocate rapid and facile solutions to complex problems gain influence and prestige at the expense of those who argue for careful thought, planning and commitment to the long haul.

The causes of this attitude undoubtedly lie deep in the American character and in the cultural, technological and historical events of the twentieth century. In much less than one-hundred years, we changed from a nation where most people lived on small farms or in small towns, shared religious and cultural norms, and felt commitment to family and community – to a nation where most people live in large cities, have pluralistic beliefs, and feel alienated from their neighbors, if not also from their family. This radical, upsetting change has brought with it an enlargement, to the point of self-defeat, of cultural characteristics which have long been part of us but which have, heretofore, been limited in their sway by opposing religious and cultural attitudes – such characteristics as our strong individuality, our personal competitiveness, our pursuit of the restless values of the frontier ('Let's cut our losses and move on').

This partial analysis of the sources of hostility to medium-term and long-term thinking is irrelevant, however, to the solutions I am proposing, for we must, so to speak, side-step the deep psychological and historical causes of our dilemma.

We must mature and now move on to deal with our problems on a conscious and rational level. In fact, we in America must move quickly from a society engaged in a mad pursuit of victory in the 50 yard dash toward a society that plans and trains for success in the marathon.

Creating an Environment Supportive of Professional Thinking: Our Political Leaders and Media.

Looking to our political leaders and the media to bring about a major shift in public attitudes toward decision-thinking and planning could be viewed as setting the fox to protect the hens. Are they not the source of much of the pressure for quick and easy solutions to intractable problems? Do the media not stimulate as well as feed the public's appetite for the sensational, the simplistic and the embarrassing? Do politicians not use the media to score points against an opposing party or individual? Do not the media manufacture scandal out of conjecture or distortion (often emanating from the leak of some public official), hoping to catch the reader's or the viewer's attention with a shocking headline? Do not politicians and the media support each other in evading real issues?

In the current frenetic atmosphere public officials and other managers often find themselves in a no-win situation. If they accept that a crisis is real and that it demands serious attention, they will need time to consider the issues, gather facts, consider options, arrive at a policy and take the necessary decisions. But time is just what the media will normally not allow them. And if those who actually have to confront the crisis are unwilling to come up with an instant opinion and an off-the-cuff solution, there will always be others who will. Only the most iron-willed can withstand the constant pressure from the media which demands an immediate answer to every problem in time for the next edition or the next news bulletin.

Given these, and many other, flaws in the relationship between the media and our public leaders, why should we look to them to take a lead in improving the public attitude toward decision-thinking and problem-coping?

One reason is that they are almost all that we have to do the job. Another reason is that they are not so much the cause of the problem as the victims of it. In the last analysis, the problem stems from public misunderstanding and confusion. The real source of the problem, as well as the key to its solution, is the level of *conscious* awareness in society about the importance and complexities of decision-thinking.

That is why I view the educational system as the fundamental point of leverage for changing the system. Before going into my recommendations in that regard, however, I want to expand on what I see as the immediate positive role that our political and media leaders should play.

The role of our political leaders, as regards professional decision-thinking, is to become the chief educators of the nation. They need honestly to admit that the problems of the world are complex and intractable. They must communicate the truth that those problems that require professional decision-thinking solutions will not be solved easily or painlessly.

They need to explain (over and over again) why instant policy-making and off-the-cuff decision making will only make things worse, that mistakes are inevitable in a world of rapid change, that issues do not pose clear choices between right and wrong or good and bad, and that the choice between the lesser of two evils often is the only choice – whether it be in developing an industrial policy or coping with black unemployment, AIDS, drug proliferation or our problems in the Middle East and Central America. Again, they will also need to explain to the public the probability and risk/reward calculations that must be made before any important decision is taken – for unless the public comes to understand these calculations, they will never come to appreciate the very real and ever-present uncertainties involved with *all* decision making.

For our part, as electors and therefore, in theory at least, our politicians' masters, we and the media must cease expecting our political leaders to have an instant policy for every issue. We should back those who are prepared to say, when a crisis does arise, that they need time to think and that they are not going to indulge the public's desire for simplistic solutions. Thus, we now need political leaders who seek to understand and explain complexities rather than hide or gloss over them.

The proper and positive role of the media is to act as a two-way channel of communication between political leaders and the public. To perform this function is a difficult task. It requires high intelligence and a dedication to treating complex matters seriously and clarifying them to assist public understanding.

By all means we should let the media continue to probe, pry and ask questions about everything and everybody – the decisions taken by those in authority concern us all and we have every right to know when mistakes have been made or wrong doing has occurred. But the media must acknowledge that they also have a responsibility to explain complexity as well as to expose villainy, to build rather than just destroy. In other words, they must help to educate the general public as to the thinking uncertainties with which our leaders must always grapple.

★

Creating Public Demand for Professional Decision-Thinking: The Role of Our Education System

Now let us turn to the crux of the matter – how to change public attitudes. If political leaders look solely to the next election, if the media are frequently frivolous, sensationalist and irresponsible, it is we, the electorate, the viewers and the readers who are ultimately to blame. If we did not create the demand for instant solutions to political issues and for entertaining drama on our nightly news programs, political leaders and journalists would soon stop supplying it.

What we must set out to do, therefore, is to create a demand for something better, and that means educating ourselves and our children to understand the decision-thinking process and to appreciate its permanent importance to human life.

Before turning to specifics, I want to mention an interesting and very real model of how the media and a sophisticated public can interact in a way that brings out the best in both writers and readers. I refer to the sports pages of the newspapers and sports news and sports programs on television. Even in sensationalist and exploitative tabloids, the coverage of sport is, generally speaking, of a high standard and is aimed at readers who are expected to appreciate many of the subtleties and complexities of the subject.

If you have trouble believing this, try reading the sports pages on any subject you do *not* normally follow. You will understand very little of what is being said, much as if you had picked up a textbook on cell biology (assuming you are not a biologist). The people who produce these pages, in other words, assume that their readers are both educated and insightful about the subject – even though they may have never aspired to be participants in the game.

But journalists, politicians and managers cannot be expected to be simple-minded idealists. They would not have got where they are, or have a good life expectancy at the top, if they were not sensitive to the market forces of supply and demand. Unless the voting citizen demands good decision-thinking, and unless there is a supply of trained decision-thinkers to help them satisfy that demand, they can hardly be expected to change their thinking priorities.

So how can we bring about a situation in which the voting citizen will be capable of discussing the decision-thinking performance of political and business leaders with the same degree of confidence, know-how and enthusiasm as he or she currently discusses the performance of a tennis player or a football coach? I think there is but one fundamental route to this goal, and that is through our vast educational system.

★

In the industrialized countries of the world, the educational system is now immensely larger than it was even twenty or thirty years ago. It now includes, in addition to schools and colleges, in-house training classes in businesses, extension classes given by public and private colleges and universities, night school classes in both metropolitan and rural systems, and classes given in lecture halls and on TV by professional groups of all kinds. To these must be added correspondence classes and educational programs operated by computer. If we take *all* of these resources as a system, we can see that it is a system capable of bringing about immense changes in public awareness and attitudes in a very short time.

What we need, then, is first for everyone in the next generation – those now in the school system and those moving into it – to be given training in decision-thinking with the *same* priority accorded to mathematics, basic science and history. At the same time, the present generation of adults should be encouraged through media coverage and television classes to gain understanding of, and experience with, the principles and processes of decision-thinking. Finally, the present generation of managers – at all levels – should be given the opportunity through advanced training seminars to have intensive experience of its theory and practice.

There are several advantages to be gained by a widespread educational program specifically aimed at both improving decision-thinking and deepening popular appreciation of its critical role in our lives. For everyone – even people without the remotest connection to managing an organization – skill in the decision-thinking process holds the possibility of improving the management of their lives, their jobs, their family and their social relationships.

For everyone, professional or not, the training would alos teach the value of working on problems in a *group* setting. Decision-thinking is normally a social process. Obtaining the insights of others, their alternative responses, their unique perspectives and views of the future – this comprises the essence of successful decision-thinking. In our overly individualistic society, introducing this communal and cooperative approach to thinking could also be of great social value.

There are two strong arguments for this participative approach. First, it increases the *cooperative* skills of students who will have to work effectively with others, if they are to succeed in their careers. Secondly, it recognizes that all of today's complex business and political thinking problems have to be solved by *teams* of thinkers rather than by isolated individuals.

Finally, the training, if done properly, would teach that no one is intrinsically a good or a bad decision-thinker. Rather, we all have thinking strengths and weaknesses, which need to be balanced in any group or organization whose purpose is practical problem-solving and coping with the future. As I have pointed out, we are often being out-thought by our enemies and competitors not so much because they are better individual thinkers, but because they are better at organizing and managing team thinking efforts. What matters now is not individual brilliance, but collective brilliance.

As for those persons who are, or will become, managers and leaders, this whole book is an argument that they must *also* become professional decision-thinkers. One of the best ways for this to come about will be through training classes and workshops devoted to the subject.

In America our fascination with (and awe of) computers could be harnessed to do some of this work. Software – varying in difficulty and complexity – could be developed to train men and women in decision-thinking skills. If teaching computer science in schools is now a matter of course, why not also teach the decision-thinking skills that will enable our children to get the best out of this formidable ally to our brain?

At more advanced levels of education, decision-thinking should also be taught as a distinct discipline. If we have Masters and Doctors of Business Administration, why should we not have Masters and Doctors of Decision-Thinking?

If this sounds extravagant or absurd, then let us pause and consider. Directly or indirectly our future depends upon the quality of the decisions made by our managers – in corporations, public institutions and the executive branches of state and federal government. Do we not have the right – and obligation – to expect that the people who make those decisions should be professionally qualified to do so?

★

To create widespread demand for good decison-thinking we need to start with the young. Even young children can quickly grasp decision-thinking theory when they encounter someone who will explain it to them with examples from childhood experience. The emphasis in the early years should be on the question – making sure that the question asked is the best question. The pupil should be introduced to the idea that questions must not be accepted in a superficial form. They should be led to the insight that it is always necessary to evaluate whether the question as first posed captures the full substance of the issue on which the decision has to be taken.

With students twelve to fifteen years old, the issues and questions worked on could be restricted to matters directly relevant to their age – family, school, and peer relationships. The next group – from sixteen to eighteen years of age – should be introduced in high school to problems that are more impersonal, problems involving policies, and plans and issues of concern to organizations and to society.

The type and subject matter of courses beyond high school would, of course, vary. For those concerned with general education, broader social or political issues would be dealt with in decision-thinking classes. For those involved with professional practice in corporate or entrepreneurial situations, the issues would be related to decisions in planning and management.

The curriculum of these advanced classes should include both a theoretical and a practical element. It would need to cover the following topics:

1. The four-stage decision-thinking process and its unique role in human affairs and in guiding us into the future;

2. The rules and principles that govern each of the stages of that process;

3. The importance of 'waste' and 'error' in the first three stages of the process;

4. How to make explicit both probability of success and risk/reward calculations;

5. How to generate alternative answers to problems (see, for example, the teaching and class curriculum on 'lateral thinking' developed by Edward de Bono);

6. The importance of planning and scenario planning to decision-thinking;

7. How decision-thinking differs from our other uses of thinking – scientific, mathematical, artistic, etc.;

8. The role of models and the passage of time in decision-thinking;

9. The role of experience, memory, imagination, intuition and reason in thinking;

10. An appreciation of the processes of the human brain;

11. Why it is not necessary to resolve philosophical conundrums about the mind in order to understand and engage in decision-thinking;

12. Individual decision-thinking and collective decision-thinking and the role of each in our lives;

13. Why professional decision-thinking almost always requires a team effort and how that team effort can best be managed;

14. How to become proficient in cooperative thinking efforts, how to become a better listener, and how to stimulate others to be better thinkers;

15. How to come to know one's decision-thinking self – how individuals vary in strengths and weaknesses in each of the four stages in the decision-thinking process and how knowledge of one's own strengths and weaknesses as a thinker and a manger of other thinkers – see the Appendix – will contribute to better decision-thinking;

16. How to recognize and reduce the damaging influence of the Ego Mind, the Rigid Mind and the Machiavellian Mind;

17. The important place of Blue-Skying and Devil's Advocacy in decision-thinking; and

18. The relevance of nutrition, sleep and exercise to good decision-thinking.

Classes covering these subjects will not only help students to understand the practical potential of their own brains and how that potential can best be realized and managed; it will also help them to understand human history as the product of a series of human decisions.

Decision-thinking skills can be driven home by practical exercises involving simulated or real problems. These can be as detailed, complex or difficult as time permits. The development of these exercises could be a project for advanced students of decision-thinking.

Furthermore, decision-thinking can also be taught, without resort to special classes, at any grade level. And this is perhaps the fastest, as well as one of the most beneficial, ways to introduce the subject in the schools. The idea would be simply to use decision-thinking as a perspective from which to view the subject matter of many different courses – those in history, economics, sociology, politics, civics, or current affairs.

Here the teacher could use a case approach to illuminate an issue, asking such questions as: What was the question considered? What were the known facts? What facts did the decision makers ignore? Why did they ignore them? What were the alternatives? What aspects of the alternatives were considered or not considered by the decision makers? What simulations were made about future consequences? What, precisely, was the decision?

For example, this approach could be used in a history class discussing the decision to use atomic weapons against Japan. An economics class might similarly examine the decision of the Federal Reserve Board to maintain slow monetary growth and high interest rates in the early eighties.

Certainly most teachers already use some variation of this approach in their classrooms. But by making the approach explicit, and with the addition of some theoretical discussions about the importance of decision-thinking, the theory and practice of it could be driven home in the schools with little fuss or fanfare.

Classes in decision-thinking for professional managers would have to have certain special characteristics. Reading in decision-thinking theory would be more intense; practical work might also be 'real' if the participants worked in an organization together; the training should also include consultations with actual businesses or government agencies; finally, some students could be encouraged to develop methodologies, cases, programs and software for teaching decision-thinking.

*

The main barrier to this proposal to introduce decision-thinking into our society through our educational institutions, or so it will be argued by some people, is that there is no demand for it. Is it not hopeless to expect our schools to introduce decision-thinking as a subject while professional decision-

thinking is not part of job descriptions and while society generally does not *consciously* appreciate the skills required?

I am optimistic about the answer to this question. Fear is
on my side. I believe that the necessary pressure can be generated
rather quickly given the problems we face, simply because it is
so much in the interest of everyone. What is needed is both a
'shove' and a 'pull': the 'shove' from leaders having insight
into the matter – political, religious, educational, media
and business leaders – and the 'pull' from individuals, both
those in organized groups (such as parents) and those who
are simply concerned about the future of our country and
civilization.

This chapter has described the often hostile and certainly
simplistic environment to serious decision-thinking in which
most of America's managers work and has outlined a program
to bring about a major change in values – a change that would
make good decison-thinking not a rarity but, rather, a part of
the managerial competence required of the ordinary professional. Both political leaders and the media can – and should
– play an important role in bringing about this change, but
the essential element in accomplishing it will be through
education.

If however this change in leadership and support is not
forthcoming, then, I am afraid, complex events and incessant
change are going to overwhelm us. More than ever before, the
words of H. G. Wells cited at the beginning of this chapter,
'Human history becomes more and more a race between education and catastrophe', are apposite.

Summary

**Better decision-thinking, and therefore better de-
cision making, requires a change in the attitude of managers. But that, by itself, will not be enough. Our society**

as a whole must also change its attitude towards its managers and their thinking responsibilities.

Three groups hold the key to bringing about this change – political leaders, the media and, most vital of all, educators.

Political leaders must set an example by shunning quick fixes and instant policy-making. They should not be afraid to think in the long term, nor to explain the real complexities of the choices they have to make.

The media should take its own high-minded rhetoric more seriously and accept that its role as an intermediary between the governed and the governors requires that it behave responsibly in reporting decision-thinking complexities.

It is however no good looking to the media to supply a fuller analysis and more informed discussion of the issues if we continue to demand coverage that is sensational and superficial.

In the long run, only education can permanently change public attitudes so as to produce a society in which the essential role of decision-thinking is both understood and appreciated.

The teaching of decision-thinking should begin in our junior high schools and continue through college or, in the case of future managers, to postgraduate level and beyond.

Courses should be both theoretical and practical, but the emphasis should always be on allowing pupils to gain 'hands-on' thinking experience.

In order to provide this experience, teachers should run regular classroom exercises in which decision-thinking principles are applied to issues which concern the students themselves.

What is asked of public officials and the media may appear unrealistic without a change in public attitudes. But by using the resources of the vast system of education and communication now in existence, we can bring about a change in public consciousness in a short time.

But it is no good for our leaders waiting to begin this program of education and communication until there is a widespread demand for professional decision-thinkers; by then it will be too late.

19

Conclusion: Action This Day – Becoming a Professional Decision-Thinker

I know damn well that whatever brains I have are of the sort which can only count for anything in so far as they are constantly fed from my humanity.

Thornton Wilder

We know that government must be as well-managed as it is well-meaning.

Walter Mondale, July 20, 1984, in his acceptance speech to the Democratic Party's National Convention

Once we become adults, our society tells us that we are personally responsible for our decisions and actions. What it does not tell us so clearly is what are the *thinking* rules and practices that we need to employ to meet that responsibility. Nor does it tell us how we should go about mastering those rules and practices. The focus has been on our decisions and their consequences, not on the rest of the iceberg – the thinking that precedes them. If this book plays some part in redressing this dangerous imbalance, it will have achieved its purpose.

For far too long we have taken decision-thinking for granted, and treated it as something like breathing and walking which everyone can do. But the truth is that decision-thinking is a particular use of thinking which must be studied in its own right, as a skill to be acquired – a skill quite separate from our other uses of thinking, such as scientific, mathematical or artistic.

In writing this book I have wished to open the way to a more profound, yet practical, analysis and understanding of the decision-thinking process. We, in America, must now learn quickly to appreciate the rules and attitudes that are required to operate that process for three main reasons:

first, so that we can strengthen and amplify our own individual decision-thinking capabilities and thereby improve our ability to make, and help others to make, better decisions;

secondly, so that we can learn how to manage, consciously and with true professionalism, the thinking capabilities of our organizations;

and thirdly, so that we can persuade our leaders in government, business and education to bring their urgent attention to bear upon the problem of how our future managers and citizens can be taught – and, if necessary, obliged – to meet their individual and collective decision-thinking responsibilities more effectively.

It is revealing that commentators on recent crises in the American political and economic system do not describe the management problems as a failure of managers to think professionally before they act. They explain the problems as arising from weaknesses of character, poor organization, or Presidential or executive inattention.

As I see it, however, none of these explanations addresses the core of the problem. The central issue is that the decision-thinking of the people at the top of public and corporate life has often not been as good as it should have been. Just when we needed their best thinking they revealed themselves to be sadly incompetent. Our nation, with the support of its noble Constitution, may be able to withstand common flaws of character and personality, but we shall not be able to survive incompetent decision-thinking.

Our hopes of moving to the next stage of human evolution, without destroying ourselves or ruining our civilization, rests upon the quality of the decisions we will make and the intelligence with which we will implement those decisions. That is why producing more professional decision-thinkers must now become a national priority.

★

Over the past decade increasing numbers of Western managers have been making the pilgrimage to Tokyo in an effort to discover the secrets of Japan's astonishing economic success. At the conclusion of one such mission, when visitors were thanking their hosts for the readiness and frankness with which they had explained their methods, one of the Westerners asked a senior Japanese executive if he was not afraid that, by speaking so openly, he was giving aid to his competitors. The Japanese was undismayed. Western visitors were always full of admiration and enthusiasm, he explained, but they never seemed to do anything about it when they got back home.

The comment may be apocryphal, but it rings all too true to anyone who has ever tried to persuade conventional or self-satisfied managers that their organizations will only achieve improved performance if they are prepared to conduct a radical re-examination of their own thinking roles and thinking responsibilities. Normally the reaction to such a proposal is an all too familiar one: 'That is an absolutely intriguing concept. I really would like to consider it very seriously – when I can find the time. Now, about next week's cost-cutting exercise . . .' And then the head goes back in the sand.

If you have found the ideas in this book relevant to your life, and if you think that they offer something to your organization, then do not, I ask of you, be content with putting those ideas away in the back of your mind as you put this book back on the shelf. If you want to grasp the principles and rules of decision-thinking and start openly applying them to the problems which concern you and your organization, then the time to begin is now.

★

When Winston Churchill fired off one of his celebrated wartime memoranda, demanding 'action this day', he did not expect by so doing to win the war at a stroke. Nor was he seeking to override careful planning efforts. Rather, he was trying to overcome the almost universal human fault of procrastination. It was a question of narrowing the gap between thought and action, not of dispensing with essential thinking processes.

How much you can achieve and how quickly you can achieve it will of course depend upon your circumstances. If you work for other people, then you are going to have to persuade them to take action, and that will require patience and tact. If you simply demand that your boss and your colleagues change their management style overnight, you are unlikely to find that your ideas get much of a welcome. But if you can quietly introduce them to the decision-thinking process, demonstrating perhaps how that process could be used systematically to clear an existing log jam in the organization's thinking, you may whet their appetite and stimulate their curiosity. And even if you cannot immediately see how to convert your colleagues and your boss to the concepts of professional decision-thinking, you can still make a start by applying them to your own thinking.

If, on the other hand, you are a manager, then you are in a position to inject these ideas and perceptions into your own organization without delay. But you will still need to start with yourself – that is, with getting to know your thinking self.

Whether you are head of an organization, the manager of a separate organizational unit or profit center, an entrepreneur in a one-man band or a member of an organization dedicated to working your way up to becoming a manager, it all begins with you. So, you will need first to evaluate yourself by using the questionnaire on pp. 173–175, and then to start working to build on your *thinking* strengths and to correct or compensate for your *thinking* weaknesses. You may not become a different person overnight, but you will find that the intelligent people you work with will respond favorably to positive changes in your thinking behavior.

For the improvement of decision-thinking along the lines recommended in this book is not a matter of simply changing organizational structures, introducing new office procedures and reassigning responsibilities. It depends above all else upon *changing attitudes*. And if you want to change other people's attitudes, you first have to change your own. Only when you are clear both about what are your own decision-thinking strengths and weaknesses and about how you intend to tackle your own decision-thinking responsibilities will you be in a position to start indicating to others what you expect of them.

★

When I speak of a need for changing attitudes, I mean something quite specific: the adoption of a new, more complete model of the relationship between a manager and the organization which he heads. In that new model thinking becomes the manager's most fundamental responsibility; the four-stage decision-thinking process is recognized as the disciplined framework (see chart on p. 31) within which all thinking meetings and managerial decisions should take place; and the proper management of that process becomes a manager's main professional concern for converting thought into action.

The summary which follows is intended to achieve two purposes. First, looking back, it brings together the main themes which have been explored in this book. Secondly, looking forward, it equips the reader who has decided to put the model and principles of decision-thinking into open practice, with a checklist which summarizes the rules of the game that he is taking up.

Because the crucial factor is a change of attitude – that is, a change in the thinking models, perceptions and rules *consciously* employed by a manager – I have in each case contrasted the worst of the old with the best of the new. I emphasize the word consciously because many excellent managers are already applying most or all of the 'new' attitudes without recognizing that, taken together, they represent a significant change in the practice of management.

For the already outstanding manager, the task now is to move these attitudes from the dim realm of intuition to the daylight of conscious choice, from the vagueness of the implicit to the clarity of the explicit. For those managers, and aspiring managers, who want to become outstanding, the task is to introduce these new attitudes into their conscious management practices and to make them habitual.

Old

'The manager is primarily a doer – an achiever of objectives. He is responsible for making decisions and ensuring that they are implemented.'

New

'The manager is primarily a thinker and a manager of other thinkers. His first responsibility is to make sure that his organization is thinking about the right issues and thinking about them in the right way. How well he manages his thinking responsibilities will prove critical in determining how well he will manage his "doing" responsibilities.'

★

Old

'I have selected a good management team and given them clear objectives. They get done what I want them to get done.'

New

'Every manager has *two* kinds of teams to manage. One is for implementing decisions and administering policies and procedures; the other is for thinking about what decisions to make. The composition of the first is more or less fixed. The composition of the second can include all or several members of the first, but it will continually change, depending on the subject under consideration. Different rules and skills apply to the professional management of the two teams.'

★

Old

'There is no single "method" for arriving at a decision. It is a question of experience, intuition and judgment.'

New

'The four-stage decision-thinking process is a clear procedure which must be consciously followed and explicitly managed whenever an important decision is to be made if we want to improve our *chances* of making better decisions. It allows us to employ our experience, intuition and judgment to best avail. Its careful use also provides the best guarantee that the right question has been asked; that every conceivable and reasonable answer to that question has been created; that the consequences of each alternative answer have been imagined and thought through; that, where contingencies can be foreseen, they have been provided for; and, finally, that the decision is based upon clearly stated and intelligent calculations of both the probabilities of success and the balance between risk and reward. Professionally managed decision-thinking helps shade the odds of success more in our favor.'

★

Old

'Imagination is an airy-fairy sort of business, best left to artists and advertising agencies. Good managers are down-to-earth people who exercise sound judgment and stick to what is practical.'

New

'Imagination is indispensable to all good decision-thinking. Every manager depends on it. Without imagination, we can never be truly innovative. Moreover seeing our way into the future and predicting the future consequences of any important decision also involves a sustained and disciplined exercise of the imagination.'

★

Old

'All questions have a single core; a good question therefore is brief and concise.'

New

'Many of the issues that confront a manager today are extraordinarily complex. There are normally many bottom lines to be considered. When we address an issue we must work to expose its complexities, not hide them. If we formulate too simple a question, we will prompt too simple an answer.'

★

Old

'We do not tolerate waste on the factory floor; why should it be tolerated in the executive suite? I have neither the time nor the patience to listen to a lot of speculative thinking and argument. We are not running a debating society around here; this is an efficient business and we all have work to do.'

New

'Of course we must meet our deadlines, but unless we look at and encourage the debate of as many alternative answers to a question as feasible, we may miss the one we need. This process will inevitably involve some "waste" – waste of time, of words, of energy. But before we make any important decision we must learn to create deliberately this so-called waste and to look upon it as unavoidable and vital to success. If we neglect this step of exploring for alternatives, we will often direct our energies to vain or ineffectual tasks. Today we need always to remind ourselves that something not worth doing is not worth doing well.'

★

Old

'There is no point in wasting time and money making detailed plans when the future is essentially unpredictable. Nor do I want my executives wasting time and money worrying about what may never happen. The best we can hope to do is to keep the shareholders and analysts happy by making sure that this year's sales and profits are ahead of last year's. And to do this I certainly don't need to have any "Chicken Littles" around here.'

New

'Every decision is in the last resort based upon a certain set of predictions about the future. We must accept that any prediction can never be guaranteed in advance to be accurate. But at the same time we must do everything possible to make sure that our own predictions, together with our acts of hedging and our contingency plans, are developed as carefully and thoroughly as possible. We need people around here who are prepared to think *and* worry about the future of this business. It is the only way we will be truly equipped to cope with the unexpected event and the uncertain future.'

★

Old

'Either you have what it takes to be a good manager or you haven't. Too much self-analysis is a waste of time. Anyway, qualities like leadership, decisiveness and determination are what matter.'

New

'Every manager needs to make a truthful appraisal of the strengths and weaknesses that characterize his own decision-thinking. Only with this knowledge will he be in a position to capitalize on his strengths, compensate for his weaknesses and surround himself with the necessary thinking talent to complement his own. For a manager, exercising the management qualities of a professional decision-thinker is today as important as exercising the qualities of leadership, decisiveness and determination – no less, no more.'

★

Old

'I am a strong leader; that is why people like working for me and carrying out my orders.'

New

'We need strong leadership in managing our organization's thinking efforts, just as much as we need strong leadership in managing our organization's working efforts.'

★

Old

'Since thinking is something each of us does most of the time in isolation or in small groups, it is meaningless to talk of the mind of the organization or of the need to manage it. Managers are there to make decisions; organizations are there to translate them into action.'

New

'A manager must conduct and manage the mind of his organization just as a professional orchestra leader must conduct his orchestra and a professional coach must manage his team. Without this ability he will not get the excellent thinking that is a prerequisite to excellent decision making. If, moreover, the decision-thinking process is so managed that the ultimate decision commands the support of the organization as a whole, the chances of effective implementation of that decision will be greatly improved.'

★

Old

'Managers should be given objectives, authority and responsibility and then left to get on with their jobs, reporting back only when necessary. Obviously it is far more important that a manager should be good at his job than that his thinking abilities should be complementary to those of his colleagues. If we talk of a management team around here, it is only in the sense that a military unit is a team in which each person knows what he has to do and does it.'

New

'Just as with decision implementing, effective decision-thinking requires a team effort. No one person can combine all the aptitudes – creativity, rigor, scepticism, patience, decisiveness and courage – which will be needed at the different stages of the decision-thinking process. The strength of any thinking team is greater than the sum of the skills and experience of its individual members. It is the ability of the team to think together as a team that will prove crucial. This means that the members of a thinking team must be picked not simply on the grounds of individual brilliance, but with the aim of building a brilliant team.'

★

Old

'A manager's life is far too busy for him to waste time listening to half-baked ideas. If someone wants to submit a new idea, I'll be glad to consider it. But they should know that I don't suffer fools gladly.'

New

'In order to manage a thinking team professionally it is necessary to perceive each member as a thinker in his own right, with a particular combination of strengths and weaknesses, and to make sure that his thinking skills are deployed to best advantage – while minimizing the damage that can be done by his weaknesses. This demands tact, courtesy and the recognition that people will only think well and give birth to their brain-children if they feel that their mental efforts are being encouraged, taken seriously and appreciated. This applies just as much to those devil's advocates who have the perseverance to find the hidden snags in a proposal as it does to those innovators who regularly come up with a brilliant, new idea.'

★

Old

'Sound thinking is something I expect all my employees to do. If I do use an idea that works out to our benefit, that's fine; but I don't intend to pass out extra praise to people who are doing what they are paid to do.'

New

'Decision-thinking, if not properly managed – particularly at Stage 2 and Stage 3 of the process – can be a thankless task. Don't ever put your thinkers in a "can't win" – no praise, but easy to blame – situation; not if you want to benefit from their best thinking.'

★

Old

'I admit that new ideas or insights sometimes come to me and my colleagues out of the blue, but these happen fortuitously. It is a waste of time trying to cultivate such things. They either happen or they don't.'

New

'For all the emphasis we put upon careful, well-reasoned thought, we have to acknowledge that there is a subconscious element in our thinking – let us call it the Eureka Factor – which is a source of originality, innovation and sound judgment. We disregard the Eureka Factor at our peril, even if we cannot explain how it operates. Rather we should try to cultivate it by discovering and reproducing the conditions which favor its appearance. Whenever possible, we need to give it an opportunity to have its say before we arrive at any important decision.'

★

Old

'If someone lets the stresses of the job get on top of him, that is a problem for the individual concerned and his doctor – not for his boss. My job is to get things done around here, not worry about stress levels.'

New

'Our capacity to think well is directly related to the health and well-being of our body. Each of us should make sure that we are physically fit, and we should avoid tackling important thinking, as well as doing, tasks when we are feeling under the weather or not at our best. As professional managers we should also be acutely aware that our colleagues' health problems, whether or not they are job-related ones like stress or fatigue, may seriously affect their decision-thinking performance and therefore their decision-making performance. Their health problems are our problems.'

★

Old

'I recognize that if expenditure is to be controlled, it must be broken down into several categories. But while I insist on monitoring what we spend on raw materials, advertising, travel and entertainment and so forth, I see no point in trying to determine what we spend on thinking.'

New

'In the long run this organization will stand or fall by the quality of its thinking. I need therefore to know on a regular basis, in terms of dollars and cents, just what resources we are *investing* in decision-thinking. Our "thinking budget" needs to be large enough to cover the costs of thinking meetings, trips and conferences, as well as the fees of those people who are specifically hired to provide us with professional advice. It must also contribute to the cost of employing those individuals who play a major part in our organization's decision-thinking. It is my responsibility to ensure that this budget is truly adequate to our needs and that we get full value for the money which we invest in our thinking resources. Furthermore, I think the day will soon come when shareholders, bankers and employees will also want to see these "thinking" expenses clearly identified in a balance sheet.'

★

Old

'Of course I try to make sure that the organization keeps on top of its problems, both from day to day and in the medium- and long-term, but I know of no procedure which will ensure that we foresee every problem that is going to arise.'

New

'By insisting on a regular audit of our organization's decision-thinking practices, priorities, contingency plans and resources, we can possibly reduce the number of surprises that occur and also ensure that, if and when an unexpected crisis does arise, our organization is fully prepared mentally to respond to it. Again, such an audit will just hedge the odds more in our favor.'

★

Old

'The Japanese have been winning during the last twenty years because they *work* harder than we do.'

New

'The Japanese have been winning because they take decision-thinking more seriously than we do, and they therefore *think* harder than we do.'

★

Old

'Let's get cracking. We don't have time to waste contemplating our navels.'

New

'When we think, we think. When we decide to act, we act.'

★

Old

'It's not my fault things went wrong. I made the best decision at the time. I never believed our competition would out-think us.'

New

'The manager gets the decision-thinking he deserves.'

★

Most managers would certainly not associate themselves with all the 'old' attitudes expressed here; you may even feel that I have exaggerated some of them. But, in fact, they all represent management diktats or observations that I have overheard or read about during the last fifteen years.

What should nevertheless be clear is that the 'new' management attitudes are radically different from most of those which generally prevail. And I hope I have persuaded you that by consciously adopting them we can dramatically improve our performance as managers and therefore our chances of solving the manifold and complex problems facing us.

Our civilization has been built over the centuries out of the thinking and the decisions of a multitude of individuals. Our ancestors also struggled to develop the basic moral values that we need to guide us into the future. What we must do now, more than ever before, is to align those values with the decision-thinking skills that will allow us to cope and to survive. Our values and our decision-thinking skills are inextricably entwined and therefore equally important. If one fails us, the other is doomed – and so are we.

It is said that the road to hell is paved with good intentions; but it is also paved with bad ones. The Nazis turned their backs on our civilization's values while running their country's military machine quite efficiently for several years, but in the end they brought their country to disgrace. On the other hand, certain of our leaders in America have espoused many of our finest values but, by the inadequate way in which they managed both their own mind and their decision-thinking responsibilities, have seriously weakened – hopefully just in the short-term – the one nation that can, today, ultimately defend those values.

In conclusion, *given* the help and guidance of our precious values, the only way we can deal with the daunting problems we and our organizations face is by thinking our way through them. To do so we shall need to improve quickly our individual *and* collective decision-thinking skills and practices far beyond the level we have achieved in a few thousand years of civilization. In this book I have focused on a hard-nosed kind of thinking, concerned with survival in the face of inescapable realities, because if we do not at least survive all other bets are off.

I therefore hope, above all, that I have convinced you that you should transform yourself into a professional decision-thinker. If you do so, you will be far better able to contribute to the future of your organization and to your own welfare. In the long run that can only be good for you, for our country and for our civilization.

Selected Bibliography

Edward de Bono, *Lateral Thinking,* Harper & Row, 1970.

Peter F. Drucker, *Management: Tasks, Responsibilities, Practices,* Harper & Row, 1974.

Loren Eiseley, *The Unexpected Universe,* Harcourt, 1972.

Loren Eiseley, *The Firmament of Time,* Atheneum, 1984.

W. Timothy Gallwey, *The Inner Game of Tennis,* Random House, 1974.

Harold S. Geneen, *Managing,* Doubleday, 1984.

William Glasser, *Take Effective Control of Your Life,* Harper & Row, 1984.

Ben Heirs and Gordon Pehrson, *The Mind of the Organization,* Harper & Row, revised edition, 1982.

Lee Iacocca, *Iacocca, An Autobiography,* Bantam Books, 1984.

C. G. Jung, *Psychological Types,* Routledge & Kegan Paul, 1971.

Niccolo Machiavelli, *The Prince,* Penguin.

Thomas J. Peters and Robert H. Waterman Jr., *In Search of Excellence,* Harper & Row, 1982.

Peter J. Prior, *Leadership Is Not a Bowler Hat,* David & Charles, 1982.

Roy Rowan, *The Intuitive Manager,* Little, Brown and Company, 1986.

Jonas Salk, *Anatomy of Reality,* Columbia University Press, 1983.

Ezra F. Vogel, *Japan as Number One,* Harvard University Press, 1979.

Richard E. Winter, *Coping with Executive Stress*, McGraw-Hill, 1983.

Pierre Wack, *Scenarios: Uncharted Waters Ahead*, Harvard Business Review, September/October 1985, pp. 73–89.

Pierre Wack, *Scenarios: Shooting the Rapids*, Harvard Business Review, November/December 1985, pp. 139–150.

Your Decision-Thinking Profile

A. Personal Decision-Thinking Characteristics

5 - 4 - 3 - 2 - 1 - 0 - 1 - 2 - 3 - 4 - 5

1.	Enjoy decision-thinking	- - - - - - - - - -	Find decision-thinking disagreeable
2.	Adventurous thinker	- - - - - - - - - -	Cautious thinker
3.	Can concentrate	- - - - - - - - - -	Mind wanders easily
4.	Easily discouraged in thinking tasks	- - - - - - - - - -	Persevering in thinking tasks
5.	Intuitively biased	- - - - - - - - - -	Analytically biased
6.	Good at working with numbers	- - - - - - - - - -	Poor at working with numbers
7.	Optimistic	- - - - - - - - - -	Pessimistic
8.	Like taking thinking initiatives	- - - - - - - - - -	Prefer reacting to the thinking of others

5 - 4 - 3 - 2 - 1 - 0 - 1 - 2 - 3 - 4 - 5

B. *Personal Factors Directly Relevant to the Four-Stage Process*

	5 - 4 - 3 - 2 - 1 - 0 - 1 - 2 - 3 - 4 - 5	
9. Tend to accept the question as posed (Stage 1)	- - - - - - - - - - -	Tend to query the assumptions underlying the question
10. Like marshalling information (Stage 1)	- - - - - - - - - - -	Dislike marshalling information
11. Dislike creating alternatives (Stage 2)	- - - - - - - - - - -	Like creating alternatives
12. Dislike thinking about future consequences (Stages 1 and 3)	- - - - - - - - - - -	Conscientious worrier about future consequences
13. Like making decisions (Stages 1 and 4)	- - - - - - - - - - -	Dislike making decisions
	5 - 4 - 3 - 2 - 1 - 0 - 1 - 2 - 3 - 4 - 5	

C. Personal Factors Relevant to Managing and Cooperating with Other Decision-Thinkers

5 - 4 - 3 - 2 - 1 - 0 - 1 - 2 - 3 - 4 - 5

14.	Self-Centered (Ego Mind) approach to thinking	- - - - - - - - - - -	Team approach to thinking
15.	Manipulative (Machiavellian Mind) approach to thinking tasks	- - - - - - - - - - -	Open and objective approach to thinking tasks
16.	Receptive to other people's ideas	- - - - - - - - - - -	Not-invented-here mentality (Rigid Mind)
17.	Poor listener	- - - - - - - - - - -	Good listener
18.	Willing to seek advice of others	- - - - - - - - - - -	Reluctant to seek advice of others
19.	Unable to accept criticism and admit thinking mistakes	- - - - - - - - - - -	Willing to accept criticism and admit thinking mistakes
20.	Poor at stimulating other people to think	- - - - - - - - - - -	Good at stimulating other people to think
21.	Not careful of other people's feelings when considering their ideas	- - - - - - - - - - -	Respectful of other people's feelings when considering their ideas

5 - 4 - 3 - 2 - 1 - 0 - 1 - 2 - 3 - 4 - 5